the well-turned phrase that will help the reader or listener get the point and remember the lesson. His aim throughout is to relate the message of Colossians and Philemon to the life and message of the church and to the experience of believers. An extra serendipity is the occasional outline and expanded comment on a theme related to the text under discussion. These will not only benefit anyone preparing a lesson or sermon, but they add a strong devotional and practical note to the commentary.

H. DERMOT MCDONALD taught at London Bible College over a long period, serving as its vice principal for 21 years. He has been a visiting professor at a number of American and Canadian institutions, including Regent College, Vancouver; Trinity Evangelical Divinity School, Deerfield, Illinois; and most recently at New College, San Francisco. Dr. McDonald received the B.A. and B.D. degrees with honors and the Ph.D. and D.D. degrees from the University of London. He is the author of several other books, including *Jesus Human and Divine,* and *Living Doctrines of the New Testament,* and commentaries on Galatians and Ephesians. His many articles have appeared in journals such as *Christianity Today, Harvard Theological Review* and *Spectrum,* and he has contributed articles to many dictionaries and symposiums. He and his wife Anne live in Sussex, England. Their three children are grown and one of his daughters is a member of Parliament.

Commentary on
Colossians
& Philemon

Commentary on Colossians & Philemon

H. Dermot McDonald

THETA

BOOKS

WORD BOOKS
PUBLISHER
4800 WEST WACO DRIVE
WACO, TEXAS
76703

COMMENTARY ON COLOSSIANS AND PHILEMON

Library of Congress Catalog card number: 79-63951
ISBN 0-8499-0088-3
Printed in the United States of America

Scripture quotations, unless otherwise noted, are from the Revised Standard Version of the Bible, copyright 1946, 1952, © 1971, 1973 by the Division of Christian Education of the National Council of the Churches of Christ in the USA, and are used by permission.

Quotations from *The New English Bible* (NEB) © The Delegates of The Oxford University Press and The Syndics of The Cambridge University Press, 1961, 1970, are used by permission.

Quotations from *The Jerusalem Bible* (JB), copyright © 1966, by Darton, Longman & Todd, Ltd. and Doubleday and Company, Inc., are used by permission of the publisher.

Quotations from *The Living Bible Paraphrased* (LB) published by Tyndale House Publishers, 1971, Wheaton, Ill., are used by permission.

Quotations from the *New American Standard Bible* (NAS) are copyright © 1960, 1962, 1963, 1968, 1971 by The Lockman Foundation.

Quotations marked Phillips are from *The New Testament in Modern English* by J. B. Phillips, published by The Macmillan Company, © 1958, 1960, 1972 by J. B. Phillips, and are used by permission of the publisher.

Quotations marked Phillips, *Letters,* are from *Letters to Young Churches* by J. B. Phillips, copyright 1947 by The Macmillan Company, and are used by permission of the publisher.

Quotations from Today's English Version of the Bible (TEV), © American Bible Society 1966, 1971, 1976, are used by permission.

Quotations from the New International Version of the Bible (NIV), published by The Zondervan Corporation, are copyright © 1973 by New York Bible Society International.

Quotations marked Weymouth are from *The New Testament in Modern Speech* by Richard Francis Weymouth published by The Pilgrim Press, 1943.

Quotations marked Moffatt NT are from *The Bible, A New Translation,* by James Moffatt, copyright, 1922, 1924, 1926, 1935 by Harper & Bros.

Quotations marked Goodspeed are from *The Bible, An American Translation* by J. M. Powis Smith, Edgar J. Goodspeed, et al., copyright 1935 by the University of Chicago.

Quotations marked Williams are from *The New Testament in the Language of the People* by Charles B. Williams, copyright 1949 by Moody Press.

Quotations marked Norlie are from *The New Testament, A New Translation* by Olaf M. Norlie, copyright © 1961 by Zondervan Publishing House.

Quotations marked ASV are from the American Standard Version, 1901, published by Thomas Nelson & Sons.

Quotations marked RV are from the Revised Version (English), published 1885.

Quotations marked KJV are from the Authorized or King James Version of the Bible.

CONTENTS

A WORD TO BEGIN WITH

It is not always the case that general users of commentaries feel compelled to read lengthy and learned pages of introduction to a biblical writing. It would sometimes, of course, obviously repay them to do so. But the fact is that they usually turn to a particular text or passage to seek what enlightenment a writer may have to give. The procedure of the present series of commentaries is to begin with a statement on, for example, such questions as where a letter originated; what its main theological interests are, and the like. That method has, therefore, been of necessity followed here. What I have written on such issues will, I believe, be of help to those who wish to get a fuller understanding of what, in this case, the Apostle Paul has to say to us in his Colossian and Philemon epistles. I have, however, sought to keep my observations on these matters to a minimum. But I have endeavored at the same time to bring into the commentary on the text, at the appropriate place, further comments which will supplement what I have to say in this introductory section. In this way the reader will be helped to face such issues in their proper context rather than having information relegated to introductions or appendices which may appear otherwise to have no real connection with the actual content and understanding of the writing, and are consequently just passed over.

Throughout the commentary I have sought to unfold Paul's essential message. As a theologian I regard myself as the servant of the church. I take it as my business to provide the preacher and the teacher with what help I can for their so important tasks. I have tried, therefore, to exegete as well as I can for their sake. And I have endeavored to cream off some of the good things in the labors of others for their use. In this regard the present commentary has sought to gather into one ring of truth many gems scattered over wide areas and periods.

The Christ and His Grace

Colossians

INTRODUCTION

Colossians

THE OCCASION OF THE WRITING

During one of Paul's imprisonments, he was visited by Epaphras (cf. 1:24; 4:10, 18), who brought him news concerning the recently formed churches of Colossae, Laodicea and Hierapolis. The news, more particularly focusing on the church of Colossae, was both good (cf. 1:3; 2:5), and disquieting (cf. 2:8–9). The good news cheered the apostle's heart. But Epaphras disclosed grave reasons for concern which plunged Paul into an agony of heart (2:1). The peril was real. Some disturbers had come into the Lycus valley—who exactly they were he does not say, but he does imply that there was a leader who tried to spoil the faith of the Christian community (2:8). The Colossian epistle is Paul's response to this news. It brings to the church, first, the apostle's message of good will; second, word of Epaphras, their minister in the gospel, who apparently elected to remain with Paul and share his imprisonment (cf. Philem. 23); and, third, more particularly the letter is concerned with the apostle's refutation of the error which had begun to afflict the church.

In this regard Colossians has the aspect of an apologetic—a defense of a basic Christian doctrine against heretical attempts to blunt its distinctiveness by blending it into an amalgam of pagan and Jewish speculations. The main thrust of the letter is, therefore, an apostolic rebuttal of a grave error central in the strange new doctrine. The epistle was apparently taken to Colossae by Tychicus who, it seems, brought with him Onesimus to restore him to his master Philemon and also, at the same time carried with him Paul's "note" beseeching the converted slave's old master to have "him back for good . . . as a man and as a Christian" (Philem. 15–16, Moffatt NT).

THE DESTINATION OF THE LETTER

The three towns Colossae, Laodicea and Hierapolis (cf. Col. 4:13) lay along the banks of the small river Lycus, a tributary of the Meander, in Western Phrygia, the Roman province of Asia, or as it is today, the west of modern Turkey. Colossae and Hierapolis were on the north of the river, with Laodicea to the south. Laodicea was about ten miles from Colossae, and some thirteen from Hierapolis, while the distance between Laodicea and Hierapolis was about six miles. They thus formed a sort of triangle, with Colossae and Laodicea as the base, and Hierapolis forming the apex. Yet in spite of its apparently more strategic setting, Colossae was in Paul's time the least commercially influential of the three. In earlier days it had been prosperous as a wool and weaving center, meriting in the fifth century B.C. the description of "a great city" (Herodotus, *Histories* vii, 30), and "a populous city, both wealthy and large" a century later (Xenophon, *Anabasis,* 1, 2.6). At the beginning of the Christian era its influence had vastly declined, so that Strabo, the first-century geographer, could describe it in his day as "a small city" (*Geography,* xii, 8, 13). It is now no more than a barren and uninhabited site. But its name remains best known because it has been enshrined for all time in an apostolic communication. The particular problem which compelled Paul to write had seemingly afflicted all three towns, as all are mentioned together in the letter (cf. 1:2; 2:1; 4:13, 15–16).

None of the places appear, however, to have been personally visited by the apostle, who had made his way westward to Ephesus by the more direct upper coast road (cf. Acts 19:1). The epistle itself makes clear that the churches of the Lycus valley were founded by Epaphras (cf. Col. 1:7, RSV; the "also" of the KJV is rightly omitted), who himself was probably won to Christian faith during Paul's long ministry in Ephesus (cf. Acts 19:10). So there is a sense in which these churches owed the gospel to Paul. He was their grandfather in Christ, a fact indicated by the true reading of 1:7, "on our behalf" (RSV), rather than the alternative "for you" (KJV). It was on Paul's initiative that Epaphras came to Colossae to open up the work of Christ there. Hence, Epaphras was, as J. B. Lightfoot says, "Paul's delegate to them, his representative in Christ."* And although the apostle was not known personally to the Colossians (2:1), yet he knew them well through Epaphras (cf. 1:4, 8), to whom he refers as "our dear fellow-servant, a trusted worker for Christ on our behalf" (1:7, NEB).

THE NATURE OF THE HERESY

The character of the teaching combatted by Paul in this epistle is described in 2:8–23. Long and learned tomes have been written on the subject of the Colossian Heresy, and from among the many

---

*Full information on commentators cited in the text is given in the bibliography at the end of the book.

statements of its precise nature and the rejection of one view by the advocates of another, it is not easy to give the doctrine a specific label. Lightfoot designates it as an early form of Essenian Gnosticism. But it is certainly not the Gnosticism of the advanced stages against which Irenaeus and Tertullian wrote. And it has been doubted whether Essenism could have reached the Lycus valley at such a time. A. S. Peake denies outright that the heresy relates to Gnosticism even in its most rudimentary form and would derive the teaching "from Judaism alone." E. F. Scott thinks that the efforts "to attach a particular label to the heresy may all be regarded as futile."

Yet there does seem to be a gnostic strand in the teaching which swept into the Colossian church. Indeed, the two streams into which later Gnosticism divided appear here in their less clean-cut forms. Basic to all Gnosticism is the thesis that matter is itself essentially evil. Starting with this assumption, one wing of gnostic teachers argued for asceticism. For, if matter is evil, then the body is evil. How then can it be kept in place but by holding it in check with utmost rigor? This view the apostle exposes by showing how valueless are ascetic practices for the attainment of the good life (cf. 2:21–23). The advocates of the opposing view, beginning from the same premise, argued for antinomianism. For again, since matter is evil, and the body is material, it is consequently destined for the dust. No good purpose can then be served by denying it the full satisfaction of its sensual desires. There must therefore be no curbing of one's instinctual passions. This folly Paul meets by insisting on the need for a clean life by the new man in Christ (cf. 3:5–6).

But the heresy was not just a simple form of Gnosticism. The fact is, rather, that "the main elements of the false teaching are such as to show that it was a fusion of pagan and Judaic speculation, which resulted in a syncretism. The features of this religious amalgam were forms of ascetic practices and disciplines, the cult of angelic worship, and the pride in superior wisdom and knowledge (Gk. *gnōsis*)" (R. P. Martin, *Colossians*).

It may be useful to set out the various elements making up the destructive compound which are to be gathered from the apostle's rebuttal. *(1)* It was at least a nominally Christian heresy, though it did not give to Christ his rightful position (2:19). *(2)* It was also partly Jewish, apparently giving recognition to circumcision (2:11) and paying attention to matters of food and drink, to festival and sabbath days (2:16; cf. 3:11). *(3)* It claimed to be a "philosophy" (2:8) so that it contained Greek, or at any rate Hellenistic elements. *(4)* It laid great stress upon asceticism, for which a number of specific rules were stated (2:16, 19, 21). *(5)* It was clearly accompanied by a considerable emphasis on angelology (2:8, 18). *(6)* It made use of such gnostic pet words as *mystery, fullness, knowledge,* which the apostle took up as the vehicle of his own profounder conceptions.

For the way that Paul met and refuted the heretical teaching, the reader must turn to chapter 2 of the letter and its comments. He was evidently well acquainted by Epaphras with its strange notions. "He did not fear them nor did he despise them, but he exposed their heresies by a richer presentation of the truth in Christ" (A. T. Robertson). He met their claim to higher knowledge by a gnosis or philosophy of religion which arched total cosmic reality.

THE THEOLOGY OF THE EPISTLE

It is against the background of the heresy that Paul develops what is the dominant theme of his letter, namely, his view of our Lord's person. It is not quite clear from the apostle's language what specific ideas the Colossian heretics held respecting Christ, but it is obviously right to assume that they were both inadequate and derogatory. The stress he puts on the Savior's eternal being and absolute sovereignty can hardly be accounted for in any other way. Whatever precisely were the notions of the false teachers, the apostle found it necessary to reiterate the Christian conviction that in Christ alone the whole divine fullness resides (cf. 1:19; 2:9).

The heresy appears basically to have been an implicit denial of Christ's twofold nature and so consequently to undercut the adequacy of his mediatorial office. The gap between God and the world had been so widened by the heretics that they required a host of angels and aeons to bridge it. They allowed Christ to be one of these emanations, albeit the highest, and thus to occupy the last rung of the ladder, next to God, by which the long ascent could be made to the spiritual realm.

The apostle meets this error by setting forth Christ as the one who, alone in himself, bridges the chasm between earth and heaven. For he is at once fully of God and fully of man; and so, as the God-man, he raises man to God and brings God to man. Thus, the chain between God and man is reduced to a single link, and through Christ the divine *plērōma* (fullness) is communicated to man (2:10; cf. 1:9).

So Christ is *(1)* related to the Father. He is set side by side with the Father to be spoken of in the same breath and so given the status of equality (cf. 1:2, 3). He is in a special sense God's Son (1:13). He is the visible manifestation of the invisible God (1:15), and in him, "the complete being of the Godhead dwells embodied" (2:9, NEB; cf. 2:3). *(2)* He is set forth in relation to the entire universe, and in his cosmic significance is involved with the Father as creator and reconciler of "all things" (1:16, 20). As God's "Other Self" he is thus in direct contact with material realities. *(3)* He is set forth, also, in relation to the church as redeemer of those who are its members (1:21; 2:13, 14). And as head of the church, he is its authority and directing intelligence (1:18; 2:19). The one great message of Colossians may, then, be summed up in the declaration of 3:11: "Christ is all that matters for Christ lives in all" (Phillips).

Although Paul's christology in Colossians has an apologetic intent, it is nevertheless profoundly related to his soteriology. For it is in Christ as the Father's "beloved Son" that redemption is secured and forgiveness of sins guaranteed (1:13, 14). He nailed to the cross the bond of legal demands which confronted us, thereby canceling their condemning thrust (2:14); and in that same cross he drew the sting of all the evil powers ranged against us, leaving them shattered, empty and defeated (2:15). Peace he made "by the blood of his cross," so to reconcile all things to God (1:20). While in "his body of flesh by his death" those once estranged and hostile in mind, doing evil deeds, have their reconciliation (1:21, 22).

Such is the Christ whom Paul declares "we preach" (cf. 1:28, KJV). And this is the Christ "received" (2:6) by "faith" (1:4; cf. 2:5, 7, 12), and who thus dwells in the believer as the hope of glory (1:27).

In him, in whom the whole fullness of deity dwells bodily, the Christian comes to his fullness (2:10). While, then, in Colossians Paul's christology and soteriology are linked, they are both the basis for his ethical declarations. As reconciled in and by such a Christ, the believer is to live and act as a redeemed person. Having received Christ Jesus the Lord, we are to live in him (2:6). There is to be death in his death to the old life of sin and self, and a rising again in his resurrection to a new life of moral worth and heavenly glory. The Christ who is our hope of glory is also "our life" (3:4) with whom our life is hid in God (3:2). But that hidden life is to be openly revealed in the many relationships of home and family (3:18–21), between master and slave (3:22–4:1), and in Christian conduct in the wider world (4:5, 6).

THE AUTHENTICITY OF THE COMPOSITION

The external evidence for the Pauline authorship of Colossians is early and strong. The epistle was known to Irenaeus, Tertullian and Clement of Alexandria at the end of the second century. It is named in the Muratorian Fragment, was accepted by Marcion before A.D. 150, and is earlier quoted by Justin Martyr. Its obvious connection with Philemon, the Pauline authorship of which is undoubted, is a presumption in favor of its composition by the same apostle.

Yet the Pauline authorship of Colossians has often been questioned, primarily on internal grounds. Four main reasons have been advanced in this regard.

1. *Because of the heresy combatted.* According to F. C. Baur (1762–1860), and the Tübingen school of which he was founder, Colossians reflects the great gnostic systems of the second century and is thus quite outside the range of Paul's time. These writers identify, for example, the "powers" with the "aeons" of the second-century Valentinus, and lay stress upon the use of such words as *gnōsis*, *plērōma*, *teleios*, which were technical gnostic expressions. The Judaistic references are explained as being due to some sort of gnostic ebionism. Others have sought to find in Colossians an attack on the docetic Gnosticism of Cerinthus (c. A.D. 100) of the last quarter of the first century. In this heresy there was certainly an emphasis on Jewish angelology and the featuring of Christian elements of a reductionist type, in which "the Christ" is said to have descended upon the man Jesus at his baptism.

But a fully sufficient reply to these theories is the fact that Colossians depicts none of these heresies in its developed form. There is evidence enough that the floating ideas with which Colossians is concerned, and which later crystallized into elaborate systems, were present in the apostolic age and have "early parallels in nonconformist Judaism" (Martin).

2. *Because of its Ephesian connection.* Even a cursory reading of the epistles to the Colossians and Ephesians will reveal that there is an intimate connection between them. On the grounds of this relationship, however, the view has been elaborated, as early as 1838 by Mayerhoff, that Colossians cannot be accepted as Pauline. In comparison with Ephesians, whose apostolic authenticity was accepted, this epistle is said to exhibit several non-Pauline ideas and presents, rather, the picture of an amateurish imitation. Against this, however, may be set the fact that for most critics it is Ephesians which is regarded as un-Pauline so that "if suspicion is cast by the comparison, it falls more naturally on Ephesians than on Colossians" (C. F. D. Moule).

Others, therefore, have reversed the order and maintain that Colossians as we have it today is indeed basically a genuine Pauline composition but has been revised and additional material interpolated by the author of Ephesians (not believed to be Paul) in an effort to relate it the more closely to his own production. Nineteenth-century German critic W. H. L. DeWette thus refers to Ephesians as a "verbose expansion" of Colossians by a disciple of Paul. The final product by the work of unknown redactors was published, with Paul's name retained because of basic material which originated from him, to constitute the Colossian epistle as it appears in our New Testament.

But there are difficulties with the theory that the author of Ephesians borrowed from Colossians to more easily pass off his epistle as Pauline. For the material supposed to be added does not in fact meet the criterion of relating Colossians the more closely to Ephesians. And however much the similarities between the two epistles are stressed, there still remain very great and important differences in emphasis sufficient to show that the author, for the ulterior purpose of having his production accepted, is not straining to keep it in line with an acknowledged apostolic document. We will consider the question whether the profound christological passage of chapter 1:15–20 is to be regarded as non-Pauline in the sense of being a prior existing hymn in honor of Christ in the commentary on that passage. All we need to say here is that the rejection of the authenticity of the epistle on the grounds that the christology is too advanced for Paul at the time the epistle was written should not be taken too seriously. Attention has been focused here on its statements on the preexistence and cosmic significance of Christ. It is surely sufficient to reply to this that all that Colossians shows is a fuller, and if the term is permitted, a more philosophical exposition of teaching implicit in Paul's earlier writings (cf. eg., Col. 1:15–17 and 1 Cor. 8:6, 15:47; Col. 1:16 and 1 Cor. 15:28; Col. 1:20, 2:9 and 1 Cor. 15:28, Rom. 11:36, etc.).

3. *Because of its elaborate angelology.* There is, it is said, little direct reference to angels in Paul's other epistles, so that the treatment in Colossians on this score rules out his authorship. The contention is not, however, quite accurate. For apart from a significant allusion by him to an angel in Acts (17:23), Paul has twelve references to angel or angels in his epistles, while there is actually only one reference to them in Colossians, and this comes in the context of the heresy he repudiates in which they were accorded a wrong regard. Yet this stern repudiation of angel-worship in Colossians is not out of harmony with what he has to say in his other epistles. If he does, in other contexts, allow them a place in God's providential ordering of human affairs, here he must insist that no created beings, not even angels, share in God's grand design for man's salvation—a right which belongs to Christ alone.

4. *Because the style is too un-Pauline.* Both the language and style of Colossians, it has been claimed, are quite unlike that of Paul, so much so, indeed, that the claim that it is his cannot be allowed. But this objection only holds if Galatians, Romans and the

Corinthian letters are regarded as the only criteria of what Paul might have written. It is certainly true that Colossians contains forty-six words not used elsewhere by the apostle. But since most of these are connected with the heresy and its refutation, their peculiarity can be accounted for by their appearance in this context. On the other hand there are eleven Pauline words found in Colossians which are not used by any other New Testament writer—a fact which can be used as an argument for the opposite conclusion. That the apostle, as we believe, wrote from Rome and that Timothy had a share in the composition of the letter provide a reason for the enlarged vocabulary. A similar instance of this expansion is noted by British classicist J. Mahaffy concerning Xenophon's later writings. They are, he has shown, full of non-Attic words picked up from Xenophon's changing surroundings, and in each many words occur only once. Nothing safe, it has been too often demonstrated, can be adduced with certainty concerning the identity of an author from the phenomenon of style.

There is therefore every justification for accepting the verdict of C. F. D. Moule that "there is nothing there, either in vocabulary or in ideas, which it seems impossible to attribute to the Paul who is known from other epistles, or even unlikely for him to have written, given the circumstances implied by the epistle." We may accept that the writing is "profound and difficult" (C. J. Ellicott), (cf. 2 Pet. 3:15, 16), "but it is Pauline to the core" (A. T. Robertson). It is "doubtless Pauline" (W. G. Kümmel, quoted by Lohse).

It may be well to append at this point a note on the relation between Colossians and Ephesians. There is a remarkable similarity between the two epistles both in language and thought. General to each are such ideas as reconciliation through the blood of Christ (Col. 1:20, 21; Eph. 2:13–16); believers as risen with Christ (Col. 3:1; Eph. 2:6); the old nature and the new (Col. 3:9, 10; Eph. 4:22–24); redeeming the time (Col. 4:5; Eph. 5:16); other similarities are noted throughout the exposition of the epistle. Colossians has, more especially with regard to our Lord's relation to the church, the complementary emphasis to that of Ephesians. In Colossians the apostle exalts Christ to the highest and supreme place in every realm. Among the "all things" over which he is supreme is the church of which he is head (1:18). In Ephesians Paul presents the church as great and glorious because of Christ, and thus called to an exalted mission and destiny in the eternal purpose of God in him. Paul's apparent purpose in Ephesians in emphasizing the glory of the church in Christ is to combat the same subtle heresy which had infected Colossae. "It was written," says H. C. G. Moule in his *Colossian Studies*, "to guard the Asian churches in general from the

Judaistic-philosophical errors against which he warns the Colossians in particular." This fact accounts in some measure for the striking similarity in the language of the two epistles. Thus, for example, in both Christ is spoken of as head of the church (Col. 1:18; Eph. 1:22), while the church is the body of Christ (Col. 1:24; Eph. 1:23). Of the 155 verses in Ephesians, 78 contain expressions which are echoed in Colossians.

THE ORIGIN OF THE PRODUCTION

The more general view of the origin of Colossians, and also the more credible, is that Paul wrote it in Rome during his imprisonment there. This is supported by the presence of Luke and Mark at the time of its writing (Col. 4:10, 14; cf. Acts 28:16; 2 Tim. 4:11). An Ephesian origin is, however, favored by Adolf Deissmann, G. S. Duncan, and some others (see Donald Guthrie, *New Testament Introduction: The Pauline Epistles*). But the arguments against this appear decisive. First, although Paul did encounter much conflict at Ephesus (cf. Acts 19:20; 1 Cor. 15:32; 2 Cor. 1:8–10), it is not stated that he was actually incarcerated in that city. And, second, it appears from Acts that neither Luke nor Mark was with the apostle during his Ephesian stay. Mark, after his earlier disagreement with Paul, had been taken by Barnabas away to Cyprus (cf. Acts 15:39). Luke does not include Paul's Ephesian period (cf. Acts 19:1–2) in the so-called "we" passages (cf. Acts 16:10–17; 20:5–21:18; 27:1–28:16) in which he suggests that he was with the apostle at those times.

Although Paul was imprisoned in Caesarea (cf. Acts 23:23, 35; 24:27), the contention of a few writers that it was from here that the letter was written is quite unlikely. It is surely more reasonable to assume that Onesimus, the runaway slave of Philemon, would have made for the capital, where he would have been less easily detected. And Paul's letter to Philemon, evidently carried by Tychicus who accompanied Onesimus to his old master at Colossae, has therefore been rightly associated with the Colossian epistle. Both are by the same hand and originate from the same place. It is, then, more in accord with all the facts as we know them to say that Colossians was written during Paul's two-year imprisonment at Rome alluded to in Acts 28:30 (cf. Col. 4:3, 10, 18). This will give us a date of about A.D. 60.

OUTLINE

Colossians

**PART ONE: CHRIST IN CHRISTIAN BELIEF
(1:1–3:4)**

I. INTRODUCTORY: THE TRUTH DECLARED (1:1–14)
  A. Presentation (1:1–2)
    1. An apostolic declaration of authority (1:1)
    2. An apostolic estimation of the believers (1:2a)
    3. An apostolic salutation for the church (1:2b)
  B. Praise (1:3–8)
    1. There is thanksgiving for their experience of the gospel (1:4–5)
    2. There is thanksgiving for the expansion of the gospel (1:6)
    3. There is thanksgiving for the evangelist of the gospel (1:7–8)
  C. Prayer (1:9–14)
    1. A prayer that centers on theology (1:9–11)
      a. Paul's habit of prayer (1:9a)
      b. Paul's requests in prayer (1:9b–11)
        (1) A deeper insight (1:9b)
        (2) A worthier walk (1:10a)
        (3) A fuller life (1:10b)
        (4) A growing knowledge (1:10c)
        (5) A greater strength (1:11)
    2. A prayer that climaxes in a doxology (1:12–14)
II. DOCTRINAL: THE TRUTH DEFINED (1:15–2:8)
  A. The Sovereignty of Christ Presented (1:15–20)
    1. The relationships of the Son (1:15–18)
      a. The Son in relation to Godhood (1:15a)
        (1) As the manifestation of God he makes the Invisible visible
        (2) As the representation of God he makes the visible intelligible
      b. The Son in relation to creation (1:15b–17)
      c. The Son's relation to the church (1:18)
    2. The reconciliation by the Son (1:19–20)

B. The Salvation through Christ Proclaimed (1:21–23)
C. The Servanthood of Christ Portrayed (1:24–2:8)
   1. Rejoicing in his suffering (1:24–25)
   2. Referring to his secret (1:26–27)
   3. Reflecting on his service (1:28–2:8)
     a. The general idea of the ministry (1:28–29)
     b. The specific concerns of the minister (2:1–8)
       (1) Admonition (2:1–3)
       (2) Warning (2:4–8)
         (a) Warning against heretical talkers (2:4–5)
         (b) Warning against spiritual immaturity (2:6–7)
         (c) Warning against false philosophy (2:8)
III. POLEMICAL: THE TRUTH DEFENDED (2:9–3:4)
A. The Statement of the Truth (2:9–15)
   1. The truth put positively (2:9–13)
     a. The theological error of the heretics refuted (2:9–10)
     b. The ceremonial error of the heretics refuted (2:11–13)
   2. The truth put negatively (2:14–15)
B. The Strength of the Truth (2:16–19)
   1. Submit not (2:16–17)
   2. Substitute not (2:18–19)
C. The Sweep of the Truth (2:20–3:4)
   1. Lessons from death with Christ (2:20–23)
   2. Lessons from life in Christ (3:1–4)

**PART TWO: CHRIST IN CHRISTIAN BEHAVIOR
(3:5–4:18)**

IV. HORTATORY: THE TRUTH DESIRED (3:5–4:1)
A. The Reconciled Life and the Self (3:5–11)
   1. Killing off the germs of evil (3:5–7)
     a. The charge (3:5a)
     b. The catalogue (3:5b)
     c. The considerations (3:6–7)
   2. Putting off the garments of evil (3:8–11)
B. The Reconciled Life and the Community (3:12–17)
   1. Robes from the Christian's wardrobe (3:12–14)
   2. Rules for the Christian's welfare (3:15–17)
     a. The ruling peace of Christ (3:15)
     b. The indwelling word of Christ (3:16)
     c. The all-hallowing name of Christ (3:17)
C. The Renewed Life and the Family (3:18–4:1)
   1. The relationship between wives and husbands (3:18–19)
     a. A word to wives (3:18)

COMMENTARY

Colossians

Part One:
Christ in Christian Belief
(1:1–3:4)

I. INTRODUCTORY: THE TRUTH DECLARED (1:1–14)

A. Presentation (1:1–2)

1. An apostolic declaration of authority (1:1)

Verse 1: Paul, an apostle of Jesus Christ by the will of God, and Timothy our brother: Not always does Paul urge his apostolic authority when he writes to a church (cf. 1 and 2 Thess., Phil. Philem.). But in the present instance he was writing to a company of believers to whom he was personally unknown (v. 4; 2:1). And he had particular need to stress his special commission as "a teacher of the Gentiles" (1 Tim. 2:7), in view of the heretical teaching which was threatening to rob Christ of his rightful place as head of the universe in nature and grace. It was imperative that the believers at Colossae heed the word of Christ's representative. For in and through Paul's words the risen and exalted Christ himself was addressing his people.

Thus, in the opening declaration Paul associated his apostleship with Jesus Christ. He is certainly Christ's apostle, but not of his own merit or choosing. He is what he is, and indeed where he is, by "the will of God." He will allude again to the divine will later (cf. v. 9; 4:12), but meanwhile such a consideration will give added solemnity to his words as God's selected spokesman. Paul finds in the will of God the source of his position in grace, as well as the secret of his success in service (cf. Acts 18:21; Rom. 1:10; 15:32; 1 Cor. 1:1; 4:19; 16:7; 2 Cor. 1:1; Gal. 1:4; Eph. 1:1; 2 Tim. 1:1). In his Galatian letter, Paul's apostolic authority was being questioned and he must boldly defend it. Here in his Colossian letter, Christ's sovereignty was being compromised, so Paul must assert himself as an apostle of Jesus Christ in order to bring the church back to the full acknowledgment of Christ's lordship. There is therefore no timidity or hesitancy in his letter. There is, rather, a holy boldness, an almost stark brusqueness both in the tone and the tempo of his writing. "Feebleness is the last charge which can be brought against this epistle" (Lightfoot). And if, as some think, the letter betrays a want of fluency, it has certainly no want of force.

But though Paul is exalted by reason of his office, he can still regard Timothy as "a brother." Paul had a high opinion of Timothy, whom he associates with himself in the opening address of 2 Corinthians (1:1) and Philippians (1:1), and with Silvanus in the letters to the Thessalonians (1:1; 2:1). Elsewhere Paul speaks of him as his "dear son" and "a most trustworthy Christian" (1 Cor. 4:17, NEB; cf. 1 Thess. 3:2; Phil. 2:19–20). At the same time, Timothy's position is distinguished from that of Paul. Paul alone is the apostle in the strict sense of the word, as one directly commissioned by the risen Lord (cf. Gal. 1 and 2). "By calling Timothy 'our brother,' Paul though *implying* that his younger associate was not in the full sense an apostle *was rather emphasizing* the closeness of his relationship between himself and his associate" (William Hendriksen). Paul and Timothy are one with those at Colossae who belong to Christ; but it is Paul "as the apostle of Jesus Christ commissioned by the will of God" (NEB) who addresses himself in Christ's name to God's people at Colossae (cf. 1:23; cf. 1:24–2:5; 4:3; 7–13).

2. An apostolic estimation of the believers (1:2a)

Verse 2a: To the saints and faithful brethren: Although the letter was sent to a Christian community at Colossae, the term *church* does not appear in the address as it does in the Thessalonian, Corinthian, and Galatian letters. Here Paul refers to the believers as *saints (hagioi;* cf. Rom. 1:7; Eph. 1:1; Phil. 1:1). But the two words do not indicate any difference of meaning (cf. 1 Cor. 1:2). Unfortunately, the designation *saints* was to become woefully misapplied both in the world and in the church. In the former the saints were regarded as the ascetics, and in the latter as the monastics. But in Paul's usage they are neither. To modern ears to speak of someone as a saint is misleading, "for the Hebrew and Greek words are concerned less with excellence of character (however much that may be implied as a *result*) than with the commitments and loyalties of the Church to the God who has made her his own" (C. F. D. Moule). The saints are those separated for and dedicated to God. The term therefore more properly designates the believers' standing in Christ rather than their present state as Christians. God sees the Christian as already holy in Christ.

However, the fact that Christians are declared holy in Christ does not mean that they should not be concerned with the attainment of personal holiness (cf. 1:22). For we are called upon to make our state like our standing, to make actual through Christ what we are potentially in Christ. "We are Christians as far as we give ourselves up to God, in the surrender of our wills and the practical obedience of our lives—so far and not one inch further. We are not merely bound to this consecration if we are Christians, but we are not Christians unless we thus consecrate ourselves" (Alexander Maclaren). All Christians then "must be saints; and if they come not under this character on earth they will never be saints in glory" (Matthew Henry). The term *saints* is, consequently, to be taken as another name for believers as the new Israel of God. The saints are "God's people" (1:2, NEB).

The saints are described as *faithful brethren,* for it is in faithfulness that saintliness is revealed (cf. Hab. 2:4; Rom. 1:17; Gal. 3:11; Heb. 10:38). It is the faithful who exercise faith; and the exercise of faith is the key to fidelity. They are not saints who are not faithful; indeed the saints are the faithful. The saints are faithful *brethren* because they are "incorporate in Christ" (NEB). The basis of sainthood is fellowship and community. We are born into God's kingdom one by one; but we come into a family, into the fellowship of the faithful, and into the community of believers. No one can be a saint on his own. The lone tree on the moor becomes bent and blasted by the wind and the weather. It is the tree in the forest that grows straight and tall; in togetherness it acquires toughness. And it is in togetherness that we are saints and faithful brethren. "The saints are faithful brethren, not by natural relation, but rather because they are joined together by God's act as members of one *familia Dei*" (Eduard Lohse). "Faith weaves the bond that unites men in the brotherhood of the Church, for it brings all who share it into a common relation to the Father" (Maclaren).

In Christ at Colossae: As in Ephesians, so here in Colossians, the phrase "in Christ" is constant. In this verse Paul uses the preposition *en* with the dative case to indicate the believers' relation both to Christ and to Colossae. The reason for the change in the translation from *in* with reference to *Christ* to *at* in reference to *Colossae* is then theological and not linguistic. It is right to read a different significance into the preposition of location to express the different relationships. Believers are *in Christ* by reason of a living, hidden unity; but they were "in Colossae" in a visible, temporary and almost accidental manner. Therefore the rendering *in Christ* and *at Colossae* may stand.

In the juxtaposition of these two statements, we have the key to the Christian's relation to the world. Every Christian has two homes; and he lives in both places at one and the same time. Of course he is *in Christ;* that makes him a Christian. But he is *at Colossae;* he has a residence in the here and now, a foothold on earth. Thus the believer has a heaven in which to breathe and an earth on which to live. Being *in Christ,* there the Christian, as an individual, lives and moves and has his being; and being *at Colossae,* there the Christian, as a human being, dwells and works and has his living. This fact of double environment carries with it a dual responsibility. Certainly the believer will acknowledge his responsibility to Christ. He will live as under the lordship of Christ. But he is also *at Colossae,* and as such he has obligations there. He must bother about his Colossae; as he accepts the rights of citizenship so must he accept its responsibilities. Yet he is *at Colossae* as one who is *in Christ.*

Difficulty often arises for the believer in relating the claims of both spheres. Sometimes there is a clash between Colossae and Christ, and the attractions of the one collide with the appeal of the other. Paul himself recognized his earthly citizenship as he realized his heavenly (cf. Acts 21:39; Phil. 3:20). He was not so otherworldly as to forget his connections with earth. The whole problem of Christian ethics lies here: to live as a heavenly citizen in an earthly situation; to effect an adjustment between being *in Christ* and *at Colossae* at one and the same time without compromising our position in either sphere. As the apostle wrote to the saints in Christ and at Colossae, he must have thought, "What a rich gain for poor Colossae that they, being in Him, were in it!" (H. C. G. Moule).

3. An apostolic salutation for the church (1:2b)

Verse 2b: Grace to you and peace: Apart from 1 Thessalonians (1:1), this is Paul's shortest opening salutation. But it is far from the merely conventional way of starting a letter. More is expressed in his words than by our "Dear So and So." In distinction from the common Greek greeting—*chairein* (cf. Acts. 15:23; 23:26)—Paul introduced his own special word *grace*—*charis*—to give to the union of the Greek (grace) and Hebrew (peace—*shalom*) form of salutation a deepened and ennobled content. As always, *grace* comes first in his thought. There is indeed "no richer word in the New Testament than 'grace' " (A. T. Robertson). Paul knew that all the blessings and bounties of God's new order derive from his sheer unmerited favor. Especially is grace the source of the *peace* which comes to the believing soul in Christ (cf. 3:15). It is by grace that peace, as the eschatological blessing of the new Israel, becomes a realized possession (cf. John 14:27; Phil. 4:7).

From God our Father: This is the divine source of all grace and peace. There is an exquisite tenderness in the word *Father* used of

God in the New Testament. In the context of this epistle it has an argumentative force. Those who were seeking to undermine the faith of the Colossians viewed God as remote, abstract, and unapproachable. In contrast, the word *Father* carries with it the sense of nearness, warmth, and intimacy.

In addition, the word *our* should be underscored. For Paul is here reminding his readers and himself of their immediate fellowship with God as Father. He has spoken of them as *brethren* in the previous verse; in this *our* he stresses the common faith and united bond which are theirs because of the peace which has come to them through the grace of God our Father. "Faith weaves the bond that unites men in the brotherhood of the Church, for it brings all men who share in it into a common relation to the Father" (Maclaren).

Paul knew well that "we enjoy peace with God and all the benefits which flow therefrom on the ground of His gracious action in Christ Jesus" (Martin); but strangely, the salutation omits any reference to Christ. This omission of his name at this point may be "in order by way of contrasting effect to single Him out for special discussion in the following verses" (Hendriksen). Certainly there is specific reference to "our Lord Jesus Christ" in Paul's immediate exposition (cf. vv. 3–7, 15–20). Since, therefore, the epistle is focused upon the unfolding of the uniqueness of Christ's person, it may be a mistake to search out theological reasons which might have led Paul to the shortening of the greeting formula (Lohse).

B. Praise (1:3–8)

Verse 3: We always thank God, the Father of our Lord Jesus Christ, when we pray for you: After Paul's greeting in the name of God, there comes his gratitude to God for the Colossians. Paul's prayers were always cradled in praise; his every supplication was shot through with jubilation. Although unknown to the Colossians personally, Paul prayed for them. And whenever he did, the note of thanksgiving was present and prior. His prayers were directed to God as the Father of our Lord Jesus Christ (cf. Rom. 15:6; 2 Cor. 1:3, 11, 31; Eph. 1:3; 3:14). This juxtaposition of God and the Lord Jesus Christ came as a reminder to the believers at Colossae of the close relation subsisting between them. There is no yawning hiatus, no unbridgeable distance, between God and Christ. It is "in Christ" that God is known as our Father; for the Father is uniquely the Father of the Lord Jesus Christ, and the Lord Jesus Christ is uniquely the Son of God (cf. v. 13; see Matt. 11:25–26). "Via Christ every spiritual blessing flows down to us from the Father" (Hendriksen). Paul's heart was glad with thanksgiving on several counts.

1. There is thanksgiving for their experience of the gospel (1:4–5)

Verse 4: Because we have heard of your faith in Christ Jesus: Evidently Epaphras, who had evangelized the area under Paul's direction, had brought news of how affairs stood with the Colossian believers. The news was good (here; cf. 2:6), and bad (cf. 2:8, Phillips). For the good news Paul will be thankful and pray on their behalf with gratitude. For the bad news he will be anxious and write on their account with concern. He expresses thanks to God because of the *faith* they "hold in Christ Jesus" (NEB). Christ had become the object, the region, and the goal of their faith. Paul's delight is that they have taken hold of Christ; his dread is that they will lose hold of him (cf. 2:19). But the fact of their *faith in Christ* is occasion for Paul's thanksgiving. "Faith in Christ stands at the head of the list for it is by faith that salvation is brought within the realm of human experience Rom. 5:1; Eph. 2:8" (Martin). "Let us hold fast this principle; in the theology of our spiritual life, let us put first faith—that is to say, Christ relied upon" (H. C. G. Moule).

And of the love which you have for all the saints: With faith goes *love,* for love is faith in expression (Gal. 5:6). "If faith is the soul's rest, love is the soul's resultant action" (H. C. G. Moule). The word *all* needs stressing. The Colossians included all the saints in their love. "We must love *all the saints,* bear an extensive kindness and good-will to good men, notwithstanding lesser points of difference, and many real weaknesses" (Henry). But such a love as this can only be by "the love of God shed abroad in our hearts" by the Holy Spirit (Rom. 5:5, KJV; cf. Col. 2:8). "As faith is the foundation of all virtue, so it is the parent of love, and as the former sums up every bond that knits men to God, so the latter includes all relations of men to each other, and is the whole law of human conduct packed into one word" (Maclaren).

Verse 5: Because of the hope laid up for you in heaven: Although the thought of *the hope laid up in heaven* was an added reason for Paul's thanksgiving to God on behalf of the Colossian believers, the main idea, according to the NEB rendering, is that both faith and love "spring from the hope stored up" for them in heaven. The hope is "stored up"; it is not locked up. It is out of physical sight but not out of spiritual reach. It is a wealth which can be cashed in in the experience of present living.

Such a hope is based on faith—on the faith that trusts God's promise in the assurance of his undying love (Rom. 5:5). "Faith provides a firm foundation for hope so that it strives forward and confidently awaits the fulfillment of what is anticipated. Hope already shapes the present through the disposition of hoping, for 'love hopes all things' " (Lohse). If, then, hope is based on faith, it is also the strength of love. Christian love "is the confidence that God's way of love 'has the last word,' " and as such it is not something stored away for a remote time to come, for "already it is the source of steadiness and of active concern for fellow-Christians. 'Hope', in this distinctively Christian sense is anything but a mere 'opiate of the people' or a mere prize 'in the sky' reserved only for the future." It is such a reality which is a "potent incentive to action here and now" (C. F. D. Moule).

At the same time the hope is "treasured" (Weymouth), that is to say, is *laid up . . . in heaven.* There it has its focus and its fulfillment. Where our treasure is there shall our heart be also (Matt. 6:20; Luke 12:34; 18:22). Christian hope reaches out beyond the present and finds its anchor in the eternal harbor of God's grace (cf. Col. 1:23, 27; Heb. 6:18,19). In this sense it may be said that faith rests on the past, love works in the present, and hope looks to the future. "Faith bases itself on the unique, eternally valid Christ-event, and confesses its binding power; love is active in the present in that it is extended to all saints. In a corresponding manner, hope is directed to the anticipated consummation" (Lohse).

Faith, love, hope—this intertwining trio of the pilgrim life of the believer is found in constant conjunction in the New Testament (cf. Rom. 5:1–5; Gal. 5:5–6; Eph. 4:2–5; Col. 1:4–5; 1 Thess. 1:3; 5:8; Heb. 6:10–12; 1 Pet. 1:3–8, 21–22). Hendriksen shows how they belong to the common stock of earlier Christianity, having an origin in the teaching of Jesus himself. "Again and again our Lord while on earth stressed the importance of faith (Matt. 6:30; 8:10, 26; 9:2, 22, 29; 14:31; 15:28; 16:8; 17:20; 21:21; 23:23, etc.). His very presence, words of cheer, bright and beautiful promises, deeds of redemption, inspired *hope* even when he did not use the very word (Matt. 9:2; 14:27; Mark 5:36; 6:50; 9:23; John 11:11, 23, 40; 1 Pet. 1:3, etc.). He placed emphasis on *love* and certainly regarded it as the very essence of both law and gospel, the greatest of the triad (Matt. 5:43–46; 19:19; John 13:34, 35; 14:15, 23; 15:12, 13, 17; 17:26; 21:15, 16, 17, etc.)."

Of this you have heard before in the word of the truth, the gospel: This assurance of hope apprehended by faith and working out in love the Colossians "learned when the message of the true Gospel first came" to them (NEB). Such a gospel was indeed the *word of the truth (toi logoi tēs alētheias),* in contrast with those false teachers whose message was an "empty deceit" and a "human tradition" (cf. 2:8). That is *the gospel,* the "good news" "so infinitely superior to all man-originated speculations, that 'authentic message of the skies' which in divine reality *(alētheia)* comes from above, instead of being

a mere echo of voices from below" (H. C. G. Moule). This *word of
. . . truth* is amplified in Ephesians 1:13 as "the gospel of your salvation." Such a gospel is a *word:* it is not idea but fact. It is divine
truth because it is the true word of him who is the very Truth of
God incarnate in historical actuality. To know him is to know the
truth, and to be in him is to be in the truth. "If we listen to Christ,
we have the truth; if we turn from him, our ears are stunned by a
Babel" (Maclaren).

2. There is thanksgiving for the expansion of the gospel (1:6)

*Verse 6: Which has come to you, as indeed in the whole world it
is bearing fruit and growing—so among yourselves:* For the apostle,
the Colossians were an illustration of the general success of the gospel. And his main thought is still thanksgiving for the blessings it has
brought to them. But everywhere the same gospel was fruitful and
growing. "More lurks under these words than appears on the surface. The true Gospel, the apostle seems to say, proclaims its truth
by its universality. The false gospels are the outgrowth of local circumstances, of special idiosyncrasies; the true Gospel is the same
everywhere" (Lightfoot). The true gospel wins and works; as it goes
it grows. The words *bearing fruit* and *growing,* echoing the language
of Mark 4:8; refer respectively to the inward energy and the outward
expansion of the gospel. "Wherever that gospel goes, it produces
Christian character, and develops it" (Phillips). The gospel is like a
plant whose "seed is in itself" (Gen. 1:11, KJV), but not one that
exhausts itself in fruit-bearing and just withers and dies. Rather, the
further the gospel extends in the world the more it enriches human
lives; its productive energy keeps pace with its external growth. The
middle voice* of the participle *bearing fruit—karpophoroumenon—*
may give special forcefulness to the verb, to convey the meaning
"fully bearing fruit." In the whole world, wherever it is heard and
believed, the gospel brings forth abundantly after its kind. And of
this fact the Colossians themselves were a signal evidence.

*From the day you heard and understood the grace of God in
truth.* The day the Colossians heard the good news was their happy
day—their day of salvation when they learned "the message of the
true Gospel" (v. 5, NEB), the gospel of grace. Once again Paul
comes back to his own "cant" words, as eighteenth-century theolo-

---

*The middle voice is peculiar to Greek, and is a form of the verb in which the sub-
ject is considered as taking part in the results of the action. For instance, ". . .
bouleuō [indicative] means *I counsel,* but *bouleuomai* [middle] means *I take counsel:*
the subject acting with a view to participation in the outcome. While the active voice
emphasizes the action, the middle stresses the agent. It, in some way, relates the action more intimately to the subject" (H. E. Dana and Julius R. Mantey, *A Manual
Grammar of the Greek New Testament,* New York, The Macmillan Company, 1949).

gian William Paley calls them. *Grace* as God's "radiant adequacy" was the very heart of his gospel. He has used the word already in the epistle (v. 2), and it will come again (cf. 3:16; 4:16, 18). From beginning to end Paul regarded the gospel as all of grace and grace for all. He read the whole life and work of Christ in terms of grace. And he saw nothing of God's saving word and deed which was not of grace. He thus equates "the gospel of your salvation" (Eph. 1:13, cf. Rom. 1:16) with "the gospel of the grace of God" (Acts 20:24).

Some read the phrase *in truth* as qualifying *the grace of God*—the grace of God "as it truly is" (C. F. D. Moule). Others take it in the adverbial sense of "truly" referring to the Colossians' hearing and understanding the gospel. But it seems preferable to take it as an adjectival phrase qualifying "word" and its synonym "gospel" (v. 5). *The grace of God* is the content of the gospel. *Grace* is the *"true"* word of the gospel, the one authentic gospel which had come to the Colossians (cf. 2 Cor. 6:7). Paul needed to emphasize that the message the Colossians heard and received was indeed the correct teaching, in view of the speculations of the false teachers. This true gospel of God's grace was the message they had heard from Epaphras with the hearing of faith and had understood with the wisdom of faith. They had mixed the word with faith to the salvation of their souls (cf. Heb. 4:2). When the true gospel came to them, they heard it and acknowledged it as God's truth. "Such acknowledgement is more than mere abstract intellectual knowledge. It is a joyful acceptance and appropriation of the truth centered in Christ. This truth concerns nothing less than the grace of God, his sovereign love in action, his favour towards the undeserving" (Hendriksen).

3. There is thanksgiving for the evangelist of the gospel (1:7–8)

Verse 7: As you learned it from Epaphras our beloved fellow servant. He is a faithful minister of Christ on our behalf: It was Epaphras who brought the gospel to Colossae as Paul's representative. And Paul gathers him up in his thanksgiving to God, for both the work he did and the good news he brought. To Paul he was a *beloved fellow servant*—"in the sacred slavery of the Lord" (H. C. G. Moule). To be a servant of Jesus Christ (cf. Gal. 1:10; Rom. 1:1; Phil. 1:1) was for the apostle the highest of all honors. He was God's chosen man sent in his service by divine commissioning. As the servant of Christ he was the recipient of his Master's secrets. "Whom God has made his servant may not declare his own thoughts and opinions, but must faithfully repeat the message entrusted to him" (Lohse). Epaphras is not only one with Paul in the same service, he is also described as *a faithful minister of Christ*. To this consistency, both his service and his supplication on behalf of the Colossians give firsthand evidence. "He works hard . . . for he prays constantly and earnestly for you" (4:12, Phillips). Nor did Epaphras avoid suffering for the Master's sake (Philem. 23). Paul's thanksgiving flowed over to include Epaphras for his own worth and work. Paul found it "an endearing consideration" that they were "in the same service" (Henry). But Paul was especially glad at the news Epaphras brought about the way the gospel was bearing fruit at Colossae.

Verse 8: And has made known to us your love in the Spirit: These words refer back to v. 4b. More is needed to love all the saints than human good will. Such a love must surely be "God-given" (v. 8, NEB). Some commentators have taken the words "in Spirit"—there is no article in the Greek—in an adjectival sense to qualify love. They then speak of the "spiritual love," or "Christian love" (Phillips) which was manifested among the Colossians. C. F. D. Moule considers this more general sense to be preferred and gives the meaning to be "your more than human love," "your spiritual, supernaturally derived love." But such a spiritual, supernatural love can only be of the Holy Spirit. It is "the mutual love implanted and fostered in their hearts by the Holy Spirit who dwelt within them and united them in a living bond" (F. F. Bruce).

The absence of reference to the Holy Spirit is a notable feature in the Epistle to the Colossians. If the Holy Spirit is in the apostle's mind at this point, then this is the only mention of him throughout. It would certainly not be uncharacteristic of Paul to allude to the third person of the Trinity after making mention of the Father (vv. 2, 3) and of Christ Jesus the Son (vv. 3, 4, 7; see Rom. 8:1–2; 2 Cor. 13:14; Eph. 1:3–4; 2:18; 3:14–15; 4:4–6; 5:18–19; cf. 1 Pet. 1:2–3). It is Paul's inspired intention in this epistle to exalt Christ as Lord, and no one can call Jesus Lord in the full Christian sense except by the Holy Spirit. (1 Cor. 12:3). We may well understand that the Spirit did not allow himself to obtrude into the picture. For the Spirit does not glorify himself but the one who is set forth as alone the world's Lord and Redeemer.

C. Prayer (1:9–14)

1. A prayer that centers on theology (1:9–11)

The burden of Paul's prayer is that the Colossians may know God—that they may indeed all be theologians. Not that they should have mere abstract ideas about the deity, or profess to some occult notions or secret gnosis which the heretics claimed. Rather that they should have that knowledge of the heart, that true knowledge of God which is essential for living. His prayer is that their knowledge of God may be experimental theology.

a. Paul's habit of prayer (1:9a)

Verse 9a: And so, from the day we heard of it, we have not ceased to pray for you: There is something compelling about the fact that Paul prayed. His prayers for his brethren were always large and profound. In fact in "some respects these are the very topmost pinnacles of his letters. Nowhere else does his spirit move so freely, in no other parts are the fervour of his piety and the beautiful simplicity and depth of his love more touchingly shown" (Maclaren). Paul took every occasion and opportunity for prayer. News about the Colossians induced him to remember them in "a love-prompted prayer" (H. C. G. Moule). But not only was Paul constant in his prayers, he was always definite. His requests "go to the heart of the soul's needs" (A. T. Robertson).

Paul has already thanked God that the Colossians had heard and understood the grace of God in truth. Now he prays that they may be filled with the knowledge of God's will in all spiritual wisdom and understanding. He has thanked God that the gospel bore fruit and was growing among them. He now prays that they may bear fruit in every good work and may increase in the knowledge of God. "On the basis of blessings already received the apostle asks for additional favours. Encouraged by evidences of God's grace already present he requests increasing proof" (Hendriksen). The apostle has "heard that they were good, and he prays that they might be better" (Henry).

b. Paul's requests in prayer (1:9b–11)

(1) A deeper insight (1:9b)

Verse 9b: Asking that you may be filled with the knowledge of his will in all spiritual wisdom and understanding: As Paul comes to his specific request, he may have had the words of Christ in his mind—"whatever you ask in prayer, believe that you receive it, and you will" (Mark 11:24). Paul has much to ask for the Colossians: that they might be *filled* with *all* (cf. Eph. 3:20). He has large requests to make of God—but then Paul has large views of God. It is our conception of God which conditions our asking. "The Lord does not want his people to ask for too little. In the *spiritual* sphere he does not want them to live frugally, parsimoniously. Let them live richly and royally in harmony with Psalm 81:1!" (Hendriksen). Paul's desire for the Colossians is that they may be filled with the *knowledge* of God's will. The apostle uses the strong word *epignōsis* to denote "a larger and more thorough knowledge" (Lightfoot) than the *gnōsis* boasted of by the false teachers (cf. Col. 1:10; 3:10). Paul wanted believers to possess this higher knowledge of God which is not

theoretical or speculative but is a knowledge born of a personal relationship between God and his people. "True knowledge is founded
in practical religion; it is that knowledge which, according to the OT,
starts with a proper attitude towards God: 'the fear of the Lord is
the beginning of knowledge' Prov. 1:7; cf. Ps. 111:10; Prov. 9:10.
Right knowledge, according to Paul, leads to right behaviour; and
right knowledge is contrasted with wrong behaviour" (Bruce). Such
a knowledge of God shows itself in the "passion for obedience" (P.
T. Forsyth). For "the will of God demands an obedience that is visible in one's actions" (Lohse). Such a knowledge consists in "all
wisdom [*sophia*] and spiritual understanding [*phronēsis*]" (KJV), or
better, "insight." Though the qualifying word *spiritual* in the Greek
follows *understanding,* it should be joined to both terms, as the RSV
so translates. For such spiritual wisdom and spiritual insight are not
the result of human achievement; they are gifts of the Holy Spirit.
The false teachers spoke of *their* wisdom and *their* insight, but they
were merely earthly and sensual. "The true antidote to the haunting
and perilous myths was simply to understand Christ better" (R. D.
Shaw). In him are hidden all the treasures of wisdom and knowledge
(cf. 2:3). Such indeed is the desire of Paul for the Colossian believers, that they may receive from God "all wisdom and spiritual understanding for full insight into his will" (NEB).

(2) A worthier walk (1:10a)

Verse 10a: To lead a life worthy of the Lord, fully pleasing to him:
Paul uses the infinitive of purpose to indicate the practical result that
should follow a life filled with the knowledge of God's will. Such a
life—and he continues to pray for the Colossians that it may be
so—should exhibit the type of behavior totally pleasing to God.
"Good knowledge without a good life, will not profit" (Henry). Paul
is requesting of God that the believers' "walk" (KJV) should conform
to their knowledge, indeed, that the two should develop together.
The word translated "walk" in the KJV is a common Pauline one for
the Christian's "manner of life" (NEB; cf. 2:6; 3:7; 4:5; see also
Rom. 6:4; 8:1; 13:13; 14:15; 1 Cor. 3:3; 7:17, etc.). The manner of life
is to be fully acceptable to God. This is the only place where Paul
uses the term *pleasing—areskeia—*without any strengthening prefix.
His usual word is *euarestos,* "well-pleasing" (cf. Rom. 12:2; 2 Cor.
5:9; Eph. 5:10; Col. 3:20; 1 Thess. 4:1). Here, however, the idea is
reinforced by *eis pasan—fully* (RSV), "all" (KJV), "entirely" (NEB);
giving pleasure "in all ways" (Lightfoot). The aim and the goal of
Christian living is to please God and thus to "bring credit to your
master's name" (Phillips). "Since this applies to *all* areas of life, the
words are "towards *all* good pleasure," for everything depends on

pleasing God (Rom. 8:8) or to be pleasing to him (2 Cor. 5:8)"
(Lohse). The God-pleasers commended here may be contrasted with
the man-pleasers condemned in 3:22.

(3) A fuller life (1:10b)

Verse 10b: Bearing fruit in every good work: The figure of the
growing tree (cf. v. 6) is used again, but here in relation to the specific Christian life of the Colossian believers. Spiritual intelligence
should lead to greater likeness to Christ, and that to further fruitfulness. In their former life the Colossians revealed the lack of a true
knowledge of God by reason of their "evil deeds" (1:21; cf. 3:7).
Now Paul continues his prayer that *every good work* consonant with
their present knowledge of God might be manifest. The apostle has
much to say about good works as the proof of fruit of the renewed
life. In Ephesians he insists that for those created anew in Christ,
good works are God's prearranged course in which they must walk
(cf. Eph. 2:10; cf. 1 Tim. 2:10; 5:10; 2 Tim. 3:17, etc.). "The only
sort of work which can be called fruit, in the highest meaning of the
word, is that which corresponds to a man's whole nature and relations; and the only work which does so correspond is a life of loving
service of God, which cultivates all things lovely and of good re-
port." "Goodness is fruit; all else is nothing but leaves" (Maclaren).

(4) A growing knowledge (1:10c)

Verse 10c: And increasing in the knowledge of God: The apostle
has made the knowledge of God the launching pad for his prayer in
verse 9; he now sees it as a "resulting characteristic" (Hendriksen)
of the life well-pleasing to God. His prayer is therefore for the Colossians that they may have "a steady growth in fuller knowledge of
God" (Williams). This paradox of spiritual knowledge is characteristic of Christian faith. Thus Paul can say with confidence, "I know
whom I have believed" (2 Tim. 1:12) and yet express the desire
"that I may know him" (Phil. 3:10). Some would take the *knowledge*
referred to here as the instrument of growth. But it seems better to
take *in . . . knowledge* as the region and realm in which the growth
is to be realized. Certainly knowledge of God makes for fruitfulness
in good works. Yet the converse is also true: fruitfulness in good
works can become the occasion for development in the knowledge of
God. "Moral truth becomes dim to a bad man. Religious truth grows
bright to a good man, and whosoever strives to bring all his creed
into practice, and all his practice under the guidance of his creed,
will find that the path of obedience is the path of growing light"
(Maclaren).

(5) A greater strength **(1:11)**

Verse 11: May you be strengthened with all power, according to his glorious might, for all endurance and patience with joy: It is Paul's sincere petition that the Colossians may be "empowered by all power" "in virtue of the power which belongs to God as he has revealed himself to men" (C. F. D. Moule, Lightfoot; cf. Phil. 4:13; 2 Tim. 4:17; see Eph. 6:10; Heb. 11:34). The participle translated *may you be strengthened* is present tense, thus denoting that the empowering is continuous, and "on the scale of the resources of His manifested Nature" (H. C. G. Moule). This divine empowering will fortify the believer against evil and fit him for service by his being made strong with the might of God's Spirit in the inward man (cf. Eph. 3:16). The word translated *might—pratos—*is referred solely to God in the New Testament (cf. Acts 19:20; 1 Pet. 5:6), unlike the more common terms *power (dunamis)* and *strength (ischus).* So God's power is measured according to the might of his glory. "The communications of strength are not according to *our* weakness, to whom the strength is communicated, but according to *his* power, from whom it is received. When God gives, he gives like himself; and when he strengthens, he strengthens like himself" (Henry). It is not our need which conditions the measure of God's supply, but the divine boundlessness of his grace and goodness. Power and glory are often associated in the New Testament in doxologies, but here they come together in an apostolic prayer for believers.

This strengthening by the might of God's glory will assure Christian *endurance* and *patience* in all circumstances and in all ways. The word *endurance—hupomonē* ("fortitude," NEB)—is usually rendered "patience" in the KJV (cf. Luke 8:15; 21:19; Rom 5:3; 8:25; 15:4, 5; 2 Cor. 6:4; 12:12; Col. 1:11, etc.). The basic idea is that of perseverance even when times are not congenial: "steering straight onward when there is not a jot of hope" (A. T. Robertson). The one who has been strengthened by God's might to endure will hold on, though the enemy may concentrate attacks on him, and even when he suffers as a consequence (2 Cor. 1:6). He will carry on in the assurance that God will not fail to fulfill his promises (Rom. 8:25; 15:4).

But while endurance will prove a defense against the opposition from without, *patience* will govern the believer's relationship with others. The word is *makrothumia* and is translated as "longsuffering" in the KJV. If the word is read with the emphasis put on the prefix *long,* the quality which the apostle wishes to convey is clear. We are to put up with and bear with others even when they are cynical or hostile. Such longsuffering is a godlike attribute (Rom. 2:4;

4:22; 1 Tim. 1:16), and thus deserves a place in Paul's hymn in praise of love (1 Cor. 13:4). Christians, then, are to "put on patience" or "longsuffering" (Col. 3:12). They can do so through the Holy Spirit—this quality is one in the cluster of the fruit of the Spirit (Gal. 5:22; cf. 2 Cor. 6:6). "Thus the words 'endurance' and 'patience' together are sure signs of the loyal Christian, for he is not swayed from his hope by any power, nor does he weary in love" (Lohse).

Paul wants to see endurance and patience revealed *with joy*. There is to be no hard-faced, stoical, grin-and-bear-it attitude. Rather the apostle wants the believers buoyant in their battling, and triumphant in their trials. "Jesus is joy" may smack today of a cheap and easy hedonistic gospel where the challenge is not great and the cost is not exacting. But in Paul's day, and for these Colossian Christians, it was otherwise. They suffered; yet they are counseled to sing (cf. Hab. 3:17–18). In their every condition and circumstance God could be their exceeding joy (cf. Ps. 43:4), for in such joy is strength found (Neh. 8:10). It is Christ's own promise that his joy will not be withheld (John 17:13; cf. 16:22, 24), and the gospel itself was announced as "good tidings of great joy" (Luke 2:10, KJV). Joy in the midst of trial (James 1:2; cf. Heb. 12:2) is possible through God (Rom. 15:13) by the Holy Spirit (Rom. 14:17).

2. A prayer that climaxes in a doxology (1:12–14)

Verse 12: Giving thanks to the Father: Some writers (Hendriksen, Lohse) take the words of the previous verse, "with joy," as the opening of verse 12 and read "with joy giving thanks. . . ." Lohse does so because he regards the whole passage from verse 12 to verse 20 as a Christian hymn incorporated by the apostle at this point. He comments, "The sound of joy ought to open the singing of this hymn." And indeed it ought. But I am not convinced either that the phrase "with joy" should be attached to verse 12, or that the whole passage bears the stamp of a communion or baptismal hymn already known to the believers as a summary of the redemption which had come to them in Christ Jesus.

I take the words of verses 12–14, then, as Paul's continuing prayer for the Colossians that they might be led to further thanksgiving to God for the saving blessings of the gospel. As the apostle prays for them, there wells up from his own heart renewed thanksgiving as he recalls that he is a sharer with them in "the grace of God in truth" (v. 6). "The opening words [of v. 12] are connected with what has gone before and form part of the apostle's prayer. The participle 'giving thanks' may possibly carry a special overtone and lead us to expect a 'Thanksgiving prayer' in the verses which follow" (Martin).

The duty of thankfulness is an apostolic appeal (cf. Rom. 14:6; Eph. 5:2; 1 Thess. 5:18). It is one that the apostle himself constantly exemplified (cf. Acts 28:15; Rom. 1:8; 1 Cor. 1:4; Eph. 1:16; Phil. 1:3; 1 Thess. 1:2; 2:13; 2 Thess. 1:2; 2:13). The Colossians are to be "abounding" therein (2:7), and to be "persistent . . . and wide awake" when they give thanks (4:2, Goodspeed; cf. Phil. 4:6). Such thankfulness should flow over into every facet and factor of Christian living. "Thanksgiving should mingle with all our thoughts and feelings, like the fragrance of some perfume penetrating through the common scentless air. It should embrace all events. It should be an operating motive of all actions" (Maclaren). Paul's usual word for "to give thanks" is *eucharisteō,* but in the Corinthian letters he also uses the word *charis,* "grace," in the sense of thanks (cf. 1 Cor. 15:57; 2 Cor. 2:14; 8:16; cf. Luke 6:32, 33, 34). Between grace and thanksgiving there is a vital connection. It is a grace to be thankful; and it is because of grace that we can be. "In Christianity, someone has said, theology is grace, and ethics is gratitude. If God's attitude and action towards us have been characterised by grace, our response to Him, in life and behaviour as well as in thought and word, should be characterised by gratitude" (Bruce). They "in whom the work of grace is wrought must give thanks unto the Father" (Henry).

Here, as in 1:13 and 3:17, Paul's thanks is directed to the Father. What follows in Paul's climactic prayer "is the summary of the doctrine of the gospel concerning the great work of our redemption by Christ. It comes in here not as a matter of a sermon, but as the matter of a thanksgiving: for our salvation by Christ furnishes us with abundant matter of thanksgiving in every view of it" (Henry). It is the Father who "in Christ" has bestowed his grace on us.

Who has qualified us to share in the inheritance of the saints in light: The word rendered *has qualified—hikanōsanti—*has the sense of "being made fit or competent," with adequate power to perform what is required (cf. 2 Cor. 3:6). By the grace of God believers have been fitted to share in the inheritance Christ has secured for them. The inheritance of Canaan and the allotment of the promised land give Paul the analogy. Through God's glorious power the new Israel has been awarded the "share [of] the lot of God's people in the realm of light" (Goodspeed, cf. 3:24). "Just as in the old dispensation the Lord provided for Israel an earthly inheritance which was distributed to the various tribes and smaller units of national life *by lot* (Gen. 31:14; Num. 18:20; Josh. 13:16; 14:2; 16:1, etc.), so he has provided for the Colossians *an allotment* or *share* in the better inheritance" (Hendriksen). Such an inheritance is God's gift by grace (Acts. 2:23; Gal. 3:18; cf. 1 Pet. 1:14). In Christ, then, we are "fit for the inheritance"—made fit "if we have ever so humbly and poorly trusted ourselves to Jesus Christ and received His renewing life into our spirits" (Maclaren).

Verse 13: He has delivered us from the dominion of darkness and transferred us to the kingdom of his beloved Son: By the grace and power of God in Christ we have been "rescued" (NEB)—*errusato*—from the thraldom of darkness. It is because of this deliverance that believers are assured of their inheritance in the kingdom of God's Son. "He has not only told us that we have a title to our Canaan; He has carried us across the border" (H. C. G. Moule). By reason of the darkness, man has lost his way (cf. John 12:35; cf. 1 John 2:11), is subject to evil powers (Eph. 6:12; cf. Luke 22:53), and is the producer of unfruitful works (Eph. 5:11). The power—*exousia*—of the darkness is arbitrary and tyrannical in contrast with the well-ordered sovereignty of God's kingdom. As a citizen by nature of the dominion of darkness, man is subject to death, and is under the wrath of God. But from both these effects of darkness Jesus has come to rescue us (Rom. 7:24, 25; cf. 2 Cor. 1:10; 1 Thess. 1:10). The phrase "jurisdiction" or *dominion of darkness* echoes the statement in Luke 22:53. Behind the hostility of the Pharisees and rulers stood the supernatural forces of Satan. That was the brief hour of their dark display; but it ended in their final defeat.

In our passage Paul has the teaching of the false innovators in view, "for those very guardians, 'the world-rulers of this darkness' as they are called in Eph. 6:10, are the principalities and powers to which the Christians of Colossae were being urged to pay some meed of homage" (Bruce). But no longer should they do so. For in the victory of the Son of God they have been rescued from the realm of evil and transferred into his eternal kingdom. The word *darkness* contrasts with the light of the previous verse: "in the contrast to the darkness which rules the godless world, the light is truth, redemption, salvation and the nearness of God" (Lohse). We who once were very darkness itself (Eph. 5:8) have come into the light of God (1 John 1:5; cf. Matt. 4:16; Luke 1:79; 2:32; John 1:4–9; 1 Thess. 5:5; 1 Pet. 2:9, etc.). "For it is the God who said, 'Let light shine out of darkness,' who has shone in our hearts to give the light of the knowledge of the glory of God in the face of Christ" (2 Cor. 4:6).

Into the kingdom of God's Son we have been *transferred.* The word—*methistēmi*—occurs here only in the Pauline letters, and twice in the Epistle to the Hebrews (11:5) in connection with the translation of Enoch. The verb is used in classical Greek for the removal of whole groups of men to make colonies or in military conquests (A. T. Robertson). "Much like a mighty king who is able to remove whole peoples from their ancestral homes and to transplant them to another realm, so God is described as taking the community from the power of darkness and transferring it 'to the dominion of the rule of his beloved Son' " (Lohse). The idea of many people being rescued links up with what the apostle has to say in verse 6. The kingdom of God's beloved Son is his rule here and now in the hearts of men, but fulfilled and finalized when he will come again to reign as Lord everlastingly (cf. 1 Thess. 2:12; Gal. 5:21; 1 Cor. 6:9–10; 15:20; 2 Thess. 1:5; see 1 Cor. 4:20; Rom. 14:17; Col. 4:11). Then shall those who have been qualified to share in the inheritance of the saints in light have in full measure their place in the kingdom of Christ and of God (Eph. 5:5). Meanwhile, by "an anticipation which is a real experience and not a legal fiction they have received here and now the glory that is yet to be revealed. The 'inheritance of the saints in light' has not yet been manifested in its infinite wealth, but the divine act by which believers have been rendered meet for it has already taken place" (Bruce).

The kingdom has, then, its twofold aspect as something realized in the present, and as a reality of the future. The apostle appears to use the phrase "the kingdom of God" for the future consummation while reserving "the kingdom of Christ" for its present phase (cf. 1 Cor. 15:24).

Verse 14: In whom we have redemption, the forgiveness of sins: Paul's thanksgiving is focused upon redemption: on the sphere of it, *in whom;* on the sureness of it, *we have;* and on the substance of it, *the forgiveness of sins.*

*Redemption—apolutrōsis—*in its simplest meaning is the act of delivering a slave from captivity by the payment of a ransom. It is to be brought back and bought back to God—a deliverance from the imprisonment and bondage of sin. Such a redemption ("release," NEB) has already been effected by Christ in the deed of the cross (cf. 1 Cor. 1:30; cf. Rom. 3:24; Gal. 3:13; 4:5; Eph. 1:7; Rev. 5:9). This redemption is to be enjoyed here and now as a present possession (here; Eph. 1:7). The verb *we have* is in the present tense, for Paul contemplates the redemption as a moment-by-moment and growing experience. It is something "we are having" as a continual communication from him with whom the believer is united by faith. The believer's redemption will be completed at the day of Christ (Eph. 1:14; 4:30; cf. Rom. 8:23). Such a redemption "is grounded in Christ, the Son of the Father's love; and it is actualized in individual experience in the consciousness of forgiveness" (Gross Alexander). Here is a "message which goes straight to the primary need of sinners" (H. C. G. Moule). Forgiveness is man's deepest and realest need. And this is what is assured in the redemption accomplished in Christ and proffered to faith's response. Paul's word for *forgiveness* means literally a "sending away" (cf. Rom. 4:7 quoting Ps. 32:1 which is the only other use of the word). "Pardon has a mighty power to banish sin, not only as guilt, but as a habit" (Maclaren). Yet Paul speaks of the forgiveness of sins only here and in the parallel passage of Ephesians 1:7. He does, however, use such ideas as justification to embrace all that is meant by forgiveness and to include other blessings besides derived from Christ's work.

According to the manuscript evidence, there is no explicit statement of the ransom price here. Other passages, however, make clear to us that it was nothing other or less than "the blood of Christ" (cf. Eph. 1:7; see Rom. 3:24–25). Yet here the redemption is assured to us "in Christ" the Son of God's love. "So that it contains in its application to the effect of Christ's death, substantially the same figure as in the previous clause which spoke of a deliverance from a tyrant, only that what we there represented as an act of Power is here set forth as the act of self-sacrificing Love which purchases our freedom at a heavy cost" (Maclaren). For the very idea of redemption carries with it that of a ransom paid.

II. DOCTRINAL: THE TRUTH DEFINED (1:15–2:8)

A. The Sovereignty of Christ Presented (1:15–20)

At this point in his letter Paul's thanksgiving prayer on behalf of the Colossian Christians merges into a magnificent presentation of Christ as Lord and Mediator of the universe in nature and grace. The word *merges* is used advisedly because there is no formal conclusion to the prayer. "It closes by rising without a break into the utterance of a wonderful *Credo,* a worshipping and enraptured confession of the glory of the Christ of God, whose Person has filled the last phrases of the prayer" (H. C. G. Moule). To be sure, the passage is "written with a definitely doctrinal purpose," but it is dogmatics born of doxology. Paul's greatest theological declarations had passed through his own glowing heart, and his profoundest christological data were shaped by his own worshiping spirit. It is thus that in this section we have "one of the great Christological passages of the NT, declaring as it does our Lord's divine essence, preexistence, and creative agency" (Bruce). Christ is set forth as at once the divine agent of all creation and the divine head of the church.

Earlier commentators have been almost unanimous in regarding the passage as Paul's own composition. They have seen a logical and theological connection and cogency in the apostle's thought as he moves from a consideration of the work of Christ realized in the lives of the Colossian believers to a proclamation of Christ as absolute Lord in view of the evident depreciation of him by the false teachers. Thus the forty-six words of the epistle not used elsewhere by Paul, and the eleven words used by no other writer of the New Testament, were usually explained as being connected with the heresy either as a summary or a refutation of its ideas. In contrast with the narrow intellectualism of the false teachers, Paul has a universal *gnosis* or knowledge. He exposed their error by a richer and fuller presentation of Christ, who is the wisdom of God, the firstborn of all creation. "As when the full moon rises, so when Christ ap-

pears, all the lesser stars with which Alexandrian and Eastern speculation had peopled the abysses of the sky are lost in the mellow
radiance, and instead of a crowd of flickering ineffectual lights there
is one perfect orb, 'and heaven is overflowed.' 'We see no *creature*
any more save Jesus only' '' (Maclaren).

Several recent writers on the epistle, however, maintain that the
passage before us had a prior existence as a christological poem in
honor of Christ (e.g. Bruce, Martin, Lohse). The hymn is said to
have been well known to Christians in Asia Minor, and the author of
Colossians took it as the point of departure for his argumentation
(Lohse). It is declared to be one of the firmest conclusions of modern New Testament study that some of the key passages dealing
with the person and work of Jesus Christ are in the form of early
Christian hymns, of which Philippians 2:6–11, John 1:1–18, and Hebrews 1:2–4 are adduced as examples (Martin, Bruce). If not then
original with Paul himself, this section of Colossians is to be seen as
part of the primitive Christian teaching "received" by the apostle
(Bruce).

The reasons advanced for this contention are mainly three. First is
the view that the verses display a rhythmic style appropriate to a
poem. Second is the observation that the section contains words
either peculiar to it or used in a special sense which seems to pre-
clude its Pauline authorship. Third is the suggestion that unlike the
verses which precede and follow, this passage does not refer directly
to the particular experience of the Colossians.

Scholars have concluded, then, that Paul's thinking of the transforming effect of Christ's work in the hearts of the believers at Colossae (1:3–14) led on naturally to his recall of a well-known hymn in
praise of such a Redeemer. Not all commentators, however, are
convinced that the considerations which have led some to adopt the
hypothesis of an earlier poem in praise of Christ, are conclusive.
The question of the conditions and influences under which the
suggested hymn is thought to have been composed need not concern
us here. It almost seems, in fact, that the advocates of one view re-
fute conclusively that of the others. But all in all, it is doubtful if the
difficulties raised by the passage, whether linguistic or logical, "warrant the conjecture of interpolation" (C. F. D. Moule). So impressed, indeed, are some by the essential Paulinity of the verses
that, while acknowledging its hymnological structure, they have advanced the thesis that it must be an earlier composition by the apostle himself.

If, however, the section is to be accepted as an early hymn of the
church in honor of Christ, this would put Paul's so-called "higher
Christology" right back into the context of the primitive church,

thus nullifying the contention of those who maintain that his christology is either different from, or an advancement on, earlier simple
ideas. Should it then be inquired how the early church came so
unanimously to speak of her Lord in such exalted terms, the answer
must surely be sought in Christ's own teaching.

Throughout the passage, Christ is portrayed in a relationship of
absolute supremacy over the whole universe as God's natural creation (vv. 15–17), and over the church as God's new moral order (v.
18). In verses 19 and 20 these two spheres are combined, and this
double sovereignty of Christ is amplified by the absolute indwelling
in him of the Divine fullness. It is in the light of this fact that all
things are declared to be reconciled and harmonized in him.

1. The relationships of the Son (1:15–18)

a. The Son in relation to Godhood (1:15a)

Verse 15a: He is the image of the invisible God: The context
makes clear that it is Jesus Christ, God's "beloved Son" (v. 13) who
is the *image* of the unseen God. Among his many usages of the term
image, Plato speaks of it as heavenly wisdom. He sees the world itself as a great god, but at the same time "an image of Him who is
greater." Such an image is indeed wisdom. The term *image* carried
with it an idea of a divine revelation, and as such was taken over by
Hellenistic Judaism to refer to "Wisdom," as a personification. In
the famous passage in Proverbs 8 (vv. 22–36), "the celestial and
pure Wisdom" (Philo) is presented as more than a mere personification, although not distinctly a person.

Philo also speaks of the *image* in terms of the Logos, the Word.
For him the Logos is described as God's "image and His agent in
creation" (Martin). The image and wisdom are identified; for "wisdom" is the "image" and "vision of God." Both "wisdom" and
"Logos" are the perfect way which leads to God.

But for Paul the Wisdom and the Word are one in Jesus Christ,
the Son of God's love. As such he is the true *image* of God. He is,
that is to say, "the perfect likeness of God, whereas carved images,
abhorred by the Jews, are blasphemous counterfeits" (C. F. D.
Moule). Man was created in God's own image (Gen. 1:26–27), but
that image became defaced by man's sin. In Christ, however, there
is no defacement of the image of Godhood, for he is "the very image
of God" (2 Cor. 4:4, NEB). "He is so the Image of God, as the Son
is the image of his Father, who has a *natural* likeness to him; and he
who has seen him, has seen the Father, his glory was the glory of
the only begotten of the Father, John 1:14; 14:9" (Henry). In his
face shines unclouded and undimmed "the light of the knowledge of
the glory of God" (2 Cor. 4:6). In him is no darkness at all. He is

God's very "character" thrown on the screen of human existence. "He reflects the glory of God and bears the very stamp [*charaktēr*] of his nature" (Heb. 1:3; cf. Phil. 2:6). His nature is, therefore, Godhood in the very depths of his being. He is not just the godlike man, but is truly the God-man. In him we see God clearly and receive God fully. As God's image he manifests God clearly and represents God fully.

(1) As the manifestation of God he makes the Invisible visible.

"No one has ever seen God" (John 1:18; cf. 1 Tim. 1:17; Heb. 11:27). Yet to speak of him as the image of God unseen, "What is this but to say that the very nature and being of God have been perfectly revealed in Him—that in Him the invisible has become visible?" (Bruce).

(2) As the representation of God he makes the visible intelligible.

In Christ, the image of God, not only is God seen but he is also declared. "God's only Son, he who is nearest to the Father's heart . . . has made him known" (John 1:18, NEB). Christ is this God "for us"; God speaking to us; God present in the here and now. Against the airy and visionary speculations of the false teachers, Paul sets forth Christ as a real, actual figure who had an existence in "bodily" form on the stage of human history (cf. 2:9). "All the great streams of teaching in the New Testament concur in the truth which Paul here proclaims. The conception in John's Gospel of the Word which is the utterance and making audible of the Divine mind, the conception in the Epistle to the Hebrews of the effulgence or forthshining of God's glory, and the very image, or stamped impress of His substance, are but other modes of representing the same facts of full likeness and complete manifestation which Paul here asserts by calling the man Christ Jesus, the image of the Invisible God" (Maclaren).

In Christ, then, the Invisible has become visible and the Unutterable knowable. He is the manifestation and the representation of God himself, in whom God—very God—can be known, loved and trusted. In him, and in him alone, the far-off, doubtful, awful God becomes near, sure and trustful. Without him and apart from him we may speculate on God and proffer guesses about God. But God, the true God, we cannot see and cannot know. We cannot see God and cannot know God except in him who is the image of the unseen Deity.

b. The Son in relation to creation (1:15b–17)

Verse 15b: The first-born of all creation: The term *first-born—prōtotokos*—was one of the catchwords of Arius in the early fourth century, who sought to bring the Son within the realm of created beings. Arius, like his modern followers the Jehovah's Witnesses, read the term in too literal a sense, and without regard to the immediate following context.

The term *prōtotokos* evidently had a messianic connotation. Psalm 89 refers to the Seed of David to be established and his throne built up forever (v. 4). Later this Figure is identified as "the first-born, the highest of the kings of the earth" (v. 27). According to Rabbi Nathan (Shemoth Rabba 19, fol. 118,4), "God said, As I made Jacob a first-born (Exod. iv.22), so also will I make King Messiah a first-born" (Lightfoot). Philo, too, used the term *prōtotokos* of the Logos, and thus suggested some sort of contrast between the Logos and creation. Paul states emphatically that it is the personal beloved Son of God who is *the first-born of all creation*.

Such a statement on the apostle's part, however, far from placing the Son as the first in the series of created beings, contrasts him with creation as its Lord (Lohse). The true meaning of the term, therefore, "is that He is the first-born in comparison with or in relation to, all creation" (Maclaren). By using an objective genitive, in which the phrase *of all creation* is considered as receiving the action of *first-born*, Paul assures that the Son is not one of the creatures, but that the whole creation exists in a relationship of "existence-in-dependence" upon him. When read, then, in the light of the succeeding verses, the two important ideas of priority in existence and sovereignty in power unite in the expression.

As *first-born* he is prior to all created things by an absolute preexistence. The term "is the scripture-way of representing eternity" (Henry). As *prōtotokos* he is sovereign over all creation. Not only does he not belong to the order of created realities, but rather the order of created realities belongs to him. It is clearly the apostle's aim in his appended declarations to indicate an essential difference between the Son and all created beings. All creation is because of him and for him (vv. 16–18; John 1:1–3; 1 Cor. 8:6; Eph. 3:9; Heb. 1:2; 2:10; Rev. 4:11; 10:6). Unlike the orders of created beings which have their cause outside themselves, he himself had no beginning: there was never when he was not. His, therefore, "is the primacy over all created things" (NEB), because "he existed before any created thing" (Williams). Thus "Christ is not only preeminent, but unique, in all that makes God real to man in every age" (R. E. O. White).

Verse 16: For in him all things were created, in heaven and on earth, visible and invisible, whether thrones or dominions or principalities or authorities—all things were created through him and for him: This verse amplifies the Son's relation to creation. The whole creation is brought into direct relation to him as at once its cause and its clue. He is the ultimate reason for the existence of the universe, and the final explanation of its riddle. In him eternally is the power and law of the becoming and being of all that "stands created" (*ektistai,* perfect tense; see commentary on 2:7 for significance of the perfect).

In him: He is the Sphere within which *all things* have their existence. The preposition *en—in—*is used here as "possibly both instrumental and local—'by means of him and within him'" (C. F. D. Moule). All that exists is "because of him." He is "the creative source, as it were, or element in which as in a storehouse or reservoir all creative forces resided, and was in a definite act put forth" (Maclaren). "In him was life" (John 1:4)—all life both natural and spiritual. The eternal preexisting Son, the Word, stands to the universe as the incarnate Son, the Word made flesh, stands to the church. All spiritual life is in him as its cause and condition; so all physical existences have their origin within the life-giving activity of his divine nature.

Through him: He is the Agency through whom *all things* have their being. It is *through (dia) him* that the cosmic whole was brought about. This declaration alone would be sufficient to mark a clear distinction between the creature and the Creator. Thus, the Son is set apart from the creation and is not confounded with the universe; while, on the other hand, it is made clear that he is the sole medium of the divine activity. In this way the apostle stresses the Son's unique relation to the inconceivable nature of the Godhead.

For him: He is the Goal unto which *all things* have their direction. *For,* or "toward" *(eis) him* the total cosmic order moves. The phrase, "toward" or "to him" indicates the end for which the universe was created. It "finds its goal in no one save Christ alone" (Lohse). "As all creation passed out from Him, so does it all converge again towards Him" (Lightfoot). The preexisting Son is, then, the goal of the universe, as he is its starting point. He is the End as he is the Beginning—both the Alpha and the Omega. As all things sprang forth at his command, so all things will return to him at his bidding. "Being created *by* him, they were created *for* him; being made by his power, they were made according to his pleasure, and for his praise" (Henry). As all the laws and purposes which guide and govern the universe reside in him, the preexisting Son, as their meeting point, so are they being directed by him to find their climax and unity in him from whom they took their rise. He is the life-source of the universe, as he is of the church; and for both he is the mainspring of all motion and the goal of all development.

Such a view of Christ should have given to the Colossians, as it should to every Christian believer, first, a right view of nature. The

One through whom, as Paul has already declared, the work of reconciliation has been accomplished is the One in and through whom
the divine act of creation took place. Thus his "mediatorial relation
to the created universe provides a setting to the gospel of our salvation which adds to our appreciation of that gospel. For a man redeemed by Christ, the universe has no ultimate terrors; he knows
that his Redeemer is also Creator, ruler and goal of all" (Bruce).

Such a view of Christ should have given to the Colossians, as it
should to every Christian, second, a right perspective on history.
History is of Christ's making; and its end is in his hands. History
has its *telos,* its end, in him, for "the helm of the universe is held by
the hands which were pierced for us" (Maclaren; cf. 1 Cor. 15:24–
27; Eph. 1:10). Maybe history does not readily show itself to be controlled by a divine purpose. It looks as if it were all loose ends—just
a random collection of unconnected events. But that is not to see the
reality of history from the standpoint of Christ's preeminence. For
the movements of historical events are held together by his strong
hand. "And that which holds them together is not Chance or Fate or
the laws of Nature or even the 'nine orbs, or rather globes' of
Scipio's Dream. On the contrary, 'all things hold together in him' "
(Hendriksen).

Whatever then is, is because of him—"not only things visible but
also the invisible orders of thrones, sovereignties, authorities, and
powers" (NEB). Nothing is excluded. Whether belonging to the
heavenly sphere or the earthly realm, everything has its genesis and
goal in him. The full meaning of *all things (ta panta)* is defined by
the phrase "everything that is in heaven and on earth. There are no
exceptions here, all things visible and invisible are included. Even
the cosmic powers and principalities were created in him. 'Thrones'
(thronoi) and 'dominions' *(kuriotētes)* (1 Cor. 8:5) were occasionally
specified in Judaism among the heavenly hosts of angels; 'principalities' *(archai)* and 'powers' *(exousiai)* are often named as being
supermundane beings and powers. In such enumerations it does not
matter whether the list is complete or whether the angelic powers
are arranged in the order of their particular classes. The emphasis is
rather that all things that exist in the cosmos were created in Christ"
(Lohse).

*Verse 17: He is before all things, and in him all things hold to-
gether:* By the use of the present tense *(he is),* Paul is declaring that
the Son's preexistence is an absolute existence. The *he* is
emphatic—Paul uses the personal pronoun in addition to the third
person singular form of the verb. *He,* this beloved Son, this Jesus
Christ, *is* (not was) before all things. "Before Abraham was, I am"
(John 8:58). His is the timeless nature of eternal being. And it is in
such a One that *all things hold together (sunestēken).* He is the

chain-band of all existence. Without him the cosmic whole would fall apart. By the action of the Son of God the universe "is preserved from disbanding, and running into confusion" (Henry). "He is the principle of cohesion in the universe. He impressed upon creation that unity and solidarity which makes it a cosmos instead of a chaos" (Lightfoot). It is, then, a Christ-caused, a Christ-centered, and a Christ-controlled universe that Paul sees (cf. John 1:3; Heb. 1:3).

c. The Son's relation to the church (1:18)

Verse 18: He is the head of the body, the church; he is the beginning, the first-born from the dead: There is an evident parallel between Christ's relation to the material creation and his relation to the church as his spiritual creation. What he was to the universe before his incarnation, he is to the church as the incarnate One. To both he exists in a relation of *first-born* (cf. v. 15). He is thus prior to and sovereign over the church, just as he is to the cosmos. He is the source, the power, and the goal of the church's life.

United in Paul's thought is the cosmic significance of Christ both in creation and redemption. "Thus the two halves of His work are as it were moulded into a golden circle, and the end of the description bends round towards the beginning" (Maclaren). Paul has four references to *the church* in this epistle (1:18, 24; 4:15, 16). He clearly intends by the term those who have experienced the redemption accomplished in Christ and who acknowledge Christ's lordship. The church is composed of those who are "in Christ"; and to be "in Christ" is to be in the church as the body of Christ. In the present passage, in view of the teaching of the heretics, Paul stresses that Christ is head of the church (cf. 1 Cor. 11:3; Eph. 1:22; 4:15; 5:23; Col. 2:19). The false teachers did not hold Christ as the head (cf. Col. 2:19). They had included him in a series by which man was supposed to reach God. By stressing Christ's lordship over the church, Paul "means that it is emancipated from evil powers which, in the current pagan thought, were believed to control the cosmos" (Martin; cf. 2:10).

Christ is also, in relation to the church, *the beginning* (*archē;* cf. John 1:1; Rev. 1:8; 3:14; 21:6; 22:13) and *the first-born (prōtotokos) from the dead* (cf. Rom. 8:29; Heb. 12:23). He is the *beginning,* but not as being the first member of the believing community. Christ was not the first Christian. Rather, it is in him and through him and unto him that any person is a Christian. He is the head and the beginning of the church by reason of his resurrection. "He is its origin, the first to return from the dead" (NEB). "His resurrection from the dead is His title to the Lordship of the Church; for 'the power of His resurrection' (Phil. 3:10) is the life of the church" (Lightfoot).

That in everything he might be pre-eminent: It is Christ's position
as the "beginning" and "first-born" which constitutes him the
"holder of the Primacy" (H. C. G. Moule). The purpose clause
(*hina,* "in order that") indicates that this supremacy belongs to
Christ by reason of his resurrection. The apostle has already proclaimed Christ first in creation; now he states that he was resurrected in order that he might be supreme in everything. "As He is
first with respect of the Universe, so it is ordained that he should
become first with respect to the church as well" (Lightfoot). The
"all things" both of the church and of creation are his by sovereign
right. "The first place in the universe is properly his alone" (Lohse),
but such, too, is his proper place in the church. Whether it is in nature or in grace, His preeminence is absolute and supreme. The end
and purpose of all the majesty of creation and of all the wonders of
grace are that he alone should stand forth as Lord (cf. Phil. 2:9–11).
"Life from nothing began through him, and life from the dead began
through him, and he is, therefore, justly called Lord of all" (Col.
1:18, Phillips, *Letters*). It is the purpose of God, then, "that the Son
who is eternally supreme may, in the realm of time and in the sphere
of revelation, become pre-eminent. This pre-eminence is to be as
wide in scope as it is possible to be. He is to be supreme in all respects, and at every point. Lord of creation and Lord of the Church,
He must be Lord in the lives of His own with a sovereignty which
brooks no rival" (H. M. Carson). As absolute in relation to God and
sovereign in relation to creation and Head in relation to the church,
"that gives him pre-eminence over all" (Moffatt, NT). To give him
that preeminence is but to comply with the divine will. "That in all
things he might have the preeminence" (KJV)—here is the declaration of the divine plan and the revelation of the divine purpose. He
is preeminent in all that pertains to nature and grace: and all that he
is he *will be*. The phrase, "in all things" (KJV) can mean "over all
creatures" or *in everything* (RSV). "This, however, is of no great importance, for the simple meaning is, that all things are subjected to
his sway" (Calvin). As yet we do not see all things subjected to him
(Heb. 2:9). But we do see Jesus crowned with glory and honor (Heb.
2:10), and "the believer knows that while the *rule* of Christ has not
been established in every human heart, the *over-rule* is an actual fact
even now (cf. Rom. 8:28)" (Hendriksen).

2. The reconciliation by the Son (1:19–20)

Verse 19: For in him all the fulness of God was pleased to dwell:
There are two questions raised by the declaration of this verse. The
first is, what, or who, is the subject of the verb *pleased* (*eudokēsen,*
the aorist or simple past tense)? The KJV attributes the pleasing to
"the Father"—"it pleased the Father that in him should all fulness

dwell." This is certainly possible, especially when reference is made to what the apostle says back in verse 2 in praise of God as the Father of our Lord Jesus Christ. But verse 2 seems a long way back to find the context, while the designation "Father" does not occur at all in the passage beginning at verse 15. Some would take *fulness* in an absolute sense, as personified and a nominative. The words would then read: "because in him all the Fulness was pleased to dwell." Others, following Tertullian, refer the good pleasure to Christ himself, and render it, "for he (Christ) was pleased that all the Fulness should dwell in him." This way of putting it is, however, generally discounted as being out of harmony with the theological drift of the whole passage. It is best, therefore, to understand *God* as the subject (Calvin, Bruce, Martin).

The reasons for doing so seem conclusive: first, because it is grammatically fitting (Lohse). And second, because it accords with the terms elsewhere translated "good pleasure" or "to be well pleased" which are generally used absolutely in reference to God (cf. Eph. 1:5, 9; Phil. 2:13; 2 Thess. 1:11). The third reason is that it is more in harmony with the requirements of the immediate context. Since Christ is presented as the image of the invisible God, it surely follows that it is God's good pleasure that in him should all fullness dwell. Furthermore, if the term *God* is supplied as subject, then the reading of verse 20 runs on smoothly. There the reconciliation of all things is declared to be accomplished by God through Christ. It is certainly a right New Testament viewpoint to ground Christ's reconciling action in the good will of God. "On that Rock-foundation of the will—the loving will of the Father—is built the whole work of His incarnate Son. And as that work was the issue of His eternal purpose, so it is the object of His eternal delight" (Maclaren). In Christ alone the fullness of the Godhead dwells. The divine powers and attributes were not distributed among the angelic hosts nor surrendered to them. "On the contrary, in accordance with God's good pleasure, from all eternity the plenitude of the Godhead, the fulness of God's essence and glory . . . which fulness is the source of grace and glory for believers, resides in the Son of his love, in him alone, not in him and the angels" (Hendriksen).

The second question raised by Colossians 2:19 concerns the significance of *the fulness*—what fullness? The use of the term in 2:9, where Paul refers to "the whole fulness of deity," would seem to settle its meaning here. What Paul is asserting, then, is that in Christ, as the incarnate Son, it was the good pleasure of God, the Triune God, that all of his own fullness—the divine "plenitude" (A. T. Robertson)—should reside. In Christ, the abundance of the Invisible God found abode "in bodily form" (2:9, NAS). The words "mean nothing else than all the divine fulness in its totality"

(Lohse). "That is, to put it in homelier words, that all the Divine nature in all its sweet greatness, in all its infinite wealth of tenderness and power and wisdom, is embodied in Jesus Christ" (Maclaren). In him the "complete being" (NEB) of God came to dwell.

Possibly the term *fulness* was used by the heretical teachers at Colossae to refer to the totality of aeons and agencies which they supposed emanated from Pure Being. In this view, the aeons were regarded as intermediaries between God and man—steps in a ladder which linked heaven and earth. Against such notions, which would deny to Christ absolute right, Paul presents the cosmic Christ as Lord of all. And he goes on to "undermine the whole of this theosophical apparatus in one simple, direct affirmation: the fulness or totality of the divine essence and power has taken up its residence in Christ. In other words, He is the one mediator between God and mankind, and all the attributes and activities of God—His spirit, word, wisdom and glory—are displayed in Him" (Bruce). Thus, Christ has no competitors and he needs no helpers. For in him all that is of God, by God's good pleasure, took up permanent residence and there dwells. Such is indeed the significance of the term *dwell* in 1:19 *(katoikēstai,* aorist; see Luke 13:4; Acts 1:20; Heb. 11:9; and cf. Matt. 23:21; Eph. 3:17).

If "all plenitude" took up its abode in bodily form in the Son incarnate, then it may surely be added that, besides all the fullness of the Godhead, there was in the Son, also, all the fullness of manhood. He was most certainly fully human, and human in the perfect fullness of humanity. Jesus Christ was the real man, the very perfection of manhood. In the incarnation of the Son of God, manhood was enriched in Godhood, and by the resurrection and ascension, manhood was elevated to the throne of God. Thus he is the fullness of all that is divine and human, the One possessor of all. So it can be said, "The cosmic fullness of Christ means for us that wherever man goes on earth or in space, he will still be confronted with Christ's challenge and ideal. Whatever man discovers will still bear the marks of the creative Mind, as Christ has helped us to read them" (R. E. O. White).

Verse 20: And through him to reconcile to himself all things, whether on earth or in heaven, making peace by the blood of his cross: It was not only the good pleasure of God that all fullness, both divine and human, should reside in Christ, the incarnate Lord, but that in him, besides, all things should be reconciled. As the plenitude of God's energy is manifested in his creative work in Christ, so too is his reconciling activity. Through Christ, God achieved his renewing purpose. Five times in the passage beginning at verse 15 the cosmic significance of Christ is underscored by the phrase *all things. Through him* was the creation of all things;

through him—is the reconciliation of all things. "The width of the reconciliation is the same as creation; they are coterminous" (Maclaren). The whole series of things, both material and spiritual, have their restitution through him. That is surely "a magnificent commendation of Christ, that we cannot be joined to God otherwise than through him" (Calvin).

It is the biblical view that at the Fall not only was man's nature affected by his sin but the whole of nature itself was also disrupted. The cosmic order became "subject to vanity" (cf. Rom. 8:18–23, KJV). But here we are assured that by God's act through Christ, sin and its effects have been measured and mastered. The universe is one reality, not only because it is created through the one personal divine Son of God, nor yet because it finds in him its principle of cohesion, but finally because, in ways past finding out, the reconciling cross reaches to its utmost heights and depths. "In reconciliation as in creation the work of Christ has a cosmic significance; as we are told in Eph. 1:10, it is God's eternal purpose to sum up all things in Christ" (Bruce).

Significantly, the order in the reconciling process is the reverse of that in the creative. When creation is in view, the order is, "in heaven and on earth" (v. 16)—the order of their creation. But when speaking of reconciliation, Paul puts it the other way round, *on earth or in heaven,* as if to indicate that those things which stand closest to the redeeming cross are the first to experience the effects of its healing power.

The reconciliation is God's act through Christ. To be reconciled *(apokatallazai)* is "to be brought back to a former state of harmony" (cf. v. 21; Eph. 2:16; see Rom. 5:10; 2 Cor. 5:18, 19). Such reconciliation is effected *by the blood of his cross.* This is an "interpretative phrase" by which "a 'theology of glory' which might view the consummation as already achieved, is corrected by the 'theology of the cross' (cf. 2:14 f.)" (Lohse). Such is the awful cost of the restitution of *all things;* "by means of that sacred blood which signifies and embodies His vicarious death, with its immeasurable merits" (H. C. G. Moule). Contrary to the speculations of the false teachers, Paul traces the restitution of all things to Christ's atoning work on Golgotha's tree (cf. 2:14; Rom. 3:8; 5:9; Eph. 1:7; 2:13; Heb. 9:12–14; 1 Pet. 2:19; 1 John 1:7; Rev. 1:5; 5:9; 7:14; 12:11; see Gal. 6:12, 14; Eph. 2:16; Phil. 2:8; Heb. 12:2). "Christ has laid the foundation for our reconciliation; for he has paid the price for it, has purchased the proffer and promise of it, proclaims it as a Prophet, applies it as a King" (Henry).

Christ is, then, the agent of the reconciliation; his blood is the means of it, and *making peace* the way of it. The compound word translated *making peace (eirēnopoiēsas)* is found only here in the

New Testament. But the idea of Christ and his work as the maker of peace is general. He came, according to Zechariah's prophecy, "to guide our feet into the way of peace" (Luke 1:79). Such peace was his dying legacy to his disciples (John 14:27; cf. 16:33; 20:19, 21, 26). There is constant reference to God as the God of peace (cf. e.g. Rom. 1:7; 15:33; 16:11; etc.); and peace is embodied for us in Christ. "For he is our peace" (Eph. 2:14). The assurance of peace with God through Christ was a central theme in the apostolic preaching (Acts 10:36).

Paul has two other references to peace in this epistle besides the declaration of this verse. In the opening paragraph he refers to the peace of God which springs from his grace (cf. 1:2). And he expresses his desire later that the peace of Christ may arbitrate in the believing heart (3:15).

B. The Salvation through Christ Proclaimed (1:21–23)

From his presentation of Christ as cosmic Redeemer, Paul turns, or rather, returns, to refer to the experience of the Colossians themselves.

Verse 21: And you, who once were estranged and hostile in mind, doing evil deeds: The apostle sets down in grim terms the effects of sin in the human heart. Once the Colossians were *estranged* (*apēllotriōmenous;* cf. Eph. 4:18; see 2:12), broken off, that is to say, from fellowship with God. The expanded passage in Ephesians 2 describes in more detail the nature of this alienation. It is a state of "fallenness" in which all men are involved. Such a state makes us begin life with our faces away from God.

Paul speaks of this pre-Christian state as one of "alienation" rather than of "being aliens." The word suggests that this was not our original condition. Alienated is something we become. Sin is not an essential element in man's nature: it is something abnormal and unnatural. It is an intruder into man's being and into the cosmic order. But it was a welcomed intruder. Man willingly allowed sin scope and place, and took up, as a result, an attitude of hostility to God. As such, sin is an "inexcusable human hostility" (Hendriksen). The consequence of such a state is the performance of *evil deeds*. The seat of this enmity against God is the *mind,* the central citadel of being where we think, imagine, reflect and will. Its sphere of manifestation is in the overt evil action. Such was the state of those Colossian believers before their experience of the reconciling grace of the gospel; and such, too, is the state of all who are as yet without God and without hope in the world.

Must we suppose that Paul paints the picture in too dark colors? Not in the least. For his account of the natural man is true to the verdict of history. Yet the essential thrust of the apostle's charge is not that every man is guilty of the most horrific deeds of evil, but that he is guilty "of practical want of affection, as manifested by habitual disobedience and inattention to God's wishes, and by indifference and separation from Him in heart and mind" (Maclaren). Man as man is estranged from God and at odds with his sovereignty. "For sin is not only disobedience to the will of God; it effectually severs our fellowship with Him, and forces us to live 'without God in the world' " (Bruce). "Once you were alienated," Paul reminds the Colossians. His purpose was to bring home to them anew the wonder of their present position as now reconciled. "You were once . . . but now you are. . . ." "The miracle of the salvation that was experienced is contrasted to the lostness from which God has freed them" (Lohse).

Verse 22: He has now reconciled in his body of flesh by his death: "But now" is how the verse really begins in the Greek, thus marking a new beginning (cf. Rom. 5:9; 7:6; 11:30–31; 16:26; Eph. 2:13; 3:5; 2 Tim. 1:10). "Against the dark foil of the past there arises a present that is all the more gleaming: 'now he has reconciled you' " (Lohse). Now all is different; they are no longer alienated. *He has now reconciled—He*—who? The NEB takes *God* to be the subject of the verb. And this is possible. The preceeding passage stresses God's initiative in the acts of creation and reconciliation (cf. Rom. 5:10; 2 Cor. 5:18, 19). Ephesians 2:4 brings God into man's hopeless situation, as the divine counterfact. God steps into the terrible quagmire of man's sin. Paul has shown us man as he is apart from God. But the situation is changed when God is brought into the picture. However, as the reconciliation is accomplished in Christ, it may be that it is Christ whom Paul would have understood by the *he.* It is through him "we have now received our reconciliation" (Rom. 5:11). But perhaps the inquiry is irrelevant, for it is, as a final fact, God—the Triune God—who acts in the deed of the cross "for us men and for our salvation" (cf. 2 Cor. 5:19; Heb. 9:14).

The reconciliation is brought about "in the body of his flesh through death" (literal). "The body of his flesh" is his actual physical body (cf. Eph. 2:15). "In the body of his flesh"—for as true man he lived and died. "In the body of his flesh"—for in it he was both a descendant of David and "was made man," one of mankind. So was he one *with* man, that he might be one *for* man. It was by the body of his flesh "through death"—thus by means of "the blood of his cross" (v. 20)—that the reconciliation was effected: "in his *body of flesh* (that was the *sphere* of the reconciliation), and through his *death* (that was the *instrument*)" (Hendriksen).

By piling up his terms in the phrase "the body of his flesh through death," is Paul indulging in a "needless exuberance of language"?

Hardly. For "it is just the right expression needed to underline the physical cost of the church's redemption, which is achieved not by a wave of the hand or some automatic process, but by the coming of God in the person of His Son to our world, His clothing Himself in our humanity and, then, suffering the bitterness and shame of a death on the cross because of His close identity with humanity in its need. Romans 8:3 provides a good parallel (cf. Phil. 2:6–8)" (Martin). By using such emphatic words Paul may have wished to distinguish the literal use of the term *body* in reference to Christ's work from the mystical sense he has given to it elsewhere in the epistle (cf. 1:18, 24; 2:17, Greek, 19; 3:5) (Lightfoot, Lohse). It seems, however, more probable that Paul has in mind the doceticism of the heretical teachers who taught that our Lord's body was only a phantasm or appearance. The apostle will stress that it was genuine human nature that the Son of God assumed at the incarnation; and it was this same genuine human body which died on the cross.

So the incarnation finds completion in the cross; and the reconciliation is focused in *his death* (cf. 1 Cor. 11:26; Phil. 2:8; Heb. 2:9, 14). In his death the incarnate Son of God met all the demands of God's holy law, so that his divine love, which prompted the reconciliation accomplished at Calvary, might flow forth to gather into its embrace of forgiveness all of sinful mankind. This is the living center of God's revelation in Christ, the holy secret of its power. He, the Word made flesh, actually gave himself up to death for the sake of estranged humanity. "Voluntarily and of His own love, as well as in obedience to the Father's will, He has borne the consequences of the sin which he never shared, in that life of sorrow and sympathy, in that separation from God which is sin's deepest penalty, and of which the solemn witness comes to us in the cry that rent the darkness, 'My God, My God, why hast thou forsaken me?' and in that physical death which is the parable in the material world of the true death of the spirit" (Maclaren).

Such is the reconciliation accomplished in Christ; a reconciliation which nevertheless we must "receive" to ourselves. "This voluntary self-identification of Christians with Christ's offering of his obedience is essential to the New Testament conception of reconciliation: Christ does for us what we could not do for ourselves; but we must do, for our part, what he will not do for us. He 'offers' us to God, but it is not the less our offering" (C. F. D. Moule; cf. 2 Cor. 5:18, 19).

In order to present you holy and blameless and irreproachable before him: Here is the grand purpose of the reconciliation, the divine climax of God's act in Christ. The words can be made to refer both to the believer's standing and to his state in Christ, both to his present life and to his position at the last day. They can thus be taken in a judicial and in a moral sense. In the view of some writers, the several words used by Paul here all have a judicial significance. Thus the *presentation* is seen, not in terms of animal sacrifice— "without blemish or spot"—but of one accused in the law courts and acquitted. The verb *to present (parastēsai)* is often used in a legal context meaning "to bring another before the court" (cf. 1 Cor. 8:8; 2 Cor. 4:14; Rom. 14:10; 2 Tim. 2:15). The word for *irreproach- able (anegklētous)* has the idea of "not being called to account" (cf. 1 Cor. 1:8; 1 Tim. 3:10; Tit. 1:6). As one accused before the judicial court hears the verdict "not guilty," so the one who has received the reconciliation is declared without blame (Rom. 8:33). As believ- ers we share in the righteousness of Christ and are accepted in the Beloved (cf. Rom. 1:17; 3:24; 10:4, 6; 1 Cor. 1:30; 6:11; Gal. 5:5; Eph. 2:18; 3:12; Phil. 3:9; Tit. 3:5, 7).

These qualities are true of believers here and now. We are, to use another of Paul's great judicial words, *justified*—we are declared righteous and perfectly acceptable "in Christ." The words *before him* in Colossians "do not primarily refer to the future day of the Lord. Rather, they express the thought that Christians' lives are lived now in God's presence" (Lohse). Such is our standing before the Lord.

At the same time, the future reference is most certainly there. "The sentence of justification passed upon the believer here and now anticipates the pronouncement of the judgement day" (Bruce). Hendriksen views the *presentation* as "definitely eschatological, that is, as referring to the great consummation when Jesus returns upon the clouds of glory." Elsewhere the apostle speaks of the day when the Lord Jesus shall "raise . . . us" up and "present us" (2 Cor. 4:14, KJV; cf. Eph. 5:27). We shall at that day be presented with him—literally, "set along side" him—without shame or blame (cf. 1 Cor. 1:7, 8; Eph. 1:7; 1 Thess. 3:13; 5:23; 1 John 2:28). For it is his purpose that we shall be *holy*—devoted to God in fullest purity; and *blameless*—as an acceptable offering; and *irreproachable*—by being absolved from every charge. "All the lines of thought in the preced- ing section lead up to and converge in this peak. The meaning of God in creation and redemption cannot be fully fathomed without taking into view the future perfection of men" (Maclaren).

The words may also be taken in a moral sense as providing for believers our present aim. Certainly, "God's act of reconciliation has already accomplished everything; perfection is thus not to be gained by one's striving. Rather, perfection is here received as God's gift to be verified in the life of Christians" (Lohse). Yet there is a striving (cf. v. 29; 1 Cor. 9:25), and a fighting (Eph. 6:11–12; 1 Tim. 6:10) required of Christian discipleship. We are called upon to make our present state before the world something akin to our present standing before the Lord. We are to become in life what we are to our Lord. Before God we are accepted as *holy and blameless and irreproachable;* before men we are to live as such (cf. 1 Pet. 1:15, 16; see Phil. 2:15; 1 Tim. 6:14). We will *be presented* fully acceptable at the last day; we are to *present* ourselves in this day as a living sacrifice, holy, acceptable to God, which is our spiritual worship (Rom. 12:1; cf. Phil. 4:18). Because the merits of Christ provide for us a full discharge, this does not permit us to be indolent, unwatchful, and fatalistic. For the next verse carries an implicit warning.

Verse 23: Provided that you continue in the faith, stable and steadfast, not shifting from the hope of the gospel which you heard: The verse begins in the Greek with an emphatic "if" *(ei ge)*—if you go on abiding in the faith, relying, that is, in full assurance upon Christ and admitting no substitute for him. The force of this double particle is to express a pure hypothesis, but the "indicative mood following converts the hypothesis into a hope" (Lightfoot). The Christian is already justified; yet "his salvation, while complete and final on the Godward side, needs his diligence and perseverance, in the manward aspect" (Martin). He must *continue* in the faith—he must keep it up. He is indeed held by the strong hand of God and Christ, but still he has to hold to him (cf. 2:19). The Christian will hold out as he holds on. On his side, God will remain steadfast in his love. But "Divine preservation always presupposes human perseverance. Perseverance proves faith's genuine character, and is therefore indispensable to salvation. To be sure, no one can continue in the faith in his own strength (John 15:5). The enabling grace of God is needed from start to finish (Phil. 2:12, 13)" (Hendriksen).

The word translated *continue (epimenein)* is a continuous form and is followed by the noun *faith* in the dative case, to indicate the basis upon and the sphere within which one must abide, so remaining steadfast and unmovable. The Colossians are urged to "continue the exercise" of their faith (Maclaren). This call to continue and abide is a constant New Testament theme (cf. John 15:4–7; Acts 13:43; 14:22; Rom. 11:22; see Acts 2:43; 2 John 9). It was a needed word for the Colossian Christians, who were being tempted by the heretical teachers to loosen their hold on Christ, and so were in constant danger of slipping away from the truth of the gospel which they had heard. Paul's fervent hope was that such should not be the case. He wanted them to continue *stable and steadfast, not shifting from the hope of the gospel.* He explains, first positively, and then negatively, what continuance in the faith means.

Positively, it is to be *stable (tethemeliōmenoi);* (cf. Eph. 3:17; cf. 1 Pet. 5:10) as a house "founded" on the rock which has a sure foundation (cf. Rom. 15:20; 1 Cor. 3:10–11; Eph. 2:20; 2 Tim. 2:19;

Heb. 11:10). The consequence of being thus well founded is that the building will stand secure amid the rains and storms. Negatively, it means *not shifting* (not "dislodged," NEB) *from the hope of the gospel.* The tense of the verb suggests the idea that the process may have been going on continually and almost imperceptibly, as when a ship gets loosened from its mooring and drifts out into dangerous waters. Such a condition must not be permitted. The Colossians must not let go. They must "not drift" nor be moved away from the *hope* on which they rest (cf. vv. 5, 27). Paul has certainly a profound theology of hope. His hope is firm and sure, summed up in Christ (v. 27; cf. 1 Tim. 1:1). "The ground of hope is Christ in the word— the evidence of hope is Christ in the heart" (Henry). *Faith* and *hope*—here are two of the great words of the gospel.

The gospel which has been preached to every creature under heaven: By the use of this phrase Paul is not, of course, suggesting that every single individual in the known world of his day had heard the good news. He is rather making the point that the gospel had gone out beyond the barriers of the Jewish nation, had broken through Judaism's narrow exclusivism to reach people of other races. Unlike the limited range of the heretics' message, whose secret word was only for the initiated few, the gospel had reached forth into "all the world" (v. 6, KJV). In all the world it was proclaimed: such is its universal perspective; and in all the world it was bearing fruit: such is its spiritual power. "The catholicity of the gospel is a token of its divine origin and power" (Bruce). Such a gospel—a gospel which declares men acceptable and makes men holy, a gospel of grace and peace and hope—is what the Colossians heard.

And of which I, Paul, became a minister: To Paul it was a constant wonder that he should have been called of God to this ministry. Before, he had been a persecutor of the believers (1 Tim. 1:13), and now, as a believer, he counted himself "the very least of all the saints" (Eph. 3:8). Yet here he is, "a minister of Christ"; this surely is grace upon grace. "Paul was a great apostle; but he looks upon it as the highest of his titles of honour, to be a minister of the gospel of Jesus Christ" (Henry). Paul never ceased to regard the ministry as a boon of God, a gift of grace (cf. 2 Cor. 3:6; Eph. 3:7); and it was ever his aim for himself, and his hope for those who served with him in the gospel, to "put no obstacle in any one's way, so that no fault may be found with our ministry" (2 Cor. 6:3). Having contemplated the glorious gospel of which Christ is the center and circumference, Paul introduces, almost abruptly, his own relationship to it. "He sees his personal ministry as closely bound up with God's gracious plan for the world" (Bruce). He will specify in greater detail in what follows what it is to be a minister of Christ. But the introduction of the term here causes him to pause and wonder at the grace which has come to him; in this way it serves as a transition point to his exposition of what is involved in being a servant of Christ.

C. The Servanthood of Christ Portrayed (1:24–2:8)

The passage begins with the few personal allusions that the apostle makes in the epistle. He has been led to refer to himself to reinforce his call to the Colossians to continue in the faith of the gospel. His connection with the gospel of Christ makes Paul's soul catch fire. He is glad to undergo suffering on its account so that others might share in its benefits. He thinks of himself, in this context of renewed praise, as a steward in God's household appointed to dispense to the Gentiles the rich bounties which God's grace has provided. No affliction can be too great to endure and no activity too demanding to fulfill what is required of him—to present every man mature in Christ. Such a ministry to which Paul has been commissioned of God is a demanding and exhausting work. As he contemplates it in relation to the Colossians, he must use words commensurate with its vast implications. Specifically, he centers his description around the three facts of his suffering, his secret, and his service. He will rejoice in his sufferings (vv. 24–25); he will refer to his secret (vv. 26–27); he will reflect on his service (v. 28–2:8).

1. Rejoicing in his suffering (1:24–25)

Verse 24: Now I rejoice in my sufferings for your sake, and in my flesh I complete what is lacking in Christ's afflictions for the sake of his body, that is, the church: The apostle refers to his sufferings for the sake of the Colossians as happenings which brought him happiness. It is doubtless easy enough to rejoice when the weather is fair and the sun shines. But it is not at such propitious times that Paul said, he rejoiced. Rather, it was when the chain chafed his wrists and the iron bit deeply into his soul. In such experiences he found reason for gladness. Paul often had occasion when writing to churches to allude to the costly nature of his service (cf. Acts 20:23; 2 Cor. 2:4; 6:4; 8:2; Phil. 1:16; 4:14; 1 Thess. 3:7). But never in so doing did he put himself at a distance from those to whom he wrote. Always, the sufferings and afflictions he underwent were for the sake of those among whom he labored. In this epistle, because he was writing to people he did not know personally, he needed to give a rationale for his suffering on their behalf. Yet what Paul had to say must come within those many things in his letters "hard to understand" (2 Pet. 3:16).

A consideration of the significance he gives to his sufferings may be approached first, negatively and then, positively. Negatively, two

things may be said. (1) The words must not be restricted as if Paul
were implying that Christ's reconciling work were somehow incom-
plete. He has already stated that all things are reconciled in the
peacemaking event of Christ's cross (Col. 1:19–20) and that the Colossians themselves have their reconciliation through the body of
Christ's flesh (v. 22). The work of Christ for our salvation is
everywhere in the New Testament presented as a completed, once-
for-all work. Thus the expression *what is lacking in Christ's afflictions,* "cannot be taken to mean that there still might be something
lacking in the vicarious sufferings of Christ which must be supplied
by the apostle. Paul and all the other witnesses of the New Testament unanimously agree that the reconciliation was truly and validly
accomplished in the death of Christ, and that no need exists for any
supplementation" (Lohse).

(2) The boldness of the words must not be softened as if the apostle were meaning that the afflictions of which he speaks were simply
those "imposed by," "endured for," or "after the style of" Christ.
He has some deeper and more profound thought in his mind.

Thus, regarding the positive approach, two observations are again
appropriate. (1) The word Paul uses for *afflictions—thlipseōs—*is
never used in the New Testament to describe the actual sufferings of
Christ on the cross. (2) There are other passages which suggest a
close connection between specific human sufferings and those of
Christ. In 2 Corinthians 1:5, for example, Paul has a similar, though
not exactly identical idea, when he speaks of the sufferings of Christ
which he shares abundantly (cf. 1 Cor. 1:6–7; Acts 9:15; Gal. 3:4;
Phil. 1:29; 2 Thess. 1:12). Paul sees a divine purpose in what he had
to endure for the sake of the Colossians. By his sufferings something
was added to the afflictions of Christ.

The word translated *complete* ("fill up" in KJV)—*antanaplēroō—*is
found only here in the New Testament, although its simple compound form *(anaplēroō)* occurs several times with the idea of a deficiency uppermost (cf. 1 Cor. 14:16; 16:17; Gal. 6:2). Some commentators would give stress to the *anti* (against) in the compound verb
used by Paul in the present verse. "It signifies that the supply comes
from an opposite quarter to the deficiency" (Lightfoot). Although
this idea is rejected by others (e.g., T. K. Abbott, C. F. D. Moule;
cf. 1 Cor. 16:17; Phil. 2:30), it is at least certain that the apostle does
wish to maintain that there is something that, as God's servant, he
can supply by way of making up for the things *lacking* in Christ's
afflictions. Evidently, then, Paul is not here thinking of Christ's
work as reconciler. Rather, he is considering him as the supreme
example of service. As the Servant of the Lord par excellence,
Christ endured "the contradiction of sinners." But all possible afflictions in this regard even he could not bear. In the nature of the case,

Christ could not have endured the full quota of sufferings which must be undertaken for the sake of his body, the church. The apostle as a minister of Christ will contribute his share. "Jesus did not exhaust all the sufferings to be endured, nor did he suffer so that his followers do not have to suffer" (A. T. Robertson). When, therefore, the apostle refers to his sufferings filling up the deficiency of Christ's afflictions, he has in mind the suffering and opposition he endured as arising necessarily out of his position as God's commissioned servant. As the Servant of the Lord, Christ's ministry is, indeed, complete in its atoning efficacy, but in its ministerial utility it has to be carried on by his servants. "That is to say, the Servant's mission of enlightenment among the nations is to be carried on by the disciples of Christ. But here Paul goes further: the Servant's sufferings are also to be carried on by the disciples of Christ—at least, by one of them, Paul himself" (Bruce). For the apostle was already bearing the afflictions of Christ in his own body (cf. Gal. 6:17; see 1 Cor. 15:42; Acts 13:45, 50; 16:19–20). There is a remarkable antithesis between the apostle's *flesh*—his physical body—and Christ's *body*—the church—for which the sufferings are endured. Paul's gladness in his sufferings derives from the knowledge that they have purpose—that they are added to the "tribulation-toils" of Christ for the sake of his body, the church.

Verse 25: Of which I became a minister according to the divine office which was given to me for you, to make the word of God fully known: The *of which* at the end of verse 23 refers to the gospel. The *of which* at the beginning of verse 25 refers to the church. As a servant of the gospel, Paul is at the same time a servant of the church. It is because he is a minister of the gospel that he suffers; and it is because he is a minister of the church that he serves. He is God's minister "by virtue of the task assigned" to him by God (NEB). This is his *divine office*, his "stewardship" (NAS). Paul's word is *oikonomia* (cf. 1 Cor. 9:17; Eph. 1:10; 3:2, 9; cf. *oikonomos*— "steward," Luke 12:42; 16:1–2; 1 Cor. 4:1, 2; Tit. 1:7; 1 Pet. 4:10). The term can be applied either to the specific office of the house manager (cf. Eph. 1:10), or to the activity of administering the household (cf. 1 Cor. 9:17). The idea of stewardship best conveys what the apostle has in mind. The steward always acts on behalf of his master. Paul knew himself to be a servant of the church commissioned by Christ to "manage" the spreading of the gospel. His ministry was something given to him, according to "the economy or wise disposition of things in the house of God. He was steward, and master-builder, and this was given to him: he did not usurp it, or take it to himself: and he could not challenge it as a debt. He received it from God as a gift, and took it as a favour" (Henry).

Paul repeatedly referred to his apostolic ministry as a "grace" *(charis)* (cf. Rom. 1:5; 12:3, 6; 15:15; 1 Cor. 3:10; 15:10; Gal. 2:9). And as such it was an office entrusted to him (1 Cor. 9:17) from which he could not withdraw, nor could he set it aside. So he wanted to be thought of as a trustworthy servant and steward of the mysteries of God (1 Cor. 4:1–2). His one consuming aim and ambition was then, "to deliver [God's] message in full" (Col. 1:25, NEB).

2. Referring to his secret (1:26–27)

Verse 26: The mystery hidden for ages and generations but now made manifest to his saints: The word which Paul "fully" proclaimed (v. 25) as God's minister was the Divine secret made known to him. This *mystery (mustērion)* or "secret" had been hidden in God throughout past ages but was now brought out into the open (cf. Rom. 16:25; Eph. 3:3, 5; 2 Thess. 2:7). Those who lived in the old dispensations before the coming of Christ could not see the meaning of what God was doing or what he had planned (cf. 2 Cor. 3:13; 1 Pet. 1:10–13). It was as though they lived surrounded by mist, in contrast with us who live in the brighter light of Christ. But now the secret is disclosed; the mist and the veil have been taken away. The Presence of God is among men in a new form, embodied and actualized in Jesus Christ. Though it was through the apostle that the mystery became known to the saints, it was not something which he himself had discovered or originated. It was "a revelation" (cf. Gal. 1:12). Below in Colossians 2:2 Paul identifies Christ as the "mystery" of God. He is God's "open secret" (Moffatt NT). Paul was the steward of this mystery for the sake of God's people—the *saints,* that is, those who hear and believingly receive the gospel (cf. Col. 1:2, 4, 12). The saints are the body of Christ; such is the church.

Verse 27: To them God chose to make known how great among the Gentiles are the riches of the glory of this mystery, which is Christ in you, the hope of glory: Here is the content of the mystery which has been made known: Christ in you. Some read the preposition *in (en)* to signify "the pneumatic indwelling of Christ in the hearts of believers" (H. C. G. Moule; cf. KJV, RSV, NEB, Lightfoot). A number of commentators prefer to render it as "among" (Martin, Lohse, NEB marg.). For them the great wonder is that Christ is proclaimed among the Gentiles (cf. 2 Cor. 1:19). The difference however is hardly material. For the emphasis surely falls upon the *you:* in *you* Colossians, Gentiles that you are, Christ dwells as the hope of glory. Thus the secret is "both Christ *and* the fact that he is among them" (C.F. D. Moule). But the surest demonstration that he was among the Gentiles was the evident fact that he was *in* the hearts of the Colossians. "Paul knew no other way by which the living Christ could be present among the Gentiles collectively but by

indwelling individual believers'' (R. E. O. White). In this reality of
Christ's indwelling, Paul saw manifest the "wonderful fact that all
barriers were broken down. He saw in that the proof and the
prophecy of the world-wide destination of the gospel'' (Maclaren). It
was just here "among the Gentiles" that "this 'mystery', this dispensation of grace, achieved its greatest triumphs and displayed its
transcendent glory'' (Lightfoot).

Such are the *riches* (cf. 2:2; see 3:16) *of the glory* (cf. 3:4; Eph.
1:18; 3:16; Phil. 4:19) *of this mystery*. What benefits and blessings
has the revealing of the mystery brought to mankind! And with them
all, Christ within the life brings "with him the hope of all the glorious things to come" (Phillips). Here is the assurance of all that we
will become; "the fact that here and now, as members of His body,
you have His life within you, affords a firm hope that you will share
in that fulness of glory that is yet to be displayed on the day of 'the
revealing of the sons of God' '' (Bruce). Glorious things belong to
the realm of *glory*. For where Christ is and where he reigns as Lord,
there is the place of divine splendor. And the believers' hope "is directed towards the 'glory' which will become manifest in the consummation (cf. 3:4). Its basis and content is Christ alone so that also
here the emphasis lies upon the content of 'hope' that shapes the
present (cf. 1:5). This content God has made known through the
worldwide proclamation of the message of Christ'' (Lohse).

3. Reflecting on his service (1:28–2:8)

a. The general idea of the ministry (1:28–29)

*Verse 28–29: Him we proclaim, warning every man and teaching
every man in all wisdom, that we may present every man mature in
Christ. For this I toil, striving with all the energy which he mightily
inspires within me:* How does Paul understand what it means to be
commissioned as a minister of Christ and a servant of the church?
The answer to that question is here compressed into two verses.

There is, first, the minister's *message. Him*—the One whom Paul
has set forth earlier in this very chapter (cf. vv. 15–18) *we proclaim.*
Christ and Christ alone is for the Colossians, and for *every man,* the
hope of glory. The apostle, knew that his was not a dead and dull
system, in contrast to that taught by the false teachers. For Paul, the
gospel focused upon the living Christ as the sole revealer of God,
the center and Lord of creation, the fountain of life of all that lives,
and the reconciler of men to God by the blood of his cross. This was
Paul's gospel; yet not his alone. For the apostle associates with himself, in the *we* of the verse, those who support him in his service.
What Epaphras had proclaimed in Colossae is the very same gospel

that he, the apostle to the Gentiles, proclaims. Theirs is the one message which God has chosen to make known. This is the authentic gospel; there is no other (Gal. 1:6–7). Having, then, "extolled the gospel in the highest terms, he [Paul] now adds, that it is that divine secret which he preaches" (Calvin).

Then there is the minister's *method*. First comes a general declaration: him *we proclaim*. The verb is emphatic (cf. Acts 13:5; 15:36; 17:13, etc.). It means "to tell out" in the certainty of the message's truthfulness and in the conviction of its effectiveness. The innovators mumbled their mysteries in secret places. But Paul, by contrast, wanted to proclaim his message to the whole world, so that everyone might understand and come to a knowledge of the truth as it is in Christ Jesus. "We are no muttering mystery-mongers. From full lungs and in a voice to make people hear, we shout our message. We do not take a man into a corner, and whisper secrets into his ear; we cry in the streets, and our message is for 'every man' " (Maclaren).

The proclamation of Christ is effected by means of *warning* and *teaching*. The word translated warning, *nouthetein,* also expresses the idea of admonition (cf. 3:16; Acts 20:31; Rom. 15:14; 1 Cor. 4:14; 1 Thess. 5:12, 14; 2 Thess. 3:15). Both must go together in setting forth the gospel. The wooing and the warning notes must be made to blend to make one music, so that grace may come as a charming sound harmonious to the ear, to use the words of Philip Doddridge. Because he knows the terror of the Lord, it is the preacher's duty to persuade men (2 Cor. 5:11). So, then, for Paul "to *admonish* meant *to warn, to stimulate,* and *to encourage.* He would actually *plead* with men to be reconciled to God (2 Cor. 5:20)" (Hendriksen).

Along with, or perhaps following, the proclamation, there is *teaching* (cf. 2:7; 3:16) or instruction. *Teaching* is put beside *warning* to stress the intense relation between pastoral care and instruction (Lohse). Such warning and teaching must be carried out *in all wisdom.* That is to say, it is directed to a practical knowledge of Christ rather than to the preoccupation with speculative notions characteristic of the heretics. For the apostle "*abstract* doctrine did not exist. Neither did Christian ethics suspended in mid-air. On the contrary, Paul's teaching was done with a view to admonishing; his admonishing was rooted in teaching" (Hendriksen).

The minister's *motive* is to *present every man mature in Christ.* The word *present* is the same as that in verse 22. In that context the divine purpose of Christ's reconciling work was set forth; here it is the apostle's purpose as the servant of the same word of reconciliation. In each case the end is the same. Paul's thought moves forward to the coming day (cf. 1 Thess. 2:19–20; 5:23) when the reconciling grace of Christ will have completed its transforming work. Then that which is *perfect* will have come; and we shall be like him for we shall see him as he is (1 John 3:2). It was in the light of such a prospect that Paul suffered and served. He was sure that his toil would end in triumph. But even in this present life there is a growth to be observed and a maturity to be attained (cf. Eph. 4:13–14; see Eph. 2:21; 2 Thess. 1:3; 1 Pet. 2:2; 2 Pet. 3:18). We are to develop spiritually and become full-grown (1 Cor. 14:20). "The demand to 'be perfect as your heavenly Father is perfect' (Mt. 5:48) is fulfilled where the will of God is done in obedience to the Lord. Whoever belongs to the exalted Christ and follows his command will be 'perfect in Christ' " (Lohse; cf. Col. 4:12). For the apostle, then, to bring men to Christ was only the first step in his ministry. It was his design and desire so to *teach* Christ that the quality of his ministry would be attested by the maturity of those he could *present* to God as His children in the faith in the day of the great consummation, when "all things" would be "brought to a head" in Christ (Eph. 1:10, literal). That was Paul's driving motive in his ministry for which he toiled "with all the energy and power of Christ at work" in him (NEB).

In this declaration there is the minister's *means* through which his task can be begun and ended aright. How can anyone accomplish a service so great? Only if he has sufficient drive and dynamic. Paul himself had that drive; and Christ had for him that dynamic. Paul strives and Christ strengthens. That is the combination which makes a ministry without fault and with fruit. *I toil*, declares the apostle, using a word which suggests an excessive expenditure of energy, "like a man tugging at an oar, and putting all his weight into each stroke" (Maclaren). I toil, *striving;* here force is added to the way Paul fulfilled his ministry. That is the key to any ministry which will count for God. But with Paul's toiling and striving there was also "the mighty strength which Christ supplies" (TEV). "The toil and the conflict are to be carried on 'according to his working, which worketh in me mightily.' The measure of our power then is Christ's power in us. He whose presence makes struggle necessary, by His presence strengthens us for it" (Maclaren).

b. The specific concerns of the minister (2:1–8)

Admonition and warning, we have noted, are the two ideas which coalesce in the one word *nouthetountes (warning)* which Paul uses in 1:28. Now he will demonstrate in what follows that concern for the believers which unites the two ideas. The *admonition* aspect of his ministry is more prominent in verses 1–3, while the *warning* aspect comes out the more sharply in verses 4–8.

(1) Admonition (2:1–3)

Verses 1–2a: For I want you to know how greatly I strive for you, and for those at Laodicea, and for all who have not seen my face, that their hearts may be encouraged as they are knit together in love: Few statements in all his writings reveal more clearly the large-heartedness of the apostle than this. Paul had not been to Colossae or Laodicea, yet, not having seen the people of God there, he loved them nonetheless—as he did all everywhere "in Christ." Here is a noble example for all of us who want to follow Christ. It is a Christian duty to be concerned for all with whom we are bound together in the same bundle of life. For we are all "one people" in Christ (Gal. 3:28). "Let us learn the lesson, that, for all Christian people, sympathy in the battle for God, which is being waged all over the world, is a plain duty" (Maclaren). For the Colossians and the Laodiceans (cf. 4:16), Paul "was in a sort of agony, and had a constant fear respecting what would become of them" (Henry). The "agony" or *striving (agōna,* "contest," "struggle") in which the apostle was engaged on behalf of the believers in the Lycus valley sprang from fears without and fears within. He was concerned that the false teachers would lead them astray and consequently the ministry be blamed. He therefore wanted to "encourage" or "confirm" their hearts. The KJV rendering "be comforted" is now too weak to convey Paul's meaning. The specific thought is "to encourage to action, not to console in misfortune" (A. T. Robertson). "The cloud that hung over the Colossian Church was not about to break in sorrows which they would need consolation to bear, but in doctrinal and practical errors which they would need strength to resist" (Maclaren). Paul's desire is, then, that they may "continue in good heart" (NEB); that they may not give way before the onslaughts of the false teaching, but that they press forward to maturity. That is the end for which he strives. But he has already declared that his striving is reinforced by Christ's strengthening (cf. 1:29). So the more Paul strives, the more Christ strengthens. And in the combination of grit and grace they can *be encouraged.*

Love is the sphere in which encouragement operates. For love alone truly unites. Only love can "bind all together and complete the whole" (3:14, NEB; cf. 1:4, 8). Unity in love gives added strength to each (cf. Eph. 4:16). It is this "compaction in love" (Maclaren) that provides the context for the "understanding" and "knowledge" which follow (in v. 2b). Thus "Paul emphasizes that the revelation of God cannot be properly known apart from the cultivation of brotherly love within the Christian community. So, in Eph. 3:17f., it is only as Christians are 'rooted and grounded in *love*' that they acquire the power to apprehend *'with all the saints'* the fulness of God's revelation" (Bruce).

To love in the human realm, it is necessary that the persons or things be known and understood. But the reverse is true of things divine. Here love is the foundation of understanding and knowledge. It is by learning "more and more how strong are the bonds of Christian love" (Phillips) that believers come to the results of love—understanding and knowledge.

Verse 2b: To have all the riches of assured understanding and the knowledge of God's mystery, of Christ: Unity in love will lead, first, to an *assured understanding* of the truth. This "full assurance" (*phērophoria;* cf. 1 Thess. 1:5; Heb. 6:11; 10:22) of *understanding* (cf. 1:9; 2 Tim. 2:7) which the apostle desires for all Christians is a wide-ranging and "clear-sighted apprehension of theological truth" (Martin). By this Paul does not mean a harsh and narrow affirmation of doctrinal statements, but an understanding born of love. Such love will assure *all the riches,* "the full wealth" (NEB) of conviction (cf. 1:27; see 3:16). The possibility of insight into the truth, in all its length and breadth and depth and height, is held out to those who are "knit together in love." Love "is here commended from its effect, because it fills the mind of the pious with true joy; so, on the other hand, the cause of it is pointed out by him, when he says, in *all fulness of understanding"* (Calvin).

The rich fullness of this insight, or understanding, is underscored by the way the term *riches (ploutos)* is combined with "full assurance." "Such a joyous stedfastness of conviction that I have grasped the truth is opposed to hesitating half belief. It is attainable, as this context shows, by paths of moral discipline, and amongst them, by seeking to realize our unity with our brethren, and not proudly rejecting the 'common faith' because it is common. Possessing that assurance, we shall be rich and heart-whole" (Maclaren).

This unity in love, which leads into an assured understanding of truth will, second, make for full *knowledge* of the *mystery.* Paul has already said something concerning this *mystery* (cf. 1:26, 27), which he asserts to be Christ "in" the Colossians and "among" the Gentiles. For the apostle, Christ is no other than, nor less than, God in the world—the image of the invisible being and the very love of God incarnate. Such is the gospel of God, and of Christ, which the first preachers proclaimed among all people. This, then, is true knowledge—to know Christ and his divine purpose for the world. And such is "full knowledge" (*epignōsis;* cf. 1:9, 10; see 3:10), in contrast with the limited and uncertain notions of the false teachers. "To understand the mystery, either what was before concealed, but is now made known concerning the Father and Christ: or, the mystery before mentioned, of the calling of the Gentiles into the Christian church as the Father and Christ have revealed it in the gospel;

and not barely to speak of it by rote, or as we have been taught it in our catechisms, but to be led into it, and enter into the meaning and design of it: that is what we should labour after, and then the soul prospers" (Henry). Here, in the last reckoning, is the key to Christian maturity: to know Christ in the full knowledge of faith. "Christian growth is into, not away from Christ, a penetrating deeper into the centre, and a drawing out into distinct consciousness as a coherent system, all that was wrapped, as the leaves in their brown sheath, in that first glimpse of Him which saves the soul" (Maclaren). To have *assured understanding and the knowledge of God's mystery* is, then, to know Christ.

Verse 3: In whom are hid all the treasures of wisdom and knowledge: This verse gathers into one sentence the four cant words of the heretics. But here the apostle asserts for his gospel what they erroneously claimed for their dreams. "Just as the right understanding of the community is dependent upon Christ alone, so also 'wisdom' *(sophia)* and 'knowledge' *(gnōsis)* have their ground only in him" (Lohse). There is no other "treasure-house of knowledge or wisdom but Christ; for the modifier 'all' excludes every other exception; and all other considerations." Stored up in him then "is the totality of all the divine attributes which are represented by those elements of the divine nature in its manward relation: 'wisdom' and 'knowledge' " (Martin). Both words are found in conjunction in Romans 11:33 to characterize God's unsearchable judgments and inscrutable ways. In the present passage they are declared to have their embodiment and home in Christ. In him *are hid* all wisdom and understanding. But they are not "hidden" in the sense of remaining forever out of sight and reach. Rather, they are hidden in him to be revealed through him. Unlike the pretended mysteries of the false teachers, whose secrets were only for a few favored souls, *God's mystery,* that is, Christ, is openly unveiled for those who have quickened minds to see the truth, and illuminated understandings to grasp it. It is hidden only that those who seek may find.

(2) Warning (2:4–8)

"Nothing needs more delicacy of hand and gentleness of heart than the administration of warning and reproof, especially when directed against errors of religious opinion" (Maclaren). This spiritual sensitiveness and sureness Paul had, like his Lord, as can be seen from this section.

(a) Warning against heretical talkers (2:4–5)

Verse 4: I say this in order that no one may delude you with beguiling speech: The phrase, "I am saying this" (literal) refers back to what Paul has already declared. He has reminded the Colossians that all knowledge is comprehended in Christ (vv. 2, 3). Christ and Christ alone is the inexhaustible storehouse of divine wisdom. By so presenting Christ the apostle aims to fortify the believers against the specious arguments of the innovators. To discover the preciousness of Christ and to explore the full meaning of his reconciling work is to be armed against error. The Colossians must not, therefore, be "tricked" *(paralogizētai;* cf. James 1:22) out of their treasure or "deluded" out of their triumph by the seductive speech of the new teachers. All that the apostle has said should prevent their being reasoned over by *beguiling* talk, persuading them "to think another path to peace and holiness more safe, more reasonable, and more honourable, than this way of Christ" (H. C. G. Moule). For to be talked out of Christ is to be "talked into error" (NEB). The apostle himself rejected the use of such plausible words of human wisdom; his message, in contrast with this high-flown wordiness of the schismatics, came rather with the power of God's Spirit (cf. 1 Cor. 2:4; Rom. 6:18).

Verse 5: For though I am absent in body, yet I am with you in spirit, rejoicing to see your good order and the firmness of your faith in Christ: Paul is physically absent from Colossae, yet he is there with his fellow believers in a spiritual manner. Were it possible for him to be among them "in the flesh," he could indeed speak directly to the situation (cf. Gal. 4:20; Phil. 1:7; 1 Cor. 5:3–5); but that was out of the question. Nevertheless, he is one in the fellowship of the Spirit with the Colossians in their common faith in Christ as Lord. And from this perspective he can rejoice to see their "orderly array and the firm front" (NEB) which their faith in Christ presents. The terms used here by the apostle are thought to have a military connotation (so Lohmeyer, Lightfoot, C. F. D. Moule, Martin). Lohse however contests this by pointing out that "the 'order' and 'bulwark' of an army would of course be requisites for the activity of soldiers, but hardly a cause of praise and joy." He would therefore see here a reference to the "well-ordered condition" which should characterize the believing community (cf. 1 Cor. 14:40), while the term *firmness (stereōma),* followed by the words *of your faith in Christ,* is then taken to specify the firm strength which supports the faith of the community. This faith is securely founded because it is directed toward Christ alone. As long as the Colossians hold firmly to him, no temptation can really endanger the Colossian church, but it will remain steadfast and strong (Lohse). So Paul can commend the faith of the Colossians "in respect of its constancy and steadfastness, meaning that it is an empty shadow of faith, when the mind wavers and vacillates between different opinions" (Calvin).

(b) Warning against spiritual immaturity (2:6–7)

Verse 6: As therefore you received Christ Jesus the Lord, so live in him: The *therefore* or "then" *(oun)* refers back to the encouragement and warning of the previous verses. In the light of all the apostle has said, he now urges the believers, as those who have received Christ, to go on living in him. They had surely *received* Christ in their acceptance of the proclamation about him made by Epaphras. They had received what they were taught (v. 7), and what they were taught was no "human tradition" (v. 8). By using the verb *(paralambanō)* which is specifically employed to indicate the acceptance of something handed down or delivered, Paul was underscoring the essential apostolic nature of the gospel they had received (cf. 1 Cor. 11:23; 15:1–5; Gal. 1:9; Phil. 4:9; 1 Thess. 2:13; 4:1; 2 Thess. 3:6). Yet what they had accepted was no mere form of words but the very Christ himself. For Christ is the gospel, the sum of apostolic tradition and the substance of Christian teaching. Paul evidently prefers to put *Christ Jesus the Lord* here rather than the term *gospel* "because the central point of the Colossian heresy was the subversion of the true idea of the Christ" (Lightfoot). In this way he strikingly illustrates the virtual identification of the facts about Christ with the believer's experience of him as the living Lord. The Colossians had received the gospel message, and in receiving that word they really had received Christ Jesus the Lord.

Paul gathers all the designations of Christ together here, as if to indicate the absoluteness and sufficiency of what they had received. A full gospel centered on a full Savior, on *Christ Jesus the Lord.* They had received "the Christ" (the Greek has the article), the promised Messiah, the One equipped with an unmeasurable enduement of the divine Spirit to fulfill all prophecy and to be the reconciler of all things. Yet this Christ is *Jesus,* the Man. He was no unreal ghostlike phantom. Jesus was a public figure who belonged to the history of the recent past. The false teachers might proclaim their misty speculations and whisper their dark secrets. But Jesus had a rootage in our human conditions and a place in our common ways. And this Christ Jesus is *the Lord*—sovereign in creation, in providence, and in grace. In this acknowledgment is the sum of Christian faith and in this affirmation the substance of Christian doctrine (cf. Mark 8:27–28; Acts. 2:21–22; 18:5; Rom. 10:9; Phil. 2:11).

Having received such a Christ they are urged to live their lives in accord with him. What had been received must be reflected. The verb *peripateite,* usually translated "walk" in the KJV (cf. 1:10; 3:7; 4:5), conveys the idea of progress, of an ongoing movement. "The inference is then clear: you have begun the Christian life by a commitment to Christ as Lord, having confessed Him as such (Rom. 6:4; cf. 8:4; Gal. 5:16). Now make good that profession and shape your life by living under this lordship, which excludes all lesser rival loyalties, especially to alien principles'' (Martin).

Verse 7: Rooted and built up in him and established in the faith, just as you were taught: Here once again comes Paul's profound *in him* which appears constantly in this epistle as in the companion one to the Ephesians. There is nothing of God for us but what is in Christ: all that is of grace and glory is *in him.* It is *in him* the believer is to "walk," to be *rooted* and *built up.* The mixture of metaphors is necessary to state all that Paul wants for the Colossian Christians. His various metaphors may "clash literally but are relevant spiritually" (R. E. O. White). Believers are to walk as live men; to be rooted like trees; and to be built up like houses; onward, downward, upward! But not backward—for no backward move must be contemplated, let alone be taken.

The change of tense of the two verbs translated *rooted* (cf. Eph. 3:17; Mark 13:6, 21) and *built up* (cf. Acts 20:32; 1 Pet. 2:15) is significant. The first is in the perfect tense to characterize it as a past action whose consequences have continuing effects. The second is continuous to emphasize that the resulting process is going on in the present. The Christian became *rooted* in Christ Jesus the Lord in the experience of faith's commitment. By faith he is brought into vital union with Christ who is henceforth that fruitful soil on which his roots may feed so that his life may flourish. And it is only if there are such roots in him that there can be fruits for him (cf. John 15:1–5). "A safe daily walk needs a heart securely rooted" (R. E. O. White).

If however the rooting is once-for-all, the building up must go on daily, hourly. Step by step and stage by stage must character be built up in him. "We are the architects of our own characters. If our lives are based on Jesus Christ as their foundation, and every deed is in vital connection with Him, as at once its motive, its pattern, its power, its aim, and its reward, then we shall build holy and fair lives, which will be temples" (Maclaren).

It is by being rooted and built up that the believer is *established in the faith.* And yet the converse is true: it is by being established in the faith that the believer becomes more firmly rooted and increasingly built up. It is the continual increase of faith that conditions all spiritual progress. Paul has already expressed his delight in the evidences of the Colossians' faith (cf. 1:4), but he encourages them to make it more evident still—to enlarge its range and increase its tenacity. For faith's grasp is never so tight that it cannot be tightened; nor its vision so clear that it cannot become further clarified;

nor its awareness so sure that it cannot become more certain. In the strengthening of faith is the strengthening of all grace, for faith is the measure of our reception of God's grace. So the believer will be established *in* his faith, as he is established *by* it. Both readings are possible, and each together brings out the truth. For faith is not only the instrument that establishes a Christian, it is also the object of instruction. The development of faith goes hand in hand with the development of the knowledge of what was *received—just as you were taught*. "Progress does not consist in dropping the early truths of Jesus Christ the Lord for newer wisdom and more speculative religion, but in discovering ever deeper lessons and larger powers in these rudiments which are likewise the last and highest lessons which men can learn" (Maclaren).

Abounding in thanksgiving: Paul adds, unexpectedly perhaps, the further note calling the believers to "overflow with thankfulness" (NEB; cf. 4:2; see 3:15, 17; 1:3, 12). For Paul himself knew how to be thankful in faith, and the theme of thanksgiving runs through all his letters. The duty of thankfulness is a constant injunction he gives to all believers. Thankfulness is a truly inescapable accompaniment of a secure and abounding Christian life. And lack of it "is very frequently the reason why we are deprived of the light of the gospel, as well as other divine favours" (Calvin). It is the trusting who are the thankful. As the believer grows in strength he will glow in thankfulness. The thankless spirit betrays a tremulous faith. "No heart is more vulnerable to doubt and spiritual delusion than an unthankful heart" (H. C. G. Moule). The inner music of the soul ceases when faith loses its hold on Christ. We can only keep the harp in tune as we keep the heart in touch. "Gratitude is that which completes the circle whereby blessings that drop down into our hearts and lives return to the Giver in the form of unending, loving, and spontaneous adoration" (Hendriksen).

(c) Warning against false philosophy (2:8)

Verse 8: See to it that no one makes a prey of you by philosophy and empty deceit, according to human tradition, according to the elemental spirits of the universe, and not according to Christ: The apostle comes now to give a specific warning to the Colossians against the insidious influence of a certain "someone" among them. He will name no names, and there is no need for him to do so, because the presence of this one must obviously be known to his readers. Besides, Paul is interested in principles rather than in personalities. His chief concern is that the Colossians should "take heed" (ASV, RV) and be on their guard (NEB). For the danger to their faith is very real. The situation to which Paul addresses himself is not a hypothetical one, nor is the adversary a shadowy figure. Unless they pay attention they may find themselves "captured" by the "hollow and delusive speculations" (NEB) which were being propagated among them. To bring out the measure of his dread and of their danger, Paul has recourse to an unusual word—one, in fact, not found elsewhere in the New Testament. In later Greek writers it has the idea of "to kidnap." The expression is, therefore, a strong one suggesting that the attack on their faith was fierce and sustained. It is the express purpose of this "someone" to make them a prey of a newfangled teaching. Such an enslavement may be set in contrast with what is said in 1:13. There it is the merciful conqueror who has transferred his conquests from sin's dark dominion into the kingdom of God's beloved Son. A blessed captivity is that to be imprisoned in the fetters of freedom!

The teaching which was designed to bring the Colossians into such tragic captivity is branded by Paul as *philosophy and empty deceit*. The phrase *empty* or "vain" (KJV) *deceit* is intended to describe the sort of philosophy Paul condemns. It is a barren and unfruitful philosophy he has in mind—a mere "intellectualism or high-sounding nonsense" (Phillips). The apostle is not bidding us set aside all philosophy as an evil thing, but philosophy of a certain kind. Philosophy as a noble pursuit is certainly not brought under Paul's condemnation. For there is a true philosophy, the proper exercise of the reasoning faculties, which reflects upon the world and thinks God's thoughts after him. Of such a philosophy it can be said with Francis Bacon, a little philosophy leads to atheism, but a depth of philosophy leads to religion. But the philosophy to which the Colossians were being subjected was a mere barren speculation, a swollen nothing, an empty fraud. There is a "show of wisdom" which is earthly and carnal; a wisdom "from below" (cf. James 3:15; see 1 Cor. 1:17–22; 2:1–13; 3:19; 2 Cor. 1:12) in contrast with that which is "from above" (cf. James 3:17; see 1 Cor. 1:24, 30; 2:7; Eph. 1:8, 17; 3:10; Col. 1:9; 28; 2:3).

This philosophy had its source in *human tradition*, and for its subject matter the *elemental spirits of the universe*. From first to last it was a teaching limited to human ideas and to earthly notions. It was altogether "a 'materialistic' teaching bound up with 'this world' alone, and contrary to the freedom of the Spirit" (C. F. D. Moule). It was *not according to Christ*. Here we reach "the sacred watch word" (H. C. G. Moule) and the touchstone by which to test all thinking about God and his world. Unlike the authentic tradition of apostolic proclamation which the Colossians had learned from Epaphras, this tradition was sheer occult verbiage transmitted in secrecy and mystery from one deluded dreamer to another. Its supreme con-

demnation lay in the place it accorded to Christ in its scheme. It
may indeed have included him in its terms; but it denied to him his
absolute place in nature and grace. It exalted created things to a
place alongside the Creator and gave to the elemental spirits a rank
beside the one Mediator. And as such it "disregards Christ" (Phillips): it is *not according to Christ*—"for Christian hearts, this is
condemnation enough" (R. E. O. White). Its whole tendency was to
loosen the believer's hold on Christ and weaken his trust in him as
the sufficient Savior. It was thus a teaching at odds with the fullness
which belongs to those who are in Christ (cf. vv. 9–10).

The Greek word rendered in the RSV and NEB by the phrase *elemental spirits* is the one plural word "elements," *stoicheia* (cf. Gal.
4:2). The limiting term *spirits* has been added by the translators.
Originally, the term signified stakes set out in rows, either to mark
off a boundary or to hang nets upon. From this developed the idea
of the letters of the alphabet placed side by side, thus connoting the
basic constituents of human speech. Two possibilities are then open
for an understanding of what the apostle means. First, there is the
physical sense, to signify those elements which constitute the material structure of the universe, as earth, air, fire and water (cf. 2 Pet.
3:10–12). Second, there is the religious use, to refer to the rudimentary ideas of a non-Christian nature which constitute the alphabet, so
to speak, of the human race, and the system of rites and ceremonies
which serve as the picture-book lessons of childhood (cf. Col. 3:20).
But whether these elements are considered to be childish teachings
or tyrannizing spirits is not possible to determine. Or, did Paul leave
it vague on purpose? What a blow to the philosophical innovators to
be told that their traditions and systems were like the picture books
of children! And what a shock for the Colossians to learn that what
they were being induced to accept belonged to the primitive fears of
the natural man! Not, then, with ideas of elemental spirits must the
Christian believer be concerned but with him who alone is the very
image of the invisible God. Christ does not need the aid of aeons
and angels to bring us to God. He alone is the Way. "The theory
that such aids make a ladder by which the soul may ascend to God
is perilously apt to be confused by experience, which finds that the
soul is quite as likely to go down the ladder as up it" (Maclaren).

III. POLEMICAL: THE TRUTH DEFENDED (2:9–3:4)

A. The Statement of the Truth (2:9–15)

The verses immediately preceeding this section may be regarded as the first shots fired by Paul in his attack upon the errors of the heretics. He has been making a long and careful preparation for his onslaught. And the warnings he has just written contain the key to the polemical portion of the epistle which now follows. Paul will maintain against the theological, ritual and ethical falsities of the innovators the sole sufficiency of Christ who alone unites God and his world. No other things, no other being, can be allowed a share in providing and guaranteeing this reconciliation. There can be no intervention of other mediators, "the supposed members of a pantheon of unseen powers, angelic and human, carrying up to the throne the distant echo of our faith, and bringing back through long channels something of the divine life" (H. C. G. Moule). One Mediator there is, and one alone, who has no competitors, and needs no helpers. For Christ is all; the Alpha and the Omega; the First and the Last; the Beginning and the End (cf. Rev. 1:8, 17; 2:8; 21:6; 22:13). In him all fullness dwells. He is the fullness of wisdom and knowledge. He is the fullness of space, for in him and through him and unto him are all things. He is the fullness of time, for he fills eternity—"before Abraham was I am"; he is the One who was and is and is to come; the same yesterday, today and forever. There is nothing beyond him—nothing before, nothing after, nothing more. He has no "before" and no "after." Jesus Christ is Ultimate. Other than Jesus will not do; less than Jesus will not suit; more than Jesus is not possible. More than all in him we find. Everything of God is to be found in him and little of God is to be found apart from him. Such must be the estimate of Christ that the apostle will set beside the heretics' teachings. In this vein Paul will take up the case for the sole sufficiency of Christ, first positively (vv. 9–13), and then negatively (vv. 14–15). Throughout he will show how Christ is supreme both because of who he is and because of what he has wrought. In this way the apostle keeps together the person and work of Christ.

1. The truth put positively (2:9–13)

a. The theological error of the heretics refuted (2:9–10)

Verse 9: For in him the whole fulness of deity dwells bodily: Christ is the very fullness of the Godhead: such is Paul's unhesitating and unequivocal declaration. The heretics had dethroned Christ to a place of one among many. The apostle enthrones him as alone the One in whom "God gives a full and complete expression of himself" (Phillips). *In him:* in the Greek, the words stand at the beginning with a special emphasis, the totality of the Divine nature resides "in a settled and congenial home" (H. C. G. Moule). By his use of words, Paul wants it understood that what was present in Christ was not a mere characteristic of the divine nature. Christ was not just a godlike man. By employing the genitive form *theotētos—of deity*—he is affirming that it is "the whole unbounded powers and attributes of Deity," "the whole essence and nature of God" (Maclaren) which dwells in him. Nothing less than "the quality of divine being" (Lohse) "has its fixed abode" (Lightfoot) in Christ Jesus the Lord. There can be few clearer assertions of Christ's absolute deity in all the New Testament than this. Christ is not just God in part but God entire; for in him *all the fulness of deity* resides.

The term *fulness (plērōma)* appears to have been one of the heretics' special words. It was used by them as a solution to the problem of the relation between God and the world—"a system of intermediate links between the two made up of the *plērōma.* Paul accepts this premise and the need for mediation, but quickly demolishes any spurious claims to a hierarchy of intermediaries (the aeons) by roundly asserting that all the *plērōma* is in Christ; and moreover this fulness is of the one divine essence so that Christ's office as a go-between is perfect since He is true God, true man" (Martin; cf. 1:19; John 1:26; Eph. 1:23). Such, then, is Paul's grand declaration concerning Christ. In him the entire fullness of deity has its abode now and forever. With this one truth Paul is able "to shiver to pieces all the dreams of these teachers about angel mediators, and to brand as folly every attempt to learn truth and God anywhere else but in Him" (Maclaren). Since Christ is all, there cannot be others to whom the Christian need look. It is therefore foolishness to turn to the elemental spirits "in whom divinity is thinly distributed, when we have Christ, *in whom the whole fulness of deity dwells bodily"* (R. E. O. White).

This fullness of deity is in Christ *bodily*. In a human body—
"incarnately" (T. K. Abbott), "embodied" (Weymouth, NEB),
"bodily-wise," "corporeally" (Lightfoot)—is the totality of the divine nature forever seen and forever secured. Here "really, not
symbolically," "actually, not apparently" is God known and man
reconciled. The *plērōma* dwells in him *bodily,* "not as the body opposed to the *spirit,* but as the body is opposed to the *shadow"*
(Henry). By Christ's humanity he shared with ours; and because of
his preexisting deity he shared eternally the very essence of the
Godhead. Yet it was not merely "into" a body that he came, but he
actually and literally became flesh and blood, by a true incarnation.
It would seem that Paul wishes to stress the reality of the Son's
union with actual human flesh in view of the heretics' repudiation of
the body as of any worth. Paul saw the reconciliation effected by
Christ as touching the whole life. Hence the stress on the *bodily* residence of the total fullness of deity in Christ.

Some commentators have laid stress on the present tense of the
word *dwell* and prefer to take the adverb *bodily* in a less specific
way, to mean "visibly" or "tangibly." Faith apprehends the divine
fullness as residing in Christ from eternity as demonstrated by his
creative and reconciling activity. Faith "sees that the entire essence
and glory of God *is concentrated in Christ as in a body.* It is in this
sense that it can be said that this fulness of the godhead *is embodied, given concrete expression, fully realized, in him.* This is but
another way of saying that from everlasting to everlasting he is 'the
image of the invisible God' " (Hendriksen).

*Verse 10: And you have come to fulness of life in him, who is the
head of all rule and authority:* As Christ is the fullness of the
Godhead, so is he the *plērōma,* the fullness of the Christian. In the
fullness of Christ the believer is filled. The *fulness of life* is ours because of his *fulness of deity.* Uniting the two thoughts is the preg-
nant term *bodily.* He in whom the deity dwells *bodily* is the One in
whom the church, as his body, shares the fullness of life. "Of his
fulness have all we received" (John 1:16, KJV). "Without Him we
must remain forever *dissecta membra*—uncompleted, unable to attain the true end of our existence. But united to Him, incorporated
in Him, we find ourselves joined in a living bond with Him in which
He and we complement each other as the body does the head and
the head the body" (Bruce).

Christ is head of all rule and authority, just as he is head over the
church (cf. 1:18). Over the church he is head by reason of a redemptive relationship, while "every power and authority in the universe
is subject to him as Head" (NEB), by reason of conquest (cf. v. 15;
Rom. 8:38; Eph. 1:21; 3:10; 6:12; Tit. 3:1). Thus did the heavenly

visitor become the earthly victor. He is the "authority over all authorities, and the supreme power over all powers" (Phillips, *Letters*). Over every principality and power he is "head, not in fully the same sense in which he is the head of the church (see on Col. 1:18), which is his body, but in the sense that he is supreme Ruler of all (1:16; cf. Eph. 1:22), so that apart from him the good angels cannot help, and because of him the evil angels cannot harm" (Hendriksen).

b. The ceremonial error of the heretics refuted (2:11–13)

Verse 11: In him also you were circumcised with a circumcision made without hands, by putting off the body of flesh in the circumcision of Christ: "There are two opposing tendencies ever at work in human nature to corrupt religion. One is of the intellect; the other is of the senses. The one is the temptation of the cultured few; the other, that of the many. The one turns religion into theological speculation; the other, into a theatrical spectacle" (Maclaren). In a very extraordinary way these two tendencies blended in that strange chaos of eccentric ideas and practices which Paul had to confront at Colossae. "Gentiles must undergo circumcision"—so went the cry of the heretics who claimed for their views the aura of Mosaic authority. Paul's counterblast is to insist that true circumcision is not a matter of outward act: it is an issue of the heart. The old ceremony was only a shadow of the true state. It prefigured the action of God on the heart. Thus, in faith's response to God, the believer undergoes the experience of a "circumcision made without hands" (cf. Rom. 2:28–29). It is in such an experience that we can say, "There God operated on me." "The new birth of the heart is Christian circumcision" (Abbott). Not the rite but the reality, not the physical transaction but the spiritual transformation, is what matters. True circumcision consists in the *putting off the body of flesh*.

To express the decisive nature of this act, Paul uses a strong word, a double compound—*apekdusis*. The body of flesh is to be "stripped quite off." "What is involved is much more than the removal of a small piece of flesh, as in the old circumcision; it is the removal of the whole 'body of flesh'—what Paul elsewhere describes as 'putting off the old man,' reckoning one's former self with its desires and propensities to be dead, as a necessary prelude to 'putting on the new man,' putting on Christ Himself in His resurrection life" (Bruce; cf. 3:9–10; Rom. 6:6; 13:14; Eph. 4:22–23; Gal. 2:20; 5:24). The *body of flesh* is, then, our human nature affected by the Fall. The phrase is akin to the ones Paul used in his letter to the Romans where he speaks about the "body of sin" (6:6, KJV) and the "body of this death" (7:24, KJV). The body which is thus to be stripped away is not the material and fleshly stuff of human nature, but the body considered as the seat of corrupt and sinful passions. From now on, as believers circumcised with a circumcision made without hands, we will not live "after the flesh, but after the Spirit" (Rom. 8:4, KJV). For the circumcision we have undergone is *of Christ*. Paul is not referring here to Christ's own circumcision but rather to a circumcision of which Christ is the author. In Christ is fulfilled all that the rite of circumcision prefigured. Indeed, the Old Testament itself suggests that the rite as such would pass away when the promise which it shadowed forth found fulfillment in the Christ that should come. As in his death all other sacrifices were rendered obsolete, so in his circumcision that rite has become antiquated. In Christ, then, "neither circumcision nor uncircumcision is of any avail, but faith working through love" (Gal. 5:6; cf. 1 Cor. 7:19). True circumcision is of the heart (Rom. 2:28), and is the possession of those who worship God in the spirit (Phil. 3:3).

Verse 12: And you were buried with him in baptism, in which you were also raised with him through faith in the working of God, who raised him from the dead: The form of the words suggest that the inner circumcision of the heart and the outward symbolic act of burial in the baptismal waters go hand in hand. There is the inward and spiritual grace and the outward and visible sign. So it can be said that "the true apostolic idea of Baptism was that of a 'sealing ordinance' " (H. C. G. Moule). In the act of baptism, we as believers demonstrate that we have the circumcision of the heart. In baptism we give expression to our oneness with Christ in his death and resurrection. We are dead in Christ's death to the old life, and alive in Christ's resurrection life to the new. For us, "baptism is the grave of the old man, and the birth of the new. As he sinks beneath the baptismal waters, the believer buries there all his corrupt affections and past sins; as he emerges thence, he arises regenerate, quickened to new hopes and a new life. This it is, because it is not only the crowning act of his faith but also the seal of God's adoption and the earnest of the Spirit. Thus baptism is an image of his participation both in the death and resurrection of Christ" (Lightfoot).

Yet the symbol is not itself the reality. The true circumcision of the heart is the reality, and without it, baptism is merely an empty form. It is not the baptism as such which brings the circumcision of the heart, but *faith in the working of God*. *Faith* is the means of our participation in Christ's burial and resurrection. Without faith it is impossible to please God (Heb. 11:6). Faith, then, is "Christ's way of circumcision" (Col. 2:11, NEB; cf. 1:4; 2:5, 7). And it must be such a faith that truly believes "in the active power of God who raised him from the dead" (NEB). Paul unites here the ideas of faith both as an objective fact and as a subjective experience. The risen

Christ, by whose operation the soul is made alive, must be believed in as the Christ who was raised from the dead. "Only by a belief in the resurrection are the benefits of the resurrection obtained, because only so are its moral effects produced" (Lightfoot).

Christ died because of the love of God for us; Christ was raised because of the working of God for him. These are facts—true in history, true for hearts. Since he died, we can live to him; since he lives we must die to our own selves. But die he did and live he does. "Thus we must die in and with Christ that we may live in and with Him, and that twofold process is the very heart of personal religion. No lofty participation in the immortal hopes which spring from the empty grave of Jesus is warranted, unless we have His quickening power raising us to-day by a better resurrection; and no participation in the present power of His heavenly life is possible, unless we have such a share in His death, as that by it the world is crucified to us, and we unto the world" (Maclaren).

Verse 13: And you, who were dead in trespasses and the uncircumcision of your flesh, God made alive together with him, having forgiven us all our trespasses: Paul begins this verse by alluding to the experience of the Colossians—*and you;* he ends by including himself among them as having being forgiven—*us.* He can remind them that in their pagan state they were, first, dead as regard to God (cf. Eph. 2:1–5). By *dead* Paul does not, of course, have in mind the mere physical condition, but rather the moral and spiritual state brought about by acts of transgression. This death is that of moral and spiritual lifelessness. Yet dead though the Colossians were, they are now alive in Christ. At the end of the previous verse Paul has referred to the physical coming to life again of Christ. Now he speaks of the spiritual coming to life of the Colossians. The two realities are brought into relation, the former being the cause of the latter. Christ was dead—a situation impossible; but God raised him from the dead. *And you . . . were dead*—a situation equally impossible; but you, too, are raised to life through the power of the resurrected Christ. The phrase *with him* is strongly emphasized; the conjunction *with (sun)* is part of the verb and is repeated with the pronoun *him.* "Being joined with Christ you are made alive with him," says Paul. "Therefore, death has been vanquished and life attained, but attained only—though here in rich fulness—where fellowship with Christ exists" (Lohse).

But the Colossians were not only dead with regard to God, they were, second, alienated with regard to privilege. They were uncircumcised Gentiles; they did not have the privilege of a covenant relation to God of which circumcision was the seal. Thus they were outside the scope of God's special promise to Israel (cf. Eph. 2:11–

12). And yet they like Paul, who was an authentic Hebrew of the Hebrews, a circumcised son of Benjamin's tribe, have been forgiven. Such is the grace of God in Christ. Now "in him," Gentiles though they are, they have been made "joint-possessors" and "joint-members" of the same body; and "joint-partakers" of the promise in Christ Jesus through the gospel (Eph. 3:6). So Paul the Jew and the Colossians the Gentiles are one in Christ. And as Gentiles they are not there by courtesy of the Jew; nor yet are the Jews there by courtesy of the Gentiles. They are both fully in one body because both are alike forgiven all trespasses in and through Christ. The Gentiles of Colossae share equally with the Jew of Tarsus "the promise of the life which is in Christ Jesus" (cf. 2 Tim. 1:1; see Rom. 15:8; 2 Cor. 1:20; Gal. 3:14, 22, 29). As Gentiles, the Colossians were "[uncircumcised] in the flesh" and so were "strangers to the covenants of promise" (Eph. 2:11–12), but now in Christ they have experienced the true circumcision of the heart. And with Paul they can rejoice in partaking of the fullness of Christ.

2. The truth put negatively (2:14–15)

Verse 14: Having canceled the bond which stood against us with its legal demands; this he set aside, nailing it to the cross: What forgiveness means is here further elaborated by Paul's picture-language about the canceling of a bond. The giving of a bond (*cheirographon*, literally "handwriting") seems to have been a common feature of his day (cf. Philem. 19). It was apparently customary to give a signed, handwritten "certificate of indebtedness" (Lohse) to the person from whom one borrowed. Such would remain as a telltale document until the debt was repaid. But in what precise way is the idea of a bond to be understood in the present context? And how can it be said to "stand against" us? And what is meant by its being "set aside"? Here are three separate questions.

First: What is the nature of the *bond?* It is generally agreed that the reference is not to "ordinances" (KJV) in the sense of "rites," but rather to "commands" or "decrees" (Abbott, Lightfoot). Our text has *legal demands* (so NEB). Ellicott renders it, "The bond which was against us by decrees." Hendriksen says emphatically, "This handwriting or handwritten document is clearly the law (cf. Eph. 2:15)." A few commentators regard the reference to be, not to legal demands, but rather to the gospel of grace. They then take the passage to mean that the handwriting, the bill of indebtedness, which was against us was set aside by the decrees of grace—that the legal system of the old dispensation is eclipsed by the new dispensation of grace (Johann A. Bengel). But these last ideas hardly fit the purport of the passage. It seems better to regard the bond as consisting of "the decrees of the law" (NEB).

Second: In what sense can such a bond be said to be *against us?* In the sense certainly that the law makes demands which none can meet. The precepts of the law are countersigned by conscience to be just and right and good. But where is the person who can measure up to the law's requirements? It is Paul's argument in Romans to show that none has done so, or can. God's law should have been man's best friend. But it comes now with stern countenance. What should have been "sweeter than honey and the honeycomb" (Ps. 19:10, KJV) is now virtually a poison. On her face the law "wears the Godhead's most benignant grace," but unable to meet her demands that she makes for our own best good, this "daughter of the voice of God," as the Jewish rabbis sometimes called the law, gathers frowns and thunders with threatening voice. Thus the requirements of the law have become an instrument of our condemnation; and so as *legal demands* they stand *against* us.

Third: In what way was the bond of legal demands *set aside?* This was accomplished by its being nailed to Christ's cross. The suggestion that there was an ancient custom of nailing up a canceled bond has no great support. Nor has that of the nailing up of a trophy above a conqueror's head. More weight can be given to the view that at a crucifixion a scroll of the victim's deeds was nailed above his head (cf. Mark 15:26). But whatever the particular allusion, one fact is clear: all that stood in the way of our full acceptance with God has been done away by the cross. On the cross Christ did all that was necessary for us, to all that which was *against us,* so that we might be forgiven all trespasses (v. 13). The scroll of condemnation that hung above our heads he took away. By his death the document of legal charge which stood against us was swept aside. "Because Christ was nailed to the cross in our stead, the debt is forgiven once for all" (Lohse).

Paul uses strong words for the effectiveness of the cross as "the instrument of our most merciful deliverance" (H. C. G. Moule). The writing having being erased (cf. Acts 3:19), the document itself was torn up and thrown away (cf. 2 Thess. 2:7). So we can rejoice that God has blotted out our transgressions, and our sins and iniquities he will remember no more (Isa. 43:25; 44:22; Jer. 31:34). "Christ has wiped the slate clean and given you a fresh start. He took the signed confession of indebtedness which stood as a perpetual witness against you, and cancelled it in His death; you might actually say He took the document, ordinances and all, and nailed it to His cross as an act of triumphant defiance in the face of those blackmailing pow-

ers who were holding it over you as a threat" (Bruce). By a completed act he dealt with the whole sin question. For Christ "has [in
accord with current practice of reusing expensive papyrus] washed
the gum and soot inkmarks from the document; he has taken it out
of our way; and he has nailed it up publicly, as so canceled, upon
his cross" (R. E. O. White).

*Verse 15: He disarmed the principalities and powers and made a
public example of them, triumphing over them in him:* This is one of
the most difficult passages in Colossians to exegete, and inevitably
opinions vary as to its exact meaning. Three questions arise.

First: What is the precise significance of the middle voice (on the
middle voice see note on 1:6) of the verb used by the apostle, *apek-
dusamenos,* and rendered in our text *disarmed* ("spoiled," KJV,
"discarded," NEB)? The same word occurs in 3:9 where it is translated "have put off" ("have done with," NEB). The cognate noun is
found in verse 11 of this chapter where it is given "putting off." The
question is, does the middle voice mean, "to strip *for* oneself," or
"to strip *from* oneself"?

The second question is, who is the subject of the verb, God or
Christ? If the former, "it can hardly mean anything but 'stripping' in
the sense of 'despoiling'—stripping a person of something that he is
wearing; but if Christ is the subject, then it may mean 'stripping off
from oneself,' 'divesting himself' of" (C .F. D. Moule). The issue
depends on how the final words of the verse *in him (en autō)* are to
be understood. They can be referred either to God's work "by
means of Christ," or to the cross (cf. RSV margin; Eph. 2:16). On the
other hand, they can be taken with Christ as subject, and so give the
idea that Christ on his cross "discarded the cosmic powers and authorities like a garment; he made a public spectacle of them and led
them as captives in his triumphal procession" (NEB).

The third question concerns the nature of the principalities and
powers. Are they good—for example, as in verse 10 of this
chapter—or *evil,* as they most frequently are?

With these questions in mind, some of the main suggestions regarding the verse may be set down. (1) Christ made a public display
of principalities and powers, having stripped himself by divesting
himself of his body (Augustine, Ambrose). (2) Having stripped from
himself the hostile powers of evil which previously encompassed
him, he flung them from him finally and forever in his cross (most
Greek commentators, Ellicott, Lightfoot, Weymouth). (3) He
stripped from *us* the hostile powers of evil by the deed of the cross
(Moffatt NT). (4) Having put off the principalities and powers—by
which he formerly made known his will (cf. 1 Pet. 3:22)—God exhibited them openly, leading them in triumph, by subjecting them to

Christ (Alford, Abbott). (5) Having spoiled from himself the dreadful hierarchy of evil principalities and powers which sought to hold men plundered from God as spoil, Christ exposed them in open disgrace by the victory of his cross (Bengel; J. H. Thayer, see *apekduomai;* H. C. G. Moule).

Most exegetes, it seems, favor God as the subject of the whole section (Lohse). But I prefer to take Christ as the subject throughout (Maclaren, Bruce, Martin). By assuming our human nature, Christ became subject to the assaults of evil which hung about him like a poisoned cloak. Of such he stripped himself in his cross. In so doing he showed himself conqueror by despoiling them of their dress and armor and parading them as captives, chained to the wheels of his triumphant chariot. "The spirit forces which accused you (he is saying) Christ has finally defeated, having divested Himself of their clinging attack. He stripped away their rule and showed them up for what they were—usurpers and tyrants, domineering over human beings and making them the plaything of fate and iron necessity in subservience of an astrological cult. The cross was the scene of their public exposure—and of Christ's resounding victory" (Martin).

Here, then, is the answer to the hazy speculations of the schismatics with their endless talk of aeons and angels, of principalities and powers. Christ the crucified is Lord; and all the hostile powers of the universe have become subjected to him. In Christ's cross the demonic hosts of evil have met their Conqueror. For "Christ's cross is God's throne of triumph" (Maclaren). At Golgotha, "far from suffering their assault without resistance, He grappled with them and mastered them, stripping them of all the armour in which they trusted, and held them aloft in His mighty, outstretched hands, displaying to the universe their helplessness and His own unvanquished strength" (Bruce).

The victory of the cross still stands. For us in our day the same sure message remains. We moderns, it is true, may not speak easily of devils and demons, of angels and aeons. But they are nonetheless real for us in new forms, though we may speak of them in another language. "These forces may be Frankenstein monsters of [man's] own creation; they may be subliminal horrors over which he has no conscious control" (Bruce). Today's men turn to black magic, to the horoscope, the drugs, to the numerous cults, to find release from the pressures of life and an answer to the problems of mind and heart. To any one of these it is easy to become a willing, and finally, a degraded slave. But the cross liberates from every bondage; for the cross is Christ's cosmic victory, his holy conquest, over every evil power and all human schemes. His scaffold is his throne; and his cross is his chariot. And so the person who has found release in

Christ's great atonement can join the chorus: "thanks be to God, who continually leads us about, captives in Christ's triumphal procession" (2 Cor. 2:14, NEB).

B. The Strength of the Truth (2:16–19)

In the light of the fact that the bond of legal demands has been canceled in the cross of Christ, and that "the sting of all the powers ranged against us" has been "exposed . . . shattered, empty and defeated, in [Christ's] final glorious triumphant act" (Col. 2:15, Phillips, *Letters*), there is no sense in the Colossians' yielding again to such tyranny. The demand made upon them to observe special feasts and fasts, ways of eating and occasions of worship, will only bring them again into bondage. Such things belong to the past as mere types of what was to come. The substance is Christ, who was proclaimed among them, and in whom they have put their trust. Those teachers among them who vaunt their wisdom, affect a false humility and boast about their visions would rob them of their status in Christ. They have substituted a host of inferior beings for the one mediator, and seek to loosen their hold on the one Christ the head. Thus they would sever the connection between him and the body in whom it has its unity, and from whom it derives its vitality. Paul urges them not to submit to a round of rituals and so lose the liberty they have in Christ (vv. 16–17), nor to substitute a number of rules supposed to lead to a higher type of spiritual life for the true growth in things divine which is from God (vv. 18–19).

1. Submit not (2:16–17)

Verse 16: Therefore let no one pass judgment on you in questions of food and drink or with regard to a festival or a new moon or a sabbath: Verse 16 asserts the reality of Christian liberty (cf. Rom. 14:5–9). It begins with a *therefore* and is consequently linked with what has gone before. In "view of such a position we hold in our sacrificed and victorious Saviour" (H. C. G. Moule), we are not to allow any one to *"take [us] to task"* (NEB) on matters of specific rituals. Elsewhere the apostle admits the need for a voluntary limitation on one's freedom for the sake of others (cf. Rom. 14:1–4, 13–16; 1 Cor. 8; 10:23–30). But here no such proviso is entered. It appears that the Colossians were being called upon to observe times and seasons as somehow necessary for their salvation. Such prohibitions the apostle must repudiate outright. They are not just harmless taboos but are harmful tyrannies. What Paul is attacking, then, is quite clearly "bad religion" (Martin). "To accept the observance of these occasions as obligatory now would be an acknowledgement of

the continuing authority of the powers through which such regulations were mediated—the powers that were decisively subjugated by
Christ. How absurd for those who had reaped the benefit of Christ's
victory to put themselves back under the control of those powers
which Christ had conquered!'' (Bruce). Absurd indeed it would be,
for the reason which Paul next states.

*Verse 17: These are only a shadow of what is to come; but the
substance belongs to Christ:* If verse 16 asserts the fact of Christian
liberty, this one proclaims its foundation. All those prescriptions to
which the Colossians were being urged to submit were only transient
shadows of what was to come. They had no intrinsic value on their
own account and were no longer of any significance. The reality
they projected and prefigured was now present. They contrasted as
"shadows with revelation, and absence with manifestation. Those,
therefore, who still adhere to those *shadows,* act like one who
should judge of a man's appearance from his shadow, while in the
mean time he had himself personally before his eyes. For Christ is
now manifested to us, and hence we enjoy him as being present"
(Calvin). The *substance (sōma,* literally, "body"), "the solid reality" (NEB) *belongs to Christ,* Christ is the "solid fact" (Phillips, *Letters*).

Yet the apostle uses the term "body" advisedly. "Since reality is
with Christ alone, the shadowy appearances have lost all right to
exist. Since the only true reality, before which the shadows must
disperse, is described here not as *eikōn* (form) but *sōma* (body), the
author of Colossians obviously wants to emphasise this term 'body'
once again: Christ is 'head of the body,' i.e., 'of the church.' The
reality which exists solely with Christ is shared only by those who,
as members of the body of Christ, adhere to the head (2:19). Therefore, for them the shadows have become completely meaningless,
and the 'regulations,' to which the arrogant exponents of the 'philosophy' refer, have lost all binding force" (Lohse).

2. Substitute not (2:18–19)

*Verses 18–19a: Let no one disqualify you, insisting on self-
abasement and worship of angels, taking his stand on visions, puffed up without reason by his sensuous mind, and not holding fast to
the Head:* Once again Paul uses the phrase, *let no one* (cf. v. 16) to
rule out every other consideration. The main drift of this difficult
verse is clear enough: Paul counsels the Colossians not to admit a
substitute for the faith of which Christ is the reality. No one must be
allowed to *disqualify (katabrabeuetō)* them. In 3:15 the simple form
of this verb occurs with the idea of "be arbiter" (NEB). There the
peace of Christ is declared to be the true "umpire" in the believer's

heart. The compound form of the verb has the idea of "deciding un-
justly against a person" (Lohse). It is to "give an adverse decision"
against someone, or to "deprive him of his rightful prize" (C. F. D.
Moule; cf. "beguile you of your reward," KJV; "rob you of your
prize," ASV, RV). Paul does not want the heretics to act the unjust
umpire's part against the Colossians and "count them out," just because they have not yielded to their detailed prohibitions and accepted their speculations.

The apostle continues his case by following the principal verb with
four participles to indicate the absurdities with which the schismatics
sought to bolster up their show of wisdom and depth of religion.

First: *Insisting on self-abasement and worship of angels*. It seems
to have been part of the heretics' rule that contentment with the
worship of angels was more commendable than a claim to immediate
knowledge of God. This, they claimed, was to display humility
which did not desire too much or aspire too high. But in reality it
was a misplaced "self-mortification" (NEB), a parade of humility
which took pride in its own form of asceticism. These people supposed themselves to be humble; too humble, alas, to venture on
God, to trust in Christ alone. It was a fantastic self-abasement which
would not take God at his word or draw near to him in his Son.
"The devil's darling vice is the pride which apes humility." "It
looked like a piece of modesty to make use of mediation of angels,
as conscious to ourselves of our unworthiness, to speak immediately
to God: but though it has a *show of humility*, it is a voluntary, not a
commanded humility; and therefore it is not acceptable, yea, it is not
warrantable; it is taking that honour which is due to Christ alone,
and giving it to the creature" (Henry).

Second: *Taking his stand on visions*. According to the strength of
manuscript evidence, the "not" of the KJV—"intruding into those
things which he hath *not* seen" must be omitted. This fact however
hardly lessens the difficulties which this short statement has posed
and which have occasioned many conjectural emendations. There is
general agreement, however, that the word sometimes translated by
the phrase "things which he had seen" (literal) has reference to special *visions* claimed by the false teachers. But what is the significance of the word translated *taking his stand on—embateuōn?* The
verb is apparently connected with the ritual mysteries of contempor-
ary cults. The NEB has the translation, "and try to enter," which is
admissable. Both ideas seem to run together. The one who would
"try to enter into some vision of [his] own" would then "take his
stand" upon the experience as evidence of attainment in the higher
"philosophy." F. F. Bruce quotes William Ramsay to show that the
word was a religious term familiar to Paul's Phrygian readers. He

then adds that these readers "would catch the suggestion that the person alluded to had formally 'entered upon' his higher experience like someone being admitted to a higher grade in one of the mystery religions, and was now appealing to that superior enlightenment in support of his teaching. The use of quotation marks may convey something of the force of the apostle's words, as when Ramsay himself translated: 'Let no one cozen you of the prize of your life's race, finding satisfaction in self-humiliation and worshipping of angels, "taking his stand on" what he has seen (in the Mysteries), vainly puffed up by his unspiritual mind, and not keeping firm hold on (Christ) the Head.' "

Thus Paul's charge against the false teachers was that by their vague visions and pretended revelations they walked "in a vain show" (Ps. 39:6) of unreal imaginings and misleading hallucinations. They were following a will-o'-the-wisp instead of living in the broad daylight of the revealed gospel of Christ.

Third: *Puffed up without reason by his sensuous mind.* Here is the third dreadful feature of the portrait. The boasted humility of the heretics was only a cover-up for their intellectual arrogance. "The heretic teacher, like a blown bladder, was swollen with what after all was only wind; he was dropsical from conceit of 'mind,' or, as we would say, 'intellectual ability,' which after all, was only the instrument and organ of the 'flesh,' the sinful self" (Maclaren; cf. 1 Cor. 8:1; 4:18).

Fourth: *And not holding fast to the Head.* This losing grip of Christ as Head must be seen as at the same time the cause and consequence of what the apostle has just outlined of the pretended religiosity and futile conceit of the innovators. By "will worship" (Col. 2:23, KJV) and making "a fair show in the flesh" (Gal. 6:12, KJV), they revealed their true position in relation to the gospel. And it was their declared desire to lead the Colossians into the same tragic state. They did not "hold fast" (*kratōn*, "keep hold of"; cf. 2 Thess. 2:15) to Christ. In fact they really disowned him by making him less than he is. And such dishonoring of Christ, Paul makes clear, is the destruction of faith. "It is the highest disparagement of Christ, who is the Head of the church, for any of the members of it to make use of any intercessors with God but Him" (Henry). If, then, anyone should "call us anywhere else than to Christ, though in other respects he were big with heaven and earth, he is empty and full of wind: let us, therefore, without concern, bid him farewell" (Calvin). For Christ is himself the head of the church by eternal right and redemptive act. And as such he not only exercises government over it but is the cohesive principle and the essential power in it. He is the Head.

Verse 19b: From whom the whole body, nourished and knit together through its joints and ligaments, grows with a growth that is from God: The idea of the church after the analogy of the human body underlies Paul's description here (cf. 1 Cor. 12:12–31). In the parallel passage in Ephesians (4:16) Paul uses the same anatomical structure to stress the need for the church to grow together into a unity of love. He is not thinking here of the world, the cosmos, by his use of the expression *the whole body (pan to sōma).* The context makes clear that he is referring to the church in particular (cf. 1:18; 3:15; Eph. 1:22–23; 4:16), and to the need for it to grow up by keeping a firm hold on Christ. It is from Christ that the whole body is *nourished (epichorēgoumenon)* and *knit together (sumbibazomenon).* Both participles are in the present tense, for the process is a continuing one. As the church draws nourishment from Christ, it becomes braced together. T. K. Abbott thinks that the term *joint* is strange in the context, because it is not the function of the joint to afford supply. He therefore prefers the idea of "touch" and suggests the meaning "through each part being in touch with the ministration" of Christ.

But Paul seems to be using the term in an acceptable physiological sense as understood by medical writers. And he had Luke, the beloved physician, with him when he wrote the Colossian letter (cf. 4:13) and would most certainly have checked with him about the legitimacy of his phraselogy. Paul may then be employing technical language to make clear the means by which the divine strengthening flows from him who is himself not only the Supplier, but also the Supply. The limbs are an integral part of the body. Severed or separated from the body, they are no longer in contact with the source from which their life and nourishment derive. The false teachers have ceased to depend on the Head; so have they ceased to function in the body. Thus cut off from Christ, they are cut off from his church. That is how closely Christ and his body are joined, and how important it is for the people of God to remain in living union with him who is their Head. "False teachers have proved themselves excluded from the church by reason of their forsaking Christ as true God and man; let the Colossians not be enticed into the same trap (2:8)" (Martin).

It may be that the particular form of the Colossian heresy has passed. But certainly the tendencies which underlay its specific characteristics are as much in vogue now as then. People today may not affect humility by a worship of angels. But there are still those who think themselves too obscure and too unworthy to be the objects of God's gracious forgiveness. They doubt his loving concern because they fancy that he can only regard the "great" and the "good." "We do not slip in angel mediators between ourselves and Him, but the tendency to put the sole work of Jesus Christ 'into commission' is not dead" (Maclaren). Other persons and other things we allow into our scheme, and we only half believe that Christ alone is sufficient for all the soul's need, and is himself the only Mediator of God's absolute grace.

And there is today, no less than in Paul's day, the claim to private religious experiences which are said to betoken a superior enlightenment. Many seek to build up an edifice of speculation on a basis of their own subjective fancies. They have moved away from the solid foundational facts of the gospel, and have drifted into a self-styled "spirituality" which only inflates pride rather than upbuilds character; or into a so-called "spiritualism" which fascinates the mind but is of no use for the instruction of faith. What the apostle had to say to the Colossians is a good word for us all. "The usual method of propagandists of some 'advanced, spiritual' theosophy is to unsettle the consciences, creating discontent and guilt, then to play upon this dis-satisfaction with specious promises of great blessing to be obtained through some new deviation. Paul urges that the Colossians shall refuse such assessments of their spiritual condition" (R. E. O. White).

All such dangerous vagueness boils down to a disbelief in the all-sufficiency of Christ, and to a weakening of grasp upon him as the one source of eternal life. In Paul's day the false teachers in their way sought to compromise the absoluteness of the Savior. Against them the apostle asserted Christ's absolute sovereignty in nature and grace. But in every age since, the person of Christ Jesus our Lord has been the central issue of Christian faith. Today there are loud voices within the church itself who, equally with those at Colossae, compromise his lordship. They, too, so qualify the church's basic doctrine of his full deity and perfect humanity that he appears as hardly more than a superman: a godlike figure, a revolutionary, a saint, or even a superstar. But anything less than that which the biblical revelation unitedly proclaims him to be—very God, very man; very God-man—is not saving faith, and cannot be Christian faith (cf. v. 9; John 20:28; Rom. 10:9).

C. The Sweep of the Truth (2:20–3:4)

Paul has exposed the doctrinal and ritual errors of the heretics. He will now uncover their ethical falsities. He will show how the truth of the gospel touches life in its total aspect, in both its outward acts and its inner attitudes. Such is the sweep of the Christian message, unlike that of the innovators whose prescriptions have to do with mere externals and cannot reach down into the hidden motives of the human heart.

If with Christ you have died (2:20), then "all the mundane relations have ceased for you" (Lightfoot). No longer need the believer be in subjection to the earthly and perishable. He has died to the heady speculations and vexatious prohibitions of the heretics which cannot curb man's natural cravings or sensuous desires. If with Christ you have been raised (3:1), then "all your aims must centre in heaven, where reigns the Christ who has thus exalted you, enthroned on God's right hand. All your thoughts must abide in heaven, not on the earth. For, I say it once again, you have nothing to do with mundane things: you *died,* died once and for all to the world: you are living another life" (Lightfoot). Such then are the far reaches of the gospel, touching man at his lowest and heaven at its highest. "Man's work in religion is ever to confine it to the surface, to throw it outward and make it a mere round of things done and things abstained from. Christ's work in religion is to drive it inwards, and to focus all its energy on 'the hidden man of the heart,' knowing that if that be right, the visible will come right" (Maclaren).

1. Lessons from death with Christ (2:20–23)

Verse 20: If with Christ you died to the elemental spirits of the universe, why do you live as if you still belonged to the world? Why do you submit to regulations . . . ? If with Christ you died—Paul assumes that such "is the case" (H. C. G. Moule), that such is a fact of which their baptism is a witness (cf. 2:11–12; Rom. 6). The apostle wishes to turn the thoughts of the Colossians back to a specific occasion when they *died* with Christ. That was when they became one with him in the commitment of faith. Then, in a very definite sense, they died in his death "to the principles of this world's life" (Phillips). So for us, Christ's death becomes ours when we die *with* him (cf. 2 Tim. 2:11). His death for us is, indeed, the ground of our acceptance with God and the basis of our full salvation. But by our death with him we are no longer alive to man-made schemes and ordinances, "whose sphere is the mundane and sensuous" (Lightfoot).

Paul uses the aorist tense* of the verb *died* to bring out the crisis nature of this act of "dying." It is a specific act which initiates a radical change of outlook and conduct. In the confession of faith in Christ, "such a change takes place upon the whole nature and relationship to externals as is fairly comparable to a death" (Maclaren). Death is a final, once-for-all, event. It separates a man from all

---

*The aorist tense in Greek looks at an action as simply occurring, as an event, without reference to time. It looks at the action as a whole, presenting it as "a point in time."

further participation in life's affairs; it makes him forever insensitive to them. Nothing of what hitherto occupied his thoughts has now his concern. So is it with the one who has taken hold of Christ as Savior and Lord. He has been cut off from all that he was. In the experience of the cross he has "died with Christ *out from under* the elements of the world" (A. T. Robertson). Elsewhere Paul sees this death as a separation from sin to God (Rom. 6:11); from law to grace (Rom. 7:6); from self to Christ (2 Cor. 5:14–15). Old things have passed away and behold all things have become new.

In the present passage the apostle maintains that, as death makes void the bond which holds a subject to a ruler, so does death-with-Christ break the links which bound the believer in his former state in servitude to principalities and powers (cf. Col. 2:15). No longer does he have to submit to "the elemental spirits of the universe" (NEB). For he has passed forever beyond their reach. "Since the presupposition is certainly correct that everyone who has died with Christ has also died to the 'elements of the universe,' it is downright absurd to accept the imposition of regulations" (Lohse). What does a dead person have to do with a legal code of taboos and rules? He has no life for such things! Yet it must be that the measure of our hold on Christ's dying for us is the measure of our experience of our dying with him. It is a case of a dying life or a living death. The former is life indeed; and the latter is death indeed. What the false teachers propose is but a savor of death unto death. Why then should the Colossians seek the living among the dead? Why indeed when no spiritual life can be derived from their list of "purely human prohibitions" (Phillips). For consider what is their end.

Verses 21–22: "Do not handle, Do not taste, Do not touch" (referring to things which all perish as they are used), according to human precepts and doctrines? Everything that can be handled, tasted, and touched belongs to this world and has its fulfillment here. Let those empiricists who would restrict all knowledge to the senses take note of that. For there is a knowledge of things eternal which comes by faith. This knowledge has its own touching, tasting and handling. There is a faith-sense that touches (Matt. 9:20; 14:36) and tastes (Ps. 119:103; Ps. 34:8) and handles (John 1:1) things unseen. But these inventions of men which the heretics presented as ways to God belong to the passing show of this world and are destined to perish. Such is the dead end of all their legalistic religion. The things "whose touching or tasting is forbidden by the taboos are things destined to be used by man. God has decreed that all of them without exception ('all'—*panta*) be consumed through man's use" (Lohse). Faith is not then a matter of food. For what has eating and drinking to do with the life of the Spirit? "Why submit to a series of

Don'ts, as if by adding enough negatives you would obtain a positive, or as if victory over sin and progress in sanctification would ever be achieved by basing all your confidence in sheer *avoidance?"* (Hendriksen). "Dives with his purple and fine linen, and the ascetic with his hair shirt, both make too much of 'what they shall put on.' The one with his feasts and the other with his fasts both think too much of what they shall eat and drink. A man who lives on high with his Lord puts all these things in their right place. There are things which do *not* perish with the using, but grow with use, like the five loaves in Christ's hands" (Maclaren).

Verse 23: These have indeed an appearance of wisdom in promoting rigor of devotion and self-abasement and severity to the body, but they are of no value in checking the indulgence of the flesh: Here is Paul's devastating verdict on the round of rituals proposed by the schismatics. Although, according to C. F. D. Moule the text is "hopelessly obscure—either owing to corruption or because we have lost the clue," the general drift of Paul's damaging characterization of the innovators "self-made" or "would-be" religion (Martin) is clear enough. It has an appearance of "wisdom"; but it is a bogus wisdom, which puffs up. It calls for *rigor of devotion,* self-mortification, and severity to the body. But to what purpose? None at all. Its list of legal demands fails to produce results. For such pretension to wisdom "in the cultivation of *will-worship,* a devoteeism invented and elaborated by human choice, and *humility,* of that plausible and spurious sort denoted above (ver. 18), and *unsparing treatment of the body;* practices which look at first sight as if they *must* be cognate to a true victory over evil, but which all the while, as compared with our glorious Secret, are not of any value against the indulgence of the flesh" (H. C. G. Moule).

The true gospel of Christ, then, is quite opposed to the "faked-religion" (Bruce) of the false teachers. These teachers move within the sphere of "elemental spirits"; but in Christ the believer is raised far above all rule and authority and power and dominion (cf. 3:1; Eph. 1:21–22). The religion of the heretics is a "will-worship" (KJV) all their own. ("Will-worship" is a literal translation of the Greek word which means "a self-made religion.") But in the faith of the gospel the Christian offers "spiritual worship," holy and acceptable to God, not as a consequence of severity to the body, but by presenting his body as a "living sacrifice" (Rom. 12:1). The apostle in this passage contrasts the innovators' stress on bodily rigor with the indulgence of the flesh *(sarx).* The *body*—the physical organism—may be subjected to ascetic practices; but the *flesh,* man's natural state over against God, is not thereby affected, nor its rebellious spirit lessened. "It is strange, and yet not strange, that

people should think that, somehow or other, they recommend themselves to God by making themselves uncomfortable, but so it is that
religion presents itself to many minds mainly as a system of restrictions and injunctions which forbid the agreeable and command the
unpleasant. So does our poor human nature vulgarise and travesty
Christ's solemn command to deny ourselves and take up our cross
after Him'' (Maclaren). All such attempts at a man-made religion are
branded by Paul as worthless. "Any system of religion which is un-
willing to accept Jesus Christ as the only and all-sufficient Saviour is
an indulgence to the flesh, a giving in to man's sinful conceit, as if
he, by his own contrivances, were able to perfect Christ's imperfect
(?) work'' (Hendriksen).

2. Lessons from life in Christ (3:1–4)

*Verse 1: If then you have been raised with Christ, seek the things
that are above, where Christ is, seated at the right hand of God:* If
you be dead—such was the presupposition of the last section (cf.
2:20). If you have been made alive is the presupposition here: "you
have been raised with Christ for a new life!" (Lohse). "The Christian who is risen with Christ has a new focal point. His spring of
motivation is set in the world of God to which he looks upward.
Paul's call is a resounding *sursum corda:* up with your hearts! No
longer is the believer earth-bound and circumscribed in his outlook
and attitudes like the 'man that could look no way but downwards,
with a muck-rake in his hand,' whom Interpreter showed to Chris-
tiana [in *Pilgrim's Progress*]" (Martin). The Colossians, the apostle
has already stated, were raised with Christ through "the working of
God, who raised him from the dead" (2:12). Their baptismal emer-
sion was the pledge and seal of their rising with "our" (the definite
article *tōi* is used) Christ (cf. 2:12, 20). In their death-with-Christ
they had severed themselves from the links that bound them to the
old order which sought to exercise its dominion over them. Now, as
risen-with-Christ, new links have been forged with the heavenly
order where Christ reigns as Lord. The call is then to *seek the things
that are above.*

"We must mind the concerns of another world more than the concerns of this. We must make heaven our scope and aim, seek the
favour of God alone, keep up our constant communion with the
upper world of faith, and hope and love, and make it our constant
care and business to secure our title to the heavenly bliss" (Henry).
Where Christ is—there is the realm of the spiritual and eternal. That
is where he went when he ascended from the here to the everywhere
(cf. John 3:13; 6:62; Luke 24:51; Acts 1:9; Eph. 1:20; Heb. 1:3; 8:1;
12:2). He was exalted from the grave to the throne—to the right

hand of the majesty on high. This is his place by eternal right. Kings placed at their right hand those associated with them in dignity and honor. No creature can be associated in dignity and honor with God except the One who has existed from eternity. God never said to one of the angelic host, "Sit at my right hand" (cf. Heb. 1:13). Having done what he came to do, Jesus returned to where he was before. As the God-man, he is forever enthroned with God the Father in the glory everlasting.

And because he is there, our hearts may have their home in the unseen realm. Because he is there definiteness and solidity are given to what otherwise would be nebulous and vague. "Without Him, there is no footing for us there" (Maclaren). But because of him we are blessed with every spiritual blessing in the heavenly places (cf. Eph. 1:3) where we "sit with him" in the rest of faith (Eph. 2:6), until the consummation of all things and we appear with him in glory (Col. 3:4). This, then, is our place and our position—"raised to life with Christ" (NEB). And on the basis of this, Paul makes his appeal to *seek the things that are above*. The verb suggests persistent and constant effort, "assiduity and intensity of aim" (Calvin). Yet it is more than "a seeking to *discover*. It is a seeking to *obtain*" (Hendriksen). The appeal is for consistency of life in view of one's high calling with Christ. "This is the strongest of all appeals to be 'spiritually minded,' i.e., to orientate all life's goals by the ascended Christ and to focus one's emotive drives upon all that belongs to God's right hand" (R. E. O. White).

Verse 2: Set your minds on things that are above, not on things that are on earth: The contrast between what is above and what is on the earth marks the contrast between what is "ultimate, essential, transcendent, belonging to God" and what is "a trivial or selfish view of life" (C. F. D. Moule). Such *above* things have their location in the "Jerusalem which is above" (Gal. 4:26), toward which goal the Christian is to press on for the prize of the upward call *(anō klēsis)* of God in Christ Jesus (Phil. 3:14). On this "realm above" the apostle would have our "thoughts dwell" (NEB). "You must not only *seek* heaven; you must *think* heaven" (Lightfoot). From this vantage point the Christian will get his perspective on life and the world; he will find his place to stand, from which to survey the whole panorama of human affairs.

To be sure, the heretics, too, sought for a higher mode of living; but it was still confined to the low levels of created existences. "But Paul has in mind a higher plane than theirs. Go in for the higher plane (he says)—higher things than the principalities and powers which dominate the planetary spheres, for Christ has ascended far above these. Don't let your ambitions be earth-bound, set on transitory and inferior objects. Don't look at life and the universe from the standpoint of these lower planes; look at them from Christ's exalted standpoint. Judge everything by the standards of that new creation to which you belong, not by those of the old order to which you have said a final farewell" (Bruce). The regulations and rules of the schismatics with their "handle not," "taste not," "touch not" never get off the ground. Paul urges us to live *above.* "Christ" says he, "calls us upward to himself, while these draw us downwards" (Calvin).

Verse 3: For you have died, and your life is hid with Christ in God: Paul repeats what he said in 2:20 regarding the state of the Colossians—*you have died.* Definite was the act of dying. (The verb is again in the aorist tense.) The thing had happened, really happened, when they identified themselves with Christ in his death. Dead, yes—but is life then extinct? By no means. For new life, divine life, Christ life, has begun: our life *is hid with Christ in God.* The old life "has come to an end with the death which we died together with Christ, and thus the past can lay no more claims. The 'life' *(zoē),* moreover, which God created in the resurrection with Christ, is and remains totally bound to Christ and is not at man's disposal" (Lohse). Removed from the sight of men, this heavenly life is a hidden life, with Christ in God—that is, "a double rampart, all divine" (H. C. G. Moule). It is *with Christ* because with him we have died and been raised to newness of life. And *in God* because Christ is the fullness of the Godhead (cf. 1:19; 2:3, 9). "Christ is at present a hidden Christ, or one *whom we have not seen;* but this is our comfort that our *life is hid with him,* and laid up safe with him. As we have reason to *love him whom we have not seen* (1 Pet. 1:8) so we may take comfort of a happiness out of sight, and *reserved in heaven* for us" (Henry).

But while the idea of a security "beyond the reach of harm" (C. H. Dodd, C. F. D. Moule) seems to lie on the surface, there may be another thought here. Paul has been arguing throughout the epistle that safety consists in "holding fast the head." He has spoken out against the secret mysteries of the heretics. Things hidden he would reject; therefore the idea of concealment may not be the thought here. "The thought of the Christian's hidden resources is more persuasive: having died to the world we draw our inspiration from heavenly places and obey a heavenly throne" (R. E. O. White).

Verse 4: When Christ who is our life appears, then you also will appear with him in glory: Paul now turns the vision of the Colossians from the present reality—their life hid with Christ in God—to the coming finality—their appearance with him in glory. Or, rather, he wants to bring both thoughts into focus for their enlightened gaze.

The verb *appears* does not refer to the manifestation to which Paul alludes in 1:26 as having already taken place. It has to do with the Second Coming of Christ which is the Colossians' hope, as it is ours (A. T. Robertson, Bruce, Lohse). Such is the Christian hope of which the New Testament has so much to say. The life that is now hidden will at "that day" be openly manifested when he appears in his glory.

Christ is our life: our eternal life (John 3:15, 16; 4:14; 5:24; 6:27, etc.); our enthroned life (Rom. 5:17); our empowered life (Phil. 1:21). Christ *is* our life. "It is not enough to have said that life is shared *with* Christ. The Apostle declares that the life *is* Christ" (Lightfoot). He is "not simply our eternal life (Meyer), or the giver of life, but the essence of life" (R. E. O. White; cf. Phil. 1:21; Gal. 2:20; 2 Cor. 4:10–11; 1 John 5:12). For the believer, Christ is at once the center and the circumference of his living; its source and its spring. The believer lives in the assurance of a grand consummation when Christ the Savior of the world will return and with him will come the new heaven and new earth in which righteousness will dwell. Then the groans of creation will cease as it shares in the glorious liberty of the children of God (cf. Rom. 8:21). For then the goal of the divine reconciliation of "all things," whether on earth or in heaven, will be brought to its grand finale (cf. Col. 1:20; Eph. 1:9–10). And in that display, when he will be manifested, his redeemed people will be revealed as "like him" (1 John 3:2), and will *appear with him in glory.*

By having this hope in Jesus Christ the Christian is called upon in the here and now to "purify himself as he is pure" (1 John 3:3). It is for his appearing we wait (Rom. 8:19–25; cf. 1 Cor. 1:7; Gal. 5:5; 1 Thess. 1:10; Tit. 2:13), and watch (Matt. 24:42–43; 25:13; 1 Thess. 5:6; Tit. 2:13), and work (1 Cor. 15:58; Eph. 2:10; 2 Thess. 2:17; 2 Tim. 3:17; Tit. 2:13–14). This will be the believer's grand day—his day of vindication, his day of transformation, his day of glorification.

"Don't we look for such a happiness as that, and should we not *set our affection* upon that world, and live above this? What is there here to make us fond of it? What is there not there to draw our hearts to it? Our Head is there, our home is there, our treasure is there, and we hope to be there forever" (Henry). In the immediate context (v. 3) Paul has the phrase "your life." He now speaks of Christ who is *our life;* he "hastens to include himself among the recipients of the bounty" (Lightfoot).

Part Two
Christ in Christian Behavior
(3:5–4:18)

IV. HORTATORY: THE TRUTH DESIRED (3:5–4:1)

A. The Reconciled Life and the Self (3:5–11)

At this point (3:5) there occurs one of Paul's significant *therefores* which signal the transition from doctrine to practice (cf. Rom. 12:1; Eph. 4:1). Paul was not, on the one hand, a mere academic theologian speculating with theories, nor, on the other hand, was he a mere general moralist, concerned with trifles. Always the apostle links up earth with heaven; yet, always, too, he sets the claim for lowly duty in the context of lofty doctrine. The apostle has been conducting us up one side of the mountain and along its panoramic pathway to reach the highest cloud-wrapped peak in 3:1–14. Now he brings us down the other side onto the lower levels of personal, community, and family living. From the exalted perspective of doctrine, we descend to the everyday perspective of duty; from the *credenda* we come to the *agenda*. And the connection of doctrine with duty, of credenda with agenda, is absolute. For in the end, we really behave as we truly believe; we finally express what we fully confess.

What, then, does Paul call us to by this clinching *therefore* of his? He makes his appeals on the basis of what he has already said about Christ's reconciliation and the individual's relation to it in the experience of dying and living with Christ. The whole drift of what he counsels is precisely this: "Live in heaven, that you may really live on earth. Live in heaven not in the sense of the poet but in that of the believer. Live in the recollecting and conscious union with Him who is there, but who is at the same time in you, your life. Live in the continual confession to your own souls that you died in His death, and live on His life, and are with Him—by the law of union—on the throne; and then bring *this* to bear upon the temptations of your path" (H. C. G. Moule).

Live by dying, Paul will say: for in dying you live. And this dying-with-Christ and living-with-Christ will show itself in the areas of personal, community, and family living It will be seen on the personal level in purity, in community relationships in love, in family affairs in caring.

1. Killing off the germs of evil (3:5-7)

a. The charge (3:5a)

Verse 5a: Put to death therefore what is earthly in you: Put to death—therefore. But wherefore? Because "you have died," because "you have been raised," because "you also will appear with him in glory." In the light of these experiences, and of these facts, the call is to put to death *what is earthly in you*. "These profound truths have the keenest edge, and are as a sacrificial knife, to slay the life of self" (Maclaren). Paul's command is a strong one; it is to "kill off." "The old man with all its members must be pitilessly slain" (Lightfoot). What has to be thus done to death is no less than "your members [*ta melē*] which are upon the earth" (KJV). The apostle is not, of course, speaking here of the parts of the body as such. For he did not share the heretics' view that sin is inherent in the material substance of physical flesh. True, some have not hesitated to credit to him such a gnostic conception. But a careful reading of what the apostle has to say about the connection between "sin" and "the flesh" prohibits such a rash conclusion. For one thing, Paul clearly distinguished sin from the flesh, and when he does treat sin's origin, he describes it as a voluntary act of transgression and in no sense the necessary outworking of human nature. The fact that the body can be cleansed and sanctified (cf. 1 Cor. 6:13, 19, 20; 2 Cor. 7:1; see Rom. 6:13; 12:1) is decisive against any identification of sin with the flesh. In Romans 8 (cf. v. 11) Paul refers to the quickening of the mortal body, and in the context he is dealing with the flesh. In all his epistles Paul declares for the resurrection of the body, and this would be inconsistent with the view that the body is essentially evil. He insists, too, on the reality and integrity of Christ's human nature, and argues at the same time for his sinlessness, a fact which suggests that in the apostle's thinking he did not consider the flesh to be sinful.

Yet "flesh"—*sarx*—is not a mere name for man's weakness as a creature of God. True, the flesh is corruptible (1 Cor. 15:53, KJV) and subject to death (2 Cor. 10:2). Nonetheless, Paul gives a more positive ethical content to his idea of *sarx*. Thus, while flesh is not itself sinful, it is that part of man's nature which gives sin its opportunity. It provides sin with its ready basis of operation. *Sarx* is that element in man upon which sin impinges and to which it attaches itself. In broad sweep, then, while Paul does not teach any gnostic notion of the essential evil of matter, he does regard the flesh as somehow permeated by the presence of evil, which issues in the "works of the flesh" (cf. Gal. 5:19; etc.). Consequently the flesh can be said to resist God (Rom. 8:8; etc.) and find satisfaction in mere outward religious ordinances (Col. 2:23). By *sarx* then is to be understood human nature as conditioned by the Fall.

What, then, the apostle "is really thinking of is the practices and attitudes to which his readers' bodily activity and strength had been devoted to in the old life" (Bruce). The association of certain vices with the "members" (KJV) make clear what Paul would have us *put to death*—that which is of the earth earthy in us. He has in mind "the 'limbs' in terms of their sinful *functions,* the transgressions which are specifically and distinctively corporeal in their conditions" (H. C. G. Moule). And the charge is specifically for those who have died with Christ and been brought to life with him (cf. 1:13; 2:3), for such have received a new nature. But the old nature is still to be reckoned with.

The reason is that "the new nature imparted by Christ does not effect the immediate annihilation of the old nature inherited from [the Christian's] ancestors; so long as he lives in 'this age,' and 'flesh' persists like a dormant force which may spring into activity at any time" (Bruce). The apostle has made it clear that the ascetic practices prescribed by the heretics are helpless in subduing the sins of the flesh. "The serpent has twined itself round my limbs, and unless you can give me a knife, sharp and strong enough to cut its loathsome coils asunder, it is cruel to bid me walk" (Maclaren). The apostle has a weapon all-sufficient, the axe of the cross and the sword of the Spirit, to cut the soul loose from binding and burdening evils.

b. The catalogue (3:5b)

Verse 5b: Fornication, impurity, passion, evil desire, and covetousness, which is idolatry: Paul lists five particular vices which must answer to the call and be carried to the guillotine. Such evils were prevalent in the society of the day, and are certainly rampant still. They are all, in the end, forms of evil self-love.

First on the list is *fornication,* or as the first edition of the RSV has it, "immorality." *Fornication* is a more precise translation of the sin Paul condemns. "Immorality" has wider connotations and covers much more than sexual deviations. But it is this latter which the apostle has in mind here. It is a vice always banned in the New Testament as essentially bad (cf. 1 Thess. 4:3; Gal. 5:19–21; 1 Cor. 5:10; 6:9; 2 Cor. 12:21; Eph. 5:3; 1 Tim. 1:9–10). Galatians 5:19 puts it first among the "works of the flesh." Elsewhere there is the injunction to "shun immorality" (1 Cor. 6:18). The second word, *impurity* (cf. Gal. 5:19; Eph. 5:5), embraces every manifestation in look, word and deed of the immoral spirit. It is thus at once a wider and subtler form than the gross physical act. The word *passion* may be used either in a good or bad sense. It obviously has the latter significance here. *Passion* and *evil desire* are the creative source of evil deeds. Galatians 5:19 refers to "the desire of the flesh" which leads to sinful actions. The last in the catalogue, *covetousness,* may seem strange. But by associating it with what we tend to consider gross forms of evil, Paul is making the point that it, like the rest, springs from the same evil root. They are all forms of self-love. The ordinary worldly nature seeks its gratification either in the pleasures of the flesh or in the passion for acquisition.

The immoral man, the impure man, the man of evil passion and evil desires, are all, like the covetous man, greedy for their own self-gratulation. All are consequently idolators. They all set up an idol of their own making in place of God, and worship the creature instead of the Creator. Idolatry is, then, the ultimate sin; it is sheer godlessness—a permanent and controlling principle of an irreligious heart and life which turns the soul from God (cf. Eph. 5:5). It is not necessary to be too precise in pinpointing exactly the specific sins the apostle is here condemning. That might too easily put some to which we are ourselves prone beyond his stricture. The catalogue has to do with the widest range of carnal misconduct—*what is earthly in you,* as he says in the opening part of the verse.

The reasons for killing off these germs of evil follow in the next verses.

c. The considerations (3:6–7)

Verses 6–7: On account of these the wrath of God is coming. In these you once walked, when you lived in them: The first consideration is the recollection of the coming wrath (v. 6). No specious arguments, no antinomian leavening of the gospel, no lighthearted regard for sin, can alter or annul this fact. The wrath of God is real. It is the same word of God which tells of God's all-embracing love that tells us of his all-consuming wrath. "If there is no wrath, there is no love; if there were no love, there would be no wrath" (Maclaren). Because of the evil things specified in the catalogue, "God's anger will come upon those who do not obey him" (TEV). This reality of the wrath of God cannot therefore be averted by the wriggling of men. From time to time in the history of the church false teachers have arisen to deny the wrath of God. But God's wrath is a fearful and terrible reality of the divine nature. In John's Gospel chapter 3—a chapter in which so much is said about the love of God—there comes the awful word, "He that believeth not the Son shall not see life; but the wrath of God abideth on him" (John 3: 36, KJV). No one can be true to the gospel of God who refuses to acknowledge its warning as well as its wooing note. The wrath of God cannot be expunged from the New Testament without doing violence to its fundamental message (cf. Rom. 1:18; Rev. 6:16, 17; 16:19; 19:15).

But God be thanked, we who were, like others, "by nature children of wrath" (Eph. 2:3) "have been saved" (Eph. 2:8), and "delivered" (1 Thess. 1:10) from the wrath of God. Those who are "sons of disobedience" (Eph. 2:2), however, are under that wrath still. It is, then, in the light of this reality of God's coming wrath that the apostle enjoins the Colossians to kill off the germs of evil. "Because if we do not kill them, they will kill us" (Henry). Paul is using this fact of the inevitability of divine wrath upon evildoers "that we may be deterred from sinning" (Calvin). "Accordingly, even such a wrath-statement is filled with mercy!" (Hendriksen).

Another consideration which the apostle adduces is the remembrance of past forgiveness (v. 7). In the specific sins of the catalogue the Colossians evidently once had pleasure. Their way of life was shaped according to its pattern. Like the Ephesians they, too, were once dead on account of trespasses (cf. Col. 2:2b; Eph. 2:1–3). Dead but walking! The unregenerate life is indeed a walking death. It is in this way of trespasses and sins that the course of their lives was set. The term *walk* is often used in the New Testament in an ethical sense to mean one's manner of life. There is a walking in sainthood (cf. 1:10; 2:6); and a walking in sinnerhood (here; cf. Eph. 2:1–3; 4:17, KJV).

By referring to what they once were, Paul is certainly reminding the Colossians of what they presently are in Christ. Theirs is a new state and status. They have now been forgiven all trespasses (2:13). Made alive with Christ, they are to "walk worthy of the Lord unto all pleasing" (1:10, KJV). But to do that they must see to it that the germs of evil are killed off. And such considerations as the recollection of coming wrath and the remembrance of past forgiveness ought to be enough to have them "put to death . . . what is earthly" (v. 5).

2. Putting off the garments of evil (3:8–11)

Verse 8: But now put them all away: anger, wrath, malice, slander, and foul talk from your mouth: Here Paul introduces into a religious context a word which had originally to do with the act of changing one's garments—*put . . . away* or "put off" (KJV). It is a metaphor of which he makes special use in this epistle (cf. 2:10, 15; 3:9). The expression is a strong one, calling for a complete putting off *from* oneself of all that pertains to the old life. Paul wants the Colossians to strip off completely those former habits which clung to them like an old garment, and to fling them away like an outworn suit of clothes. Such attire is no longer becoming for those who have been given new life in Christ. The idea is substantially equivalent to that of verse 5—"put to death"—but less vehement. There the vices listed were conceived of as members of the self; here they are thought of as the garments of the soul.

Off, then, must go the deeds of the "old nature" (v. 9)—"all these" (v. 8, KJV)—those things mentioned in verse 5 and those which he will now specify. Indeed, the apostle desires that "all [vices] of whatever kind" (Lightfoot) be stripped right away.

Paul lists five particular evils here—the same number as in verse 5. But the second list goes in the opposite direction to the first. That began with actions and went upstream to desire: this one begins with emotions and comes down to actions—those which specifically belong to the old uniform the Colossians had worn when serving in the sad regiment of evil.

Anger (orgē) is the first named for removal. The word is used of God in verse 5, and the verb is found in Ephesians 4:26 for the righteous anger of man. Here it depicts that outburst of passion and temper which springs from personal resentfulness and provocation. Associated with such anger is *wrath (thumos)*, or vengeful rage. When anger boils up there is wrath; when it cools down there is *malice*. "Anger and wrath are bad; but malice is worse, because it is more rooted and deliberate, it is anger heightened and settled" (Henry). " 'Malice' represents a general term for moral evil (Greek *kakia*) and is used in passages which depict the havoc to human society caused by evil-speaking (1 Pet. 2:1; James 1:21; Eph. 4:31)" (Martin).

Wicked love shows itself in deeds, while wicked hate is expressed in words. So next comes *slander.* The word in the Greek text is *blasphēmia,* the essential nature of which is the use of speech with intent to injure. As such it may be directed either against God or against man. Hate readily expresses itself in the speech which hurts. "The heated metal of anger is forged into poisoned arrows of the tongue" (Maclaren). Almost inevitably, therefore, the apostle adds *foul talk* to the list. The word used here occurs only in this place in the New Testament, but its meaning is spelled out in what James has to say about the use of the tongue (cf. James 3:1). In Ephesians 4:29 Paul charges believers to *put away* falsehood. For such is part of the filthy garment of the old nature, and does not belong to the wardrobe of the renewed life. Falsehood he regards as no more than a hood under which all sorts of equivocating thoughts lurk, waiting an opportunity to burst forth, and he associates "bad language" (NEB) with lying and deceitful talk (cf. Eph. 5:4–6). There, as here in Colossians, the reference is to the type of speech that is tainted by moral decay. Such talk is not just worthless, it is also hurtful, in contrast with the speech that edifies, the speech that is seasoned with salt (Col. 4:6).

Verses 9–10a: Do not lie one to another, seeing that you have put off the old nature with its practices and have put on the new nature: Consideration of one another is the great obligation of love. "A lie ignores my brother's claim upon me, and my union with him" (Maclaren). Lying is contrary to the law of truth and the life of love. It is both unjust and unkind, and works to destroy faith and to weaken fellowship. "Lying is a part of the devil's image in the soul" (Henry). For the devil is the "father of lies" (John 8:44; cf. 1 John 2:21; Rev. 21:27; 22:15). No wonder, therefore, that Paul counsels the Ephesians to "leave no loop-hole for the devil" (4:27, NEB). The devil will take every opportunity to squeeze into our lives and cause us to lie to one another. And if he once gets standing room, he will quickly have sitting room; if he gains an entry, he will soon become an occupier. He must, therefore, not be allowed "that sort of foothold" (Eph. 4:27, Phillips). No lying can be tolerated, just because it is an unbecoming article of dress for those who have put off the old rags and put on the new robe. The *old nature* has been doffed, and the *new nature* donned. Lying belongs to the old garments, whereas truthfulness is an item of the new. It is part of the believer's outfit who has been to the investiture of the King (see Matt. 22:1–14). To lie is to belie one's new nature; falsehood is not of faith, and what is not of faith is sin.

It seems natural to refer the acts of putting off and putting on to the original commitment of the Colossians. At that time they clothed "themselves with the new man, when they entered in the second Adam on their state of acceptance and spiritual victory" (H. C. G. Moule). But there are other ideas. So the question can be posed: Do the verbs regarding the putting off and putting on refer back to the baptismal experience of the Colossians and so provide a reason for not lying? Or are they to be taken as imperatives and thus as following on the command not to lie to one another? The latter suggestion is favored by Lightfoot. Lohse, although declaring that "the verb forms 'put off' *(apekdusamenoi)* and 'put on' *(endusamenoi)* emphatically stress the relationship to baptism," still asserts that "it is far more plausible to understand the verb forms as imperatives continuing a sequence of admonitions." So understood, the injunction of the verse is a call to stop lying and to rid oneself of falsity by stripping off the old nature with all its clinging evils. Those who see in the passage a reference to baptism point to the apostle's statement in Galatians 3:27 for support—"as many of you as were baptized into Christ have put on Christ." They thus regard the putting off and the putting on to be associated with the baptismal experience. The reason, then, to have done with lying, it is concluded, is that in baptism the believer expressed his death-with-Christ and his determination to walk in newness of life (cf. Rom. 6:4). "The link with the reminder of having divested oneself of the old nature is clear from 2:11, 12, just as the summons to live in the light of the new investiture matches Paul's teaching elsewhere (Rom. 13:12, 14; Eph. 4:24, though other texts are more general in scope: 1 Thess. 5:8; Eph. 6:11, 14)" (Martin).

Perhaps, however, it is best to see a combination of ideas here. An entire change is taken for granted by the apostle as having already taken place. It was something done when the Colossians put their faith in Christ the reconciler and when, in their baptism, they sealed and symbolized their trust. Yet, is it not true to Christian experience that what has been done, has to be constantly renewed? The paradox is this: we must put off the vices of the old nature precisely because we have put off the old nature with its vices. At the same time we must put on the virtues of the new nature because we have put on the new nature with its virtues.

Some commentators see in *the new nature,* or as in the Greek, "the new man" *(naos anthrōpos)* a reference to Christ rather than to "the regenerate man formed after Christ" (Lightfoot). Bruce points out that the first Adam is regarded by the apostle as the "'old man' who must be discarded, in order that the believer may put on the new man, the second Adam" (cf. 1 Cor. 15:45). The "second Adam," the "new man," is then, in this reading of the verse, Christ (cf. Gal. 3:27; Rom. 13:14). It is with Christ that the believer is dressed; we are clothed in his righteousness.

Verse 10b: Which is being renewed in knowledge after the image of its creator: The Greek verb used by the apostle and translated *renewed (anakainoō)* indicates continuous action. The new nature "is ever being renewed" (Lightfoot). But this renewing is not worked up by man, so Paul's word is in the passive voice (cf. Eph. 2:10; Tit. 3:5). The "renewing is not merely effected by us, nor due only to the vital power of the new man, though growth is the sign of life there as everywhere, but is 'the renewing by the Holy Ghost,' whose touch quickens and whose indwelling renovates the inward man day by day" (Maclaren). There are two verbs translated "to renew" used by Paul. One derives from the adjective *kainos* meaning fresh, unused, unprecedented (cf. Matt. 26:60; Mark 1:27; Heb. 8:13; etc.). The other form has the idea of young, recent, youthful (cf. Tit. 2:4) deriving from *naos* new. The two adjectives come together in Matthew 9:17 where the new—*naos,* freshly made, young—wine must be poured into new—*kainos,* fresh, unused—bottles. In 2 Corinthians 4:16 the verb formed from *kainos* is employed to describe the new creation in Christ Jesus. Here in Colossians it comes as a contrast with the old, as that which is distinctive, fresh, of a type hitherto unknown (cf. Eph. 2:15).

The new man *is being renewed* by a continuous increase of *knowledge*. The schismatics were given to saying much about knowledge. But for the apostle growth in knowledge marks the development within the believer of the new nature. The knowledge of which Paul speaks is not "a simple and bare knowledge," but "the illumination of the Holy Spirit, which is lively and effectual, so as not merely to enlighten the mind by kindling it up with the light of truth, but transforming the whole man" (Calvin). The new man is being renewed "unto knowledge" (literal); for an increase of knowledge of God goes together with an advance in spiritual renewal. "The new man is said to be renewed in knowledge; because an ignorant soul cannot be a good soul. Without knowledge the heart cannot make good, Prov. xix:2. The grace of God works upon the will and affections by renewing the understanding" (Henry). The new nature, then, will reveal an increasing knowledge of divine realities by a deepening communion with God, and a growing recognition of his ways, and a fuller approximation to his will.

The renewing in knowledge of which Paul speaks is described further as *after the image of its creator*. The declaration of Genesis 1:27 where the first man is said to have been created by God "after his own image" comes immediately to mind. If the apostle intends a parallel between the Genesis statement and what he affirms here in Colossians, then it is God who is to be regarded as the Creator, who will renew his lost image in reconciled man. Man still, in some measure, carries within himself "the image of his first purity" (Francis Bacon), though darkened and "carved in ebony." But it will become fully clear when at length the believer attains complete knowledge in the day of his perfecting. "The standard or yardstick and the aim of the renewal is God's image, the likeness of the very One who created this new man in the hearts and lives of believers, just as he once created the first Adam as his own image (Gen. 1:26, 27)" (Hendriksen).

But it seems more to accord with the christological thought of the whole passage to suggest that Christ is the image into whose likeness the believer is being transformed (cf. Rom. 8:29; 2 Cor. 3:18; 4:16). Christ has been designated earlier in the epistle as "the image of the invisible God" (1:15). But he is also the "image of true manhood," "the second Adam" (cf. Rom. 5:12–21; 1 Cor. 15:44–49). He is the representative Man, the head of a new, that is of a reconciled, humanity. He was raised and ascended; therefore at the right hand of

God is the true man, the real man, in flesh glorified. To be renewed after his image is the aim and end of his work for us and in us. "From the first moment in which the supernatural life is derived from Christ into the regenerated spirit, that new life is like its source. It is kindred, therefore it is like, as all derived life is" (Maclaren). As the image "is known to us in Christ, we may speak of his image as the pattern (1:15; Rom. 8:29; 2 Cor. 3:18)" (R. E. O. White).

Verse 11: Here there cannot be Greek and Jew, circumcised and uncircumcised, barbarian, Scythian, slave, free man: Here—where? "In this regenerate life, in the spiritual region into which the believer is transferred in Christ" (Lightfoot). *Here*—for those who have begun "a brand new kind of Life" (v. 10, LB)—there no longer exists those surface distinctions of national superiority, religious affiliation, or social class. For Christ, as the "last Adam" (1 Cor. 15:45) and head of a new humanity, has broken down all dividing walls. He has forever rendered void racial prejudices, nationalistic differences, class distinctions, religious bigotry, and personal dislikes, by welding together all into one Body. Every "wall of partition" (Eph. 2:14, KJV) which would separate man from man in the world has been abolished.

In Galatians 3:28 the apostle gives a wider catalogue of clashing differences which parted the ancient world; of race—Jew and Greek; of status—slave and free; and of sex—male and female. The Galatians are reminded that in the faith which they have declared in baptism no room is left for any apartheid. In Christ every wall has tumbled; all barriers have been swept away. No particular claim can now be entered, and no special disabilities can now debar, because before God none counts for anything. For in Christ all partitions have been leveled, curtains pulled aside, borders made to cease, frontiers between peoples and peoples swept away, and segregation of color from color made to cease.

For the Colossians, the apostle modifies his list somewhat, probably in reference to the particular declarations of the false teachers. But he insists that in the new life in Christ there are no distinctions between Greek or Jew. National pride is out of place here. No iron or bamboo curtain, no high wall of today divides people so absolutely as did the cleavage which existed between Gentile and Jew in the first century. Yet here is Paul, Hebrew of the Hebrews as he once was, now commissioned of God "an apostle to the Gentiles" (Rom. 11:13) declaring that the ancient hostility has been removed (cf. Eph. 2:14). In the fellowship of Christ racial distinctions of white and black, national and immigrant, are no more. "Not only does the distinction not exist, but it *cannot* exist" (Lightfoot).

Gone, too, in Christ are all claims to religious privilege. The circumcised and the uncircumcised are on the same level. There is no special class in grace. Sin levels all men to the same low position; grace lifts all men to the same high privilege. Sin puts us under the table as slaves; grace puts us at the table as sons. And all seats are of equal status. Not only are all one who are "in Christ Jesus," but conversely, all who are "in Christ Jesus" are one (cf. Gal. 3:28). Christ has by his cross nullified the former privileges of the circumcised Jew (cf. Rom. 2:25–29; Gal. 6:15) by introducing a circumcision "made without hands" (cf. Col. 2:11; Phil. 3:3) by which the uncircumcised Gentile becomes one with the Jew in the new Israel—"the Israel of God" (Gal. 6:16). No longer is there any special advantage, as far as the operation of grace is concerned, in being born a Jew; and no longer, therefore, is there any need for one to become a Jew on the supposition that it is a help in the securing of the grace of God (Gal. 5:6).

The terms *barbarian* and *Scythian* come in here, by way not so much of an antithesis as of a climax. They suggest a contrast of supposed cultural inferiority to the Greek. For the Greek, the rest of the world was considered as uncivilized and underprivileged, and consequently *barbarian*. In Jewish eyes likewise, the Scythian was equally abhorrent. According to Josephus they were thought of as "little better than wild asses." By speaking, then, of *barbarian* and *Scythian* the apostle had in mind those judged to be the low and lawless sections of human society. But these despised groups he brings within the renewing and equalizing grace of Christ. They have, with Greek and Jew alike, share and status in the gospel. Christ was, indeed, the first to blot out the word *barbarian* from the Christian's vocabulary and substitute in its place the term *brother*. So, too, was Christ the first to take away the reproach of *Scythian* by receiving them on the same terms with the rest as sons of God.

Paul adds as a final antithesis *slave, free man*. The gulf which separated slave and master in the ancient world was certainly wide—too wide for sympathy to span and understanding to cross. But not too wide, alas, for hatred to stride and bitterness to bridge. The apostle was aware of the awful miseries for which the institution of slavery was responsible in the social structure of his day. Later he will add a word about the relationship of master to slave. But meanwhile he puts in this clause to stress that the distinction between slave and free man has no significance in the light of the cross. In the all-embracing love of God, slave and free man are as one; and in the Christian community the slave as much as the free man is a brother for whom Christ died. There is, then, "no question" (NEB) of national superiority, of religious affiliation, of social status, or of economic position holding a special claim on God: for in Christ "there is no room for distinction" (JB) to be drawn between any one group and its opposite. "Christ is all that matters, for Christ lives in all" (Phillips).

But Christ is all, and in all: Here is Paul's grand climax and the last word on the matter. For *Christ is all:* and more than Christ is not possible. But since Christ is *in all*—in the Greek and the Jews, circumcised and uncircumcised, barbarian and Scythian, slave and free man, other than that is not necessary. It is in him, and in him alone, they are all one. "The words 'but Christ is all, and in all' contrast the new reality that obtains in Christ with that which divides men in the world" (Lohse). This statement must not be referred to the future realm in which God will "be everything to everyone" (1 Cor. 15:28). It relates specifically to the present order, so that in his perfected reconciliation Christ is to, and for, every believer, "all in all." "Christ is the Christian's all, his only Lord and Saviour, and all his Hope and Happiness. And to those who are sanctified, one as well as another, and whatever they are in other respects, he is *All in all,* the *Alpha* and the *Omega, the Beginning and the End:* he is *All* in *all* things to them" (Henry).

B. The Reconciled Life and the Community (3:12–17)

The distinctive community aspect of this section comes out in the three occurrences of the phrase "one another"—twice in verse 13 and once in verse 16. Significant, too, are the terms "God's chosen ones" (v. 12) and "one body" (v. 15). This latter phrase has already appeared in the epistle as Paul's typical description of the church (1:18; cf. 1:24; 2:17, 19). In the first part of this present passage the apostle turns his readers' thoughts back, by "the logic of inference," to what he has said earlier about the putting off and the putting on of the garments of the soul. The "therefore" (KJV) of verse 12 has in view these parallel exhortations, but its more immediate context are the words, "but Christ is all, and in all." Because of the new nature put on in Christ, believers should therefore array themselves in becoming garments. Because Christ is all, we should therefore all be clothed in the complete robes of brotherly graces, in harmony with the unity which is ours through their common possession of Christ. The apostle goes on from this requirement to add a number of loosely connected injunctions designed to amplify something of the all-sufficiency which is in Christ. These further statements can be focused on aspects of Christ's relationship to the believer's welfare—his peace, his word, and his name.

1. Robes from the Christian's wardrobe (3:12–14)

Verse 12: Put on then, as God's chosen ones, holy and beloved, compassion, kindness, lowliness, meekness, and patience: Paul now sets out the items of the Christian's clothing which are to be *put on.* But first he states another reason for his appeal. Those who are in possession of the "new nature," he declares to be *God's chosen ones,* his "picked representatives of the new humanity" (Phillips, *Letters*). They have been chosen in Christ (cf. Eph. 1:4), according to the foreknowledge of God (1 Pet. 1:2) and constituted by him a "chosen race" (1 Pet. 2:9). God's choice is the foundation and first cause of all the benefits we have "in Christ." Yet God is not to be thought of as choosing from among those who are not "in Christ" with a view of bringing them into union with him; rather, the elect are those "in Christ," and by virtue of being "in him" they come into the possession of all those spiritual blessings which in God's eternal purpose it was decreed before ever the world was created, were theirs to enjoy. For Paul, the doctrine of God's absolute choice was never an idle speculation but was a living experience. "In Christ" is the assurance of all God has determined before the foundation of the world.

As God's chosen ones, believers are *holy and beloved—holy,* because they are dedicated to God by being chosen in Christ; *beloved* because of "having being loved" (perfect passive participle) by him into a living relationship with himself. The call to *put on* comes as a reminder to the Colossians that because they know themselves to be God's chosen ones, and thus *holy and beloved,* they are not exempt from the necessity of right living. Paul's word is the same as that of Peter's: "Set your minds, then, on endorsing by your conduct the fact that God has called and chosen you" (2 Pet. 1:10, Phillips). Holy you are; so holy you must become; beloved you are, so as sons beloved you must live. "Those who have been sanctified by God are called to 'holiness' (*hagiasmos,* 1 Thess. 4:3). They have experienced God's love in his act of election and therefore should deal with other men in terms of 'love' (*agapē*)" (Lohse).

And how best will that holiness and love be displayed? Clearly by putting on the garments fitting for the renewed life. In keeping with the numbers specified in verses 5 and 7, Paul lists five. *Compassion,* or better "a heart of compassion" (*splagchna oiktirmou*) comes first. The expression is formed by the union of two separate words which are found in Philippians 2:1 joined by a conjunction and there rendered "affection and sympathy." The phrase is really a Hebraism. Among the Greek poets, the *splagchna,* inward parts, viscera—the bowels, liver, lungs, and heart—were considered the seat of different emotions. More particularly, the bowels were regarded as the basis of the more violent passions—anger and love. But to the Hebrews, the bowels were the special seat of the tenderer affections, such as kindness and compassion (cf. "the bowels of Jesus," Phil. 1:8, KJV; "bowels of mercies," here and Phil. 2:1, KJV; cf. 2 Cor. 6:12; 1 John 3:17; and see on Philem. 7, 12, 20). The idea is that of a ready and open sympathy which finds evidence in outward deeds of goodness. Arndt and Gingrich translate the phrase "heartfelt compassion." *Kindness* is a term associated with God in Titus 3:4; with Christ in Ephesians 2:7; and with the Holy Spirit in 2 Corinthians 6:6. Here it forms a pair with *lowliness* (cf. Eph. 4:2; Phil. 2:3), to describe the Christian temper in its two main aspects; of one's relation to others *(kindness)*, and one's relation to oneself *(lowliness)*. Lowliness is when the "I-ness" is laid low; and the lower we get the higher we go.

With lowliness the apostle associates *meekness*. Meekness has to do with that disposition of mind which shows itself uncomplaining and unresentful. It is in this spirit we are to receive the word of God (James 3:21). It especially refers to the attitude of "easiness" and "mildness" by which we treat other people (cf. 1 Cor. 4:21; Gal. 6:1; 2 Tim. 2:25; Tit. 3:2). Meekness, however, is not weakness. For the person of gentle spirit is the person who has control of himself under Christ. Such a person finds strength for his meekness in the meekness of Christ's strength (cf. Matt. 11:29). It is the meek who inherit the earth (Matt. 5:5; cf. Ps. 37:11). The *"King* cometh . . . *meek"* and lowly (Matt. 21:5, KJV): that was the paradox both Jew and Greek failed to understand. In the thinking of the Jew, loftiness was alone the sign of lordliness; and in the teaching of the Greek, sovereignty was displayed in strength. But for the Christian, meekness is the badge of mightiness. Thus Jesus revealed to the Jew that which in his own Scriptures the Jew failed to reveal; and thus Paul demanded of the Christian that which Jesus so fully demonstrated— that "the Lord lifteth up the meek" (Ps. 147:6) and he "will beautify the meek with salvation" (Ps. 149:4).

The word translated *patience* (cf. Eph. 4:2) is in the KJV translated "longsuffering" (cf. Heb. 6:12; James 5:10). Underlying the word is the thought of "slowness in avenging wrong" (Abbott). To be longsuffering is to suffer long; there is no limit. It is used of God's relation to man (Rom. 2:4; 9:22; 1 Pet. 3:20; 2 Pet. 3:15), and of Christian behavior in relation to others (2 Tim. 4:2; cf. Eph. 4:2). It is essentially the fruit of the Spirit (Gal. 5:22).

Verse 13: Forbearing one another and, if one has a complaint against another, forgiving each other; as the Lord has forgiven you,

so you also must forgive: The imperative participles *forbearing* and
forgiving once again underline the supreme importance of right action within the Christian community. Yet they do not come in here
as new virtues. Rather they are the qualities of meekness and patience in action. Patience, we have seen, is slowness in avenging
wrong; and meekness is the disposition to be unresentful. The patient person is not ever quickly angry; while the meek person is not
ever wrongly angry. Forbearance is patience demonstrated. The forbearing person will remain calm whatever the provocation, and will
keep clear of unkind reactions. The forgiving person must go even
further, and wipe clean from his heart all bitterness and irritation.
Forbearing one another and forgiving one another are then the high
charge of Christian duty—the outworking of the virtues put on.

Yet there does not seem to be a specific situation envisaged in this
call to forbearance and forgiveness; for "the 'if' *(ean),* puts, as it
were, reluctantly, a case just supposable" (H. C. G. Moule). Rather
the admonition expresses "something that is universally valid for the
community's life together" (Lohse). And, certainly, there are always
occasions enough within the fellowship of the church "for the exercise of these peace-making attitudes as we seek to curb our impa-
tience with that person and to show a charitable and forgiving spirit"
(Martin).

The pattern and motive of forgiveness are given particular emphasis in the phrase *as the Lord has forgiven you. As* Christ forgave—
who can measure that? (Cf. 1:14; 2:13.) In the parallel passage in
Ephesians 4:32, forgiveness is based on the fact that "God in
Christ" (RSV) or "for Christ's sake" (KJV; see also Phillips) forgave
us. The experience of God's forgiveness in Christ should be enough
to make us not only ready but eager to forgive. The natural outflow
of the forgiven heart is "love" (cf. Eph. 4:2). When Simon, in
whose house Jesus was a guest, protested at the presence of a
woman who was "a sinner," Jesus replied that "her sins, which are
many, are forgiven her, for she loved much" (Luke 7:47). Jesus was
not, of course, declaring that her love was the ground, or condition,
of her forgiveness. The force of the "for" is rather "because"
(hoti)—because you see this lavish outpouring of her love, you may
know she has been forgiven much. Nor is there any limit to the forgiveness we must show to others (cf. Matt. 5:43; 18:22). There is a
close connection between our willingness to forgive others and
God's forgiveness of us (cf. e.g., Matt. 6:12–13). It is only the one
who can forgive who can be forgiven. This is no *lex talionis*—no law
of retaliation. Jesus does not say that God will show mercy only
when we show it to others. The point is rather that God cannot for-

give the one who will not forgive, for an unforgiving spirit reveals an unrepentant heart. And where there is no full repentance there is no real forgiveness. In the present context, the word Paul uses for *forgiving* is not the common one generally translated either as "to remit" or "to let off." It is a word of richer content with the basic meaning of "give freely or graciously" and rendered "frankly forgave" in Luke 7:42 (KJV).

Such, then, "is the apostle's outline sketch of the Christian character in its social aspect, all rooted in pity, and full of soft compassion; quick to apprehend, to feel, and to succour sorrow; a kindness, equable and widespread, illuminating all who come within its reach; a patient acceptance of wrongs without resentment or revenge, because a lowly judgement of self and its claims, a spirit schooled to calmness under all provocations, disdaining to requite wrong by wrong, and quick to forgive" (Maclaren).

Verse 14: And above all these put on love, which binds everything together in perfect harmony: Above all these things does not mean here "more important than all." The idea is rather that of "over" in its simple local sense. The apostle has in mind the flowing garments of his day which had to be kept together by a girdle. Over the other garments which the Christian has *put on* must be added the silken sash of love to bind them securely about himself. For love is "the bond of perfectness" (KJV; cf. 1:4, 8; 2:2). "The grace which binds all these other graces together [is] the crowning grace of love" (Bruce). Love is the uniting principle which keeps all the other virtues in their proper place. It is, indeed, the very fullness of Christian living. So Paul, in Ephesians bids Christians "live in love" (5:2, NEB). Love is the law of the Christian road. "In the present context it is especially *mutual* love, love for one another within the Christian community, that is thought of, though it is true that such love overflows its boundaries (1 Thess. 3:12)" (Hendriksen). In Colossians 3:13 Paul has called upon Christians to manifest the forgiving spirit. He now broadens the injunction to that of *love*. It is love that brightens the day and lightens the load. The special requirements of verses 12 and 13 are now brought under this one positive command, "to crown all" (NEB) with love, and to be "truly loving, for love is the golden chain of all the virtues" (Phillips, *Letters*).

2. Rules for the Christian's welfare (3:15–17)

We noticed earlier how these verses focus upon three realities of Christ—his peace, his word, his name. These are treated by Maclaren under the headings "The Ruling Peace of Christ" (v. 15), "The Indwelling Word of Christ" (v. 16); "The All-hallowing Name of Christ" (v. 17).

a. The ruling peace of Christ (3:15).

Verse 15: And let the peace of Christ rule in your hearts, to which indeed you were called in the one body: The manuscript evidence supports the particular reading of the RSV, *the peace of Christ,* (the KJV, following later manuscripts has "the peace of God"). The expression is not without suggestive parallels. Recalled at once will be Christ's own words, "Peace I leave with you, my peace I give to you" (John 14:27). Christ's peace is his legacy. But it is not something possessed apart from himself. To have his peace is to have himself. "For he is our peace" (Eph. 2:14). He is "the Lord of peace" who can give peace at all times (2 Thess. 3:16). He made peace by "the blood of his cross" (Col. 1:20), thus reconciling us to himself so that we may through him "continue at peace with God" (Rom. 5:1, NEB). Thus every believer can enjoy the calm of Christ's ruling peace amidst fightings without and fears within. For here is peace subsisting at the heart of endless agitation.

The appeal is to *let* the peace of Christ rule our hearts. It must be allowed scope and rule. And the surest way to have the peace of Christ always at flood tide is to maintain fellowship with him. "The fulness of our possession of His gift of peace depends altogether on our proximity to the Giver" (Maclaren). It "diminishes with the square of distance" from its source. This peace of Christ is to *rule* the heart. The verb—*brabeuein*—occurs only here in the New Testament; but it carries the idea of "to arbitrate" (cf. NEB, Bruce), "to umpire" (Lightfoot), "to hold sway" (Lohse).

It is, however, within the context of the community that Christ's peace must be allowed to act as umpire. The *your* is plural. So the apostle's word is "let the plea for self-assertion be ever met and negatived by the decision of that umpire *(brabens)* in favour of love. For that 'peace of Christ' is given to you not for yourselves as individuals, but for the community" (H. C. G. Moule). Within the church, the peace of Christ must "give the verdict" on every occasion and in every situation where differences threaten to disturb its fellowship and destroy its unity. "For if the members are subjected to Him, the peace which He imparts must regulate their relations with one another. It is not to strife but peace that God has called them in the unity of the body of Christ" (Bruce). The Colossians *were called in the one body,* to share the peace of Christ. So were they knit together by the possession of a common gift.

Thus summoned to be joint-partakers of so precious a possession, they must now give that peace of Christ the right to "be arbiter" (NEB) in molding their common life. It would be a contradiction, indeed, if having being brought into one body by becoming joint-sharers in the peace of Christ, they yet refused to allow that peace to bind them all together into one fellowship of love. The peace of God will garrison the heart of the individual believer and keep at a distance the hostile forces which seek an entry (Phil. 4:7). But the *peace of Christ* will be its umpire for the fellowship of "God's chosen ones" as its right is acknowledged and its reign allowed. "Let the ruling principle in your hearts be Christ's peace, for in becoming members of one body you have been called under its sway" (Goodspeed). "We are called to peace, to peace with God as our privilege, and peace with our brethren as our duty" (Henry).

In Colossians 1:2 the apostle has wished "grace and peace" for the church. There he puts *grace* first, as if to say that peace has its source and stay in grace. "Nothing is more desirable," says Calvin in a comment on Romans 1:7, "than to have God propitious to us, and this is signified by *grace;* and then to have prosperity and success in all things flowing from him, and this is intimated by *peace.*" Grace and peace, the words belong together as the two experiences go hand in hand. The reception of grace is the realization of peace.

And be thankful: Literally, "become thankful." Thankfulness is nothing other than "the response of gratitude to the grace of God" (Bruce). However, Paul is not asking that the Colossians may begin to express gratitude; rather he wants them to "become more and more thankful." Thankful in some measure he knew them to be (cf. 1:12). He wanted them to "be filled with gratitude" (NEB) and to "always be thankful" (LB). The failure to glorify God and give him thanks was the indictment brought against the pagan world in Romans 1:21. If, therefore, thanks is due from all men, how much more should it come from those who possess the "peace of Christ." The measure of our thanks is the depth of our trust. The praiseless heart is still a pagan spirit. To be without a Savior is to be without a song. But our gratitude must grow until there is praise in every part. The apostle himself is the best illustration of a life which never forgot to be thankful for what God had done. Paul was apt to catch fire whenever he thought of God's fathomless grace. His characteristic style is to give expression to a sudden burst of gratitude whenever his thought led him to the sunlit heights from which to catch sight of God's miracle of love in Christ. This interjected precept in Colossians 3:15 is one more instance of Paul's sudden jets of praise. For his own great heart was certainly overflowing with the peace of Christ about which he had just written. And as he recalls what he has disclosed already about this Christ which reached its sum in his declaration, "Christ is all, and in all" (v. 11), how can the Colossians be other than thankful? *And be thankful*—who of us cannot but be? "And to crown all forget yourselves in thankfulness towards

[Christ]" (Lightfoot): let us bracket ourselves in with Christ, and be thankful.

Always be thankful for everything, he says to the Ephesians (cf. 5:20). He may seem to be asking a hard thing here as there. And he is. But he himself demonstrated his precept with the most astonishing fullness. He suffered the strain of his work, but he offered the strain of his heart. The duty of thankfulness is one of Paul's constant themes. And it is to be always—whatever the situation; and for everything—whatever the condition (cf. 2:7; 1 Cor. 15:27; 2 Cor. 2:4; 8:16; Eph. 5:4; 1 Tim. 4:3, 4). Sing, then, we must with "grace" or "thanksgiving" *(charis)* in our hearts (cf. Col. 3:16). For it is a grace to express gratitude.

b. The indwelling word of Christ (3:16)

Verse 16: Let the word of Christ dwell in you richly, teach and admonish one another in all wisdom: The apostle has just encouraged thanksgiving. And here is one of the ways that such thanksgiving may be manifest; by hearing and appropriating the *word of Christ.* Reference has already been made to "the word of God" (1:25), which for Paul is the "word of truth," the gospel (1:5). As he has been dealing with the things of Christ in the immediate context, Paul can identify that "word" and "gospel" with the *word of Christ.* For the gospel is Christ's as it is God's (cf. Gal. 1:7; 1 Cor. 9:12; 2 Cor. 2:12; etc.). This *word of Christ* is to *dwell in* each member of the church. Those truths which have their sum and substance in Christ are to dwell "as a permanent part, always present" in the believer (H. C. G. Moule).

Since Paul has the total Christian community in view as he sets down these injunctions, the word *in* may be rendered "among" (NEB). In this case the *word of Christ* will refer more particularly to "what Christ taught" (LB) or his "message" (NEB). The apostle wants the great affirmations of gospel truths to have a home among the believers so that they will have a sure reference point for their faith. The "message of Christ must be allowed to 'keep house' *(enoikeito);* not as a servant in the family, who is under another's control, but as a master, who has a right to prescribe and direct to all under his roof" (Henry). But whether in the individual or in the community, the word of Christ is to dwell there *richly;* "not with scanty foothold, but with a large and liberal occupation" (J. Eadie). It is to have an abundant entrance "in all its richness" (NEB). And rich it can be, since "God chose to make known the riches of his glory" (1:27), and with hearts "knit together in love" believers may "have all the riches of assured understanding in the knowledge of

God's mystery, even Christ" (2:2). The *word of Christ* in this verse parallels the "peace of Christ" of the previous one. The peace of Christ will rule in hearts as the word of Christ overrules in lives.

Insofar as the word of Christ dwells richly in and among believers, they will have the necessary message for mutual helpfulness. Such mutual teaching and admonition "would contribute very much to our furtherance in all grace; for we sharpen ourselves by quickening others, and improve our knowledge by communicating it for their edification" (Henry). The RSV attaches the phrase *in all wisdom* to the preceding words to amplify the character of this teaching and admonition. It is probably right to do so. For the measure in which the word of Christ is known and appropriated is the measure of spiritual wisdom available to and manifest within the community. Christ is not divorced from his word. True, to know the mere letter of Scripture is not to know Christ. Yet, Christ cannot be known except through the word. He comes livingly to faith "in all the scriptures" (Luke 24:27). Thus to know Christ in his word is to have *wisdom* indeed (cf. 1:9, 28; 2:27). "The word should manifest the rich abundance of its indwelling in men by opening their minds into 'every kind of wisdom'" (Maclaren).

And sing psalms and hymns and spiritual songs with thankfulness in your hearts to God: Here is the further way in which thanksgiving may be manifest—not only by teaching the word in all wisdom, but by singing the word with all thanksgiving. Praise is a wonderful healer, and a great persuader. For there is nothing so contagious as a singing heart and a praising tongue. The community context of the present injunction can be gathered from the use of the phrase *one another* in the preceding clause. Praise is, then, a means by which the body is edified and God glorified. This singing of *psalms, hymns,* and *spiritual songs* has its counterpart in Ephesians 5:19, on which Bruce comments, "If we are to distinguish between the three kinds of musical composition, 'psalms' may refer to the Old Testament Psalter, which provides a perennial source of Christian praise from earliest times; 'hymns' may denote Christian canticles such as have been recognized in several places in the New Testament; 'spiritual songs' may be unpremeditated words sung 'in the Spirit' voicing praise and holy aspirations." But in whatever way voices are raised it must be with heartfelt thanksgiving. To sing heartily may be a matter of temperament; but to sing from the heart will be the measure of our thankfulness. It is the presence of the peace of Christ, and the possession of the word of Christ which opens the lips and thrills the soul with melodies of grateful thanksgiving. Paul's word here for *thanksgiving* is the same as that for *grace (charis)*. And to give thanks is certainly one of its primary meanings (cf. Luke 6:32,

33, 34; 1 Cor. 15:27; 2 Cor. 2:14; 8:16; 9:15; 1 Pet. 2:19). But elsewhere in the epistle the apostle uses the word *grace* with its enriched content to signify God's unmerited favor and sheer good will toward us in Christ (cf. 1:2, 6; 4:18). Thus grace and thanks are linked, not only linguistically, but more importantly, experimentally. It is because of grace that we can be grateful. "Thanks be unto God for his unspeakable gift," says Paul (2 Cor. 9:15, KJV); there is Paul's gratitude for God's grace.

c. The all-hallowing name of Christ (3:17)

Verse 17: And whatever you do, in word or deed, do everything in the name of the Lord Jesus, giving thanks to God the Father through him: This is an all-inclusive injunction. *Whatever you do, in word or deed*—not only that which relates to the narrow circle of religious worship, but everything which belongs to the round of daily living is to be brought under the same motive and Master (cf. v. 23; 1 Cor. 10:31). "That expresses emphatically the sanctity of common life, and extends the idea of worship to all deeds" (Maclaren). In biblical word and spiritual worship the Christian will show his thanksgiving. In no less measure is he to do so in all the affairs of everyday living.

"He has to make the praise of God resound by listening to and spreading the word, in song and prayer, but especially in his daily life and dealings with his fellows" (Lohse). So must the Christian's walk and talk be consonant with his confession. The hymns of the Lord's day must harmonize with the life of everyday. Ephesians 4 begins Paul's more detailed outline of what is becoming in the Christian's talk and befitting in his walk. Here all is subsumed under one grand principle: "Whatever you are doing, whether you speak or act, do everything in the name of the Lord Jesus" (NEB).

Jesus' name will hallow every ordinary thing and give significance to the small and meaning to the monotonous. " 'In the name' means, accordingly, 'in vital relation with him,' that is, in harmony with his revealed will, in subjection to his authority, in dependence on his power" (Hendriksen). In the preceding two verses the apostle has the name *Christ*—"the peace of Christ," "the word of Christ." Here it is *the Lord Jesus.* As *Jesus* he belongs to the real world of human concerns. For he worked as a carpenter and lived in an ordinary home. He knows all about the talk and toil of everyday life, and he showed us how life is to be lived and its affairs conducted. It is this same Jesus who is the Christian's *Lord.* In the everyday world where we labor and love, we place ourselves under the lordship of Christ. To do anything which would bring disgrace on the fair name of Christ is to compromise his sovereignty. Rather, we are to aim every day and in every way to honor the name of the Lord Jesus. For his is the name above every name that is named (Eph. 1:21; Phil. 2:9), and as such to him shall every knee bow (Phil. 1:10). Paul sometimes used Jesus' name as a plea for harmony (1 Cor. 1:10; cf. 2 Thess. 3:6) and holiness (1 Cor. 5:4) in the church. He also appealed to Jesus' name to induce right living in the world; for those who know his name are to "depart from iniquity" (2 Tim. 2:19, KJV)—as Christians they are to "give up evil" (Goodspeed). The name of Jesus Christ the Lord is the source of saving grace and of sustaining power. This was the name the Colossians had "put on" when they had themselves baptized. Now they are urged to conduct the whole course of their lives under the authority and in the power of that name. For to acknowledge his sovereignty in all things, to depend upon his sufficiency in everything, is to make his name glorious in life's daily round and common tasks.

To each of the three injunctions concerning the Christian's welfare Paul attaches a reference to the duty of gratitude (Col. 3:15, 16, 17). Christians are to let the peace of Christ rule in their hearts with thanksgiving (v. 15); to let the word of Christ dwell in them richly with thanksgiving (v. 16); and to let the name of the Lord Jesus be honored in everything with thanksgiving (v. 17). Thanksgiving is, then, the recurring note of the believer's life. Our words are to have a note of praise. Love is to shine through our language; praise is to permeate our parlance; and thanksgiving is to be in our talk. Our actions, also, will show a new attitude. For here, too, love will control our labors; there will be thanksgiving in our toil; and our work will be a form of worship. The stamp and the standard of all the Christian does is the name of the Lord Jesus through whom we can give thanks to God the Father.

C. The Renewed Life and the Family (3:18—4:1)

Paul turns now to the application of Christian principles to the family structure of his day. He will state how the renewed life affects the three ordinary relationships of the household: wife and husband, children and parent, servant and master. The apostle is concerned to make clear the proper reciprocal attitudes which should exist between these. Each one of these relationships is to be reared on the basis of cooperation and partnership. This was a totally revolutionary concept. The gulf between the several groups is here bridged by an altogether new understanding of the mutual need of each other and of respect one for the other. Running through all he has required is an appreciation of the worth and value of the single individual under God which Jesus Christ introduced into the world.

Paul, of course, could only accept the existing structure of society as he found it, but he laid down the principles which would inevitably destroy its glaring inequalities and gross injustices. For a husband to love his wife, and for a master to treat his slave as a human being—that would be socially reforming enough. True, codes governing such ethical relationships were not unknown in pagan antiquity. And especially among the Jews and Stoics, parallel summaries to those of the New Testament have been adduced. "But to say that the mere addition of such phrases as 'in the Lord' (vss. 18, 20) to the formularies already existing 'Christianizes them in the simplest possible way' is really to say everything, for a new and powerful dynamic is now introduced. If the Stoic disciple asked why he should behave in this particular way, his masters would no doubt tell him that this was the way which accorded with the nature of things; when a Christian convert asked the same question, he is told that this is behaviour which 'is fitting in the Lord': he must live thus for Christ's sake. The added words may be exceedingly simple, but they transform the whole approach to ethics" (Bruce).

The apostle is apparently led to refer to these domestic relationships here because he has, in the previous verse, made it clear that the Christian life must be expressed outside the restricted area of the believing community. In the outside world, as well as within the believing community, every deed and word is to be in accord with the Spirit of Christ. And there is no greater test of that accomplishment than within the home. It is here, within the family circle and among those closest to us, that we indicate most surely the quality of our Christian commitment. It is here that the controlling influences of Christ's *peace,* and *word,* and *name* on character and conduct ought to be the most obviously manifest. That is where the apostle urges that it should, in this short section where he sketches the outline of the ideal Christian household.

1. The relationship between wives and husbands (3:18–19)

a. A word to wives (3:18)

Verse 18: Wives, be subject to your husbands, as is fitting in the Lord: Here Paul introduces the wife's relationship of "submission" to her husband which Ephesians 5:21–22 makes clear is a particular instance of a general principle that is binding on all believers. Such mutual submission denies any superiority of one over the other. The postulate of the relationship between wife and husband and the pattern for the Christian home is a mutual deference of wife to husband and of husband to wife. This is genuine partnership; this is true peace. The Christian home is the masterpiece of the gospel, the greatest of its gifts to the social fabric. Without this mutual submission, the home easily becomes anarchistic or despotic. In every branch of life God works for harmony, while the devil works for disunity. The mutual relationship of wife and husband is "in the name of our Lord Jesus Christ" (Eph. 5:20, KJV). Christ is at once the starting point and the goal for harmonious domestic life.

We may well suppose that the situation at Colossae demanded such a word to wives. For the first time women were learning that they were of account and equal in God's sight with men. That was for them a startling revelation. In Christ's name they had, all in an hour, it seemed, attained a new dignity and status. The thought of such freedom in the gospel may well have pushed them to excess. Paul must put the brake on by applying specifically to wives the general principle of mutual subjection. Such "subjection," *as is fitting in the Lord,* must ultimately be part of the "everything" done "in the name of the Lord Jesus" (Col. 2:17). To the apostle, human and earthly relationships were the patterns of things in the heavens. Thus he saw the union of man and wife in the marriage bond as fashioned after the likeness of that more mysterious relationship of Christ and his church (cf. Eph. 5:23–30). Christ has entered into a relationship of love with his church. That love for his church and the church's response to him in willing service was for Paul the analogy by which to understand the wife's "subjection" to her husband. It is not enforced from the husband's side: it is given lovingly from the wife's. In such a "subjection," anything harsh or degrading has no place. For the "submission" of which Paul speaks is not the sullen submission of a demand, but the willing submission of a devotion. So you wives, says the apostle, who would do what is fitting in the Lord must "adapt yourselves to your husbands" (Eph. 5:22, Phillips).

b. A word to husbands (3:19)

Verse 19: Husbands, love your wives, and do not be harsh with them: The call to husbands to love their wives must have come as something quite revolutionary. Here, indeed, is a declaration which raises the wife to a position of equal partnership with her husband. She is no longer a chattel, a thing to be used. Only as this statement is read in the light of 1 Corinthians 13 is its full significance understood—there is no question there of another's inferiority and one's own superiority. All that is gone—lost in love. Paul uses the verb *agapaō* for the love that is required of husbands (cf. Eph.

5:25); not *erao* that expresses the deep sexual passion of man for woman; not even *phileo* which is the usual verb used for affection within the family. *Agapao* love is the highest love of all, a veritable Godlike thing, which puts another's welfare above our own. Such is the love which is to govern all Christian relationships (cf. 1:4, 8; 2:2; 3:14, all of which use the noun *agape*); and the husband is charged to be and express in the home, in his relationship with his wife what he is required to show and professes to be in relationship with others of the household of faith. The verb translated *be harsh* can also mean "make or become bitter." Harshness that would spoil harmony the Christian husband must renounce. For love puts a ban on all bitterness.

2. The relationship between child and parent (3:20–21)

a. A word to children (3:20)

Verse 20: Children, obey your parents in everything, for this pleases the Lord: The word used by Paul for the obedience required of children is not the same verb translated "be subject" in verse 18. The child's submission cannot, like the wife's, be "tempered by equality." A full obedience is demanded of the child—"in everything," for such "is pleasing to God and is the Christian way" (NEB). It may be, as Bruce thinks, that Paul has a Christian family in view, and that he does not contemplate the situation where parental orders might be contrary to the law of Christ. Whether this is so or not, the principle of obedience of children to parents still stands. Unruly children are an evidence of social disintregration and moral bankruptcy (cf. Rom. 1:10; 2 Tim. 3:3). To obey one's parents is right and proper according to the ordering of things. Paul could almost say here what he says elsewhere, "Does not nature itself teach you that . . . ?" (1 Cor. 11:14). The obligation arises out of the very nature of the relation between parent and child, and must follow wherever that relation exists.

b. A word to fathers (3:21)

Verse 21: Fathers, do not provoke your children, lest they become discouraged: The plural form *pateres* is thought by some commentators to include both parents, rather than merely fathers as such. Certainly both parents must equally share in the upbringing of children. Paul's word translated *provoke (erethizete)* in our text (cf. its use in a good sense in 2 Cor. 9:2) is well put in the NEB: "Fathers, do not exasperate your children." Fathers specially need counsel in this particular. For they can easily become tyrannical and unreasonable, bullying where they should be blessing, and infuriating when they should be inspiring, sometimes imposing silly restrictions which can only lead to exasperation, or impossible demands which can only make them "disheartened" (NEB). Therefore, "Fathers, don't over-correct your children, or they will grow up feeling inferior and frustrated" (Phillips, *Letters*).

3. The relationship between slaves and masters (3:22–4:1)

a. A word to slaves (3:22–25)

Verse 22: Slaves, obey in everything those who are your earthly masters: Paul belonged to a society in which slavery was an accepted institution. He could not deny its existence, nor could he abolish it. But he could, and he did, lay down principles which would one day make the whole system impossible. Meanwhile slavery was there, but as a reality of the temporal order. In this section Paul has more particularly in mind the Christian slave, many of whom had come into the household of faith. Yet what he has to say to both parties holds principles which can be applied to employees and employers in every sphere and every age. In the spiritual realm there is no distinction between the Christian slave and the Christian master. Both stand on a common platform in God's sight, both equally in need of grace and both equally the objects of it. But in daily activity the slave is not to take advantage of his equal status in Christ; he is to accept direction and obey. He must acknowledge his earthly master, just as both alike must own one heavenly Lord. And even should the earthly master be a pagan, the Christian slave is not exempt from honest service. He must rather do his duty all the more willingly and faithfully as befits his Christian profession; for in so doing he will be Christ's servant and witness.

Not with eye-service, as men-pleasers: " 'Those who want to please men' *(anthrōpareskoi)* only take into account men and their authority, not God" (Lohse). Paul seems to have coined the word *eye-service, ophthalmodouleia* (which he uses only here and in Eph. 6:6, and nowhere else), to refer to those who only work "when seen of men." Such are they who seek human applause, but when they are out of the master's eye they become idle and mere self-pleasers. The eye-pleaser, like the modern clock watcher, will do as little as he can get away with, putting up a show of eagerness when under observation. The Christian slave of the first century is reminded that he is primarily Christ's servant. And the same fact holds for the Christian employee of the twentieth century. He, too, is to be no eye-server, but a Christ-server.

But in singleness of heart, fearing the Lord: As a servant of Christ he will set himself to fulfill his task "with single-mindedness" (NEB).

The phrase *singleness of heart* is parallel to that of Ephesians 6:5 (cf. Matt. 6:22; Acts 2:46). The idea is honesty of purpose which sometimes runs into liberality—doing more than is demanded. *Singleness of heart* is "onefoldness" of heart, as opposed to "twofoldness." As the men of Zebulun who gathered to David at Ziklag were "not of double heart" (1 Chron. 12:33, KJV; cf. Ps. 12:2; James 1:8; 4:18), so must the slave serve his master. Such men did not have a "heart and an heart" (1 Chron. 12:33, literal), one for David and one for Saul; they had but one heart and that entirely for David's cause. So must the slave serve with one heart, *fearing the Lord*. This fear is not mere frightfulness of his master as such, but fear of God (cf. 2 Cor. 7:1; Eph. 5:21).

Verse 23: Whatever your task, work heartily, as serving the Lord and not men: Paul's actual word translated here *heartily* is *psuchē* (soul), (as in Eph. 6:6) which he uses as an equivalent for *kardia* (heart), to mean the seat of the desires and affections. But sometimes in the New Testament the two words are distinguished, as in Mark 12:30 ("with all your heart [*kardia*], and with all your soul [*psuchē*]"). But the word *heart* is used in the translation to bring out the inner nature of the service. It is a service which springs from the inner being in contrast with that "outward show of service" intended merely "to curry favour with men" (NEB). Whatever the service which has to be rendered, it is to be done with the "whole heart" (NEB), for that is to work *heartily* or "whole-heartedly" (NEB in Eph. 6:6). Paul "goes on to transfigure the squalor and misery of the slave's lot by a sudden beam of light—'as to the Lord'—your true 'Master,' for it is the same word as in the previous verse—'and not unto men'" (Maclaren). The slave must remember that in the final reckoning, service rendered in a human situation is "for the Lord, and not for men" (NEB). This puts a high value upon ordinary toil and, indeed, can make drudgery divine. And this is the difference which makes all the difference. To work for men merely as unto men would hardly call forth the response of the heart. But to work for men in the recognition that one is "serving the Lord Christ" (v. 24) can stimulate wholeheartedness. "As the innermost part of man, the heart which determines his thought and conduct should be single and sincere. If this is the case, everything a man does will be guided not by false, ulterior motives, but will be done to God" (Lohse). "In spirit people cease to be slaves as soon as they begin to work for the Lord, and no longer in the first place for men" (Hendriksen).

Verse 24: Knowing that from the Lord you will receive the inheritance as your reward: However their earthly masters may reward them, Christian slaves may be sure of this, that there is a Master who will give them a just recompense. It is the fashion of men to give short measures. But not so God. He does everything for those who fear him on a large scale. Of course, the "reward of inheritance" is not to be understood as an inheritance gained as a reward. The Colossian believers, and evidently there were several slaves among them, already knew that through grace they had been qualified to share "the inheritance of the saints in light" (1:12; cf. Acts 20:32; Eph. 1:12). This qualification is not by the works of the law (cf. Gal. 3:18) but is authenticated to faith in the heart by the Holy Spirit (Eph. 1:14). The slave was truly poor in this world's coinage; but he can work on in the assurance of faith that the "riches of the glory" of God's inheritance (Eph. 1:18) are his; and that he is destined to an inheritance kept for him in heaven "that nothing can destroy or spoil or wither" (1 Pet. 1:4, NEB). And something of the riches of the glory of that inheritance believers, the slave included, already enjoy (Eph. 1:18), but of its fullness they have not yet received. That will be theirs at the appearance of Christ at his Second Coming, when we together with them shall be made perfect.

You are serving the Lord Christ: The word *Lord* before Christ is significant. Earthly masters are not "lords" in their own right. Theirs is a borrowed and a passing authority. Their title of "master" is acquired. But Christ is *Lord* in his own right. Those who are slaves serve mere human masters, but in reality as Christians they "serve as their master *the* great *Master Christ*" (Lightfoot). In the translation, the declaration is in the form of an indicative; but some would take it as an imperative (e.g., Lohse), an admonition: *Do* serve the Lord Christ. The indicative, however, seems to suit the context better. For the slave is being assured that what he does for his earthly master wholeheartedly, with "reverence for the Lord" (v. 22, NIV), is really service to the Lord Jesus.

Paul can think of nothing more glorious and more rewarding than service to the Lord Christ. Often he refers to himself as a "servant of Christ" (cf. Rom. 1:1; 2 Cor. 4:5; etc.). But here he speaks of the Christian slave who fulfills required duties as Christ's servants. In this way Paul exalts ordinary duty to the high status of spiritual activity and eliminates the distinction between the sacred and the secular. Those who do only a slave's task must remember that they "are actually employed by Christ" (Phillips, *Letters*).

Verse 25: For the wrongdoer will be paid back for the wrong he has done, and there is no partiality: The verse begins with a *For,* and immediately raises the question as to the identity of the persons addressed. Some think that Paul has the masters in view in this reminder of the inviolable law that wrongdoing will receive its just punishment. Commentators who take this line go on to make the point that the apostle is warning masters against unjust treatment of their slaves. And by Paul's putting it here in close connection with his word to slaves, the slaves would find comfort in the rebuke of their owners if they were victims of ill treatment. On the other hand, seeing that the masters are not directly addressed until 4:1, others regard it as more probable that Paul is still addressing the slaves. "If they trespass against their masters, they will have to give account of themselves to God. They should not suppose that since they are miserable slaves they would not be responsible for their actions or would be granted indulgence because of their extenuating circumstances" (Lohse). Certainly Paul would not regard right action to be affected by the circumstances. For him goodness is goodness and is not altered by changing social conditions. "A superior's injustice does not warrant an inferior's breach of the moral law, though it may excuse it" (Maclaren).

But the question may be put as to how it possibly can be supposed that a slave would wrong his master. The answer to that question is surely there in the context. It is by his failure to obey in everything, and by his acting the part of a man-pleaser, by doing the least he can and working only when seen. It may be, however, that the apostle desires all, whether slave or master, employer or employee, to recognize the moral principle governing all relationships: "whatever a man sows, that he will also reap" (Gal. 6:7). The vital issue for every person is not his status in the eyes of the world, but rather whether he has done the will of God. That is the ultimate test for everyone. The good that we do is known of the Lord and has his approval for its goodness alone, and not on account of our position here below.

And there is no partiality. Significantly in Ephesians this affirmation about God's impartiality comes in the word the apostle has to say to the masters (6:9). Here it is linked to his word to slaves. The reminder is necessary for both, for both have the same heavenly Master (cf. 4:1; Eph. 6:9) whom, in Christ, they may address as "Our Father who art in heaven." And before him there is no distinction of class. There is no partiality in God's assessments (cf. Acts 3:25). And since he is not partial, no more dare we be.

b. A word to masters (4:1)

Verse 1: Masters, treat your slaves justly and fairly, knowing that you also have a Master in heaven: The slave-owner is required by this Christian ethic to be just and fair. And that is urged upon him as a "responsibility" (Phillips, *Letters*). "The masters should treat their slaves in as humane a way as possible. This requirement would include fairness of treatment and an honest remuneration (perhaps implied in the verb rendered 'treat,' literally 'grant'), with the possibility that there should be no unduly harsh measures of repression or victimization of those in a helpless position" (Martin). Here in Colossians, in the context of his word to masters, as noted above, Paul puts his declaration: *you also have a Master in heaven.* "This is not a stimulus, but a pattern" (Maclaren). Masters, too, must reckon on that, for they likewise will appear before the judgment seat of Christ to give account. The hearty acceptance of that principle should control the attitudes of those for whom they are responsible. The slave is not his own; but neither are masters. They must not forget they have a "Heavenly Employer" (Phillips, *Letters*). They are "slaves" of Christ, yet sons of God. Let them, therefore, treat their slaves as sharers with them in that sonship. So will both find with equal delight that "all duty is elevated into obedience to Him, and obedience to Him, utter and absolute, is dignity and freedom" (Maclaren).

This was a needed word for the day; for the laws of the time were heavily loaded in favor of the masters. And even when their excess of cruelty in the treatment of their servants compelled the emperors to enact restraints of their tyranny, the slave was left outside the protection of the royal edicts. But Paul has a word from God for the masters in their relation to their slaves—an insistence that they do not go beyond what can be subsumed under the law of love. And Paul means exactly what he says. Slaves are to be treated on the principle of equality with their masters, because as men, and more so as men accepted of God, they are equals. Fair treatment for the slave is called for. That must have come almost as a revolutionary precept—the slave to be treated as a man, a husband, a parent, having equal rights with his master. It was something unheard of hitherto. Doubtless, even the Christian master found it hard to take; but take it he must.

There is, however, as has been noted, no command of Paul for the wholesale freeing of slaves; and in the nature of the case there could not be. For Paul to have issued such a directive would have been merely to have plunged the slave into deeper distress and brought upon him even harsher treatment. But Paul takes the better way. He enunciates those principles which will sooner or later so affect the consciences of men that they will not be able to continue to treat their fellows as tools and things. Yet the immediate result of Paul's teaching must, in many cases, have brought easement to the slave's lot. Legally the slave was part of the household, and if once the master took to heart what the apostle had counseled, the slave must have found himself treated as more than a legal piece of household property (cf. Philem. 12, 17, and comments).

But slavery is still slavery, however congenial the arrangement; as such it could not survive in a society where the gospel had taken hold. It was indeed the very principles that Paul proclaimed which led to its abolition, and which have an ever-abiding application, for they arise out of the one eternal gospel of Christ. As such they can be applied to the structure of human society in every age, and so speak to the conditions of the present time as they did to the first century.

V. PERSONAL: THE TRUTH DISPLAYED (4:2–18)

A. Special Precepts That Assure It (4:2–6)

As the apostle comes to the end of his epistle, there are a few precepts he must underline so that the renewed life may be maintained and manifest. And there are a number of persons whom he can mention as living illustrations of that life. The practical exhortations have to do with the inner attitudes and the outward activities of the Christian life. In this regard Paul makes reference to the need for prayer; but he wants himself included in the Colossians' intercession. "Don't forget us," he says, "whenever you pray for yourselves." In Colossians 1 he has given them his prayer for them. Now he tells them what in particular he wants them to pray for him. He wants a door of opportunity open to him and boldness in speech for the occasion. The apostle, however, knew all too well that proclamation and practice must go hand in hand in the work of God's kingdom. And not in his case only, but for all believers who must be about the King's business. Thus, as he thinks of his own speaking in the name of Christ, he adds that their speech, too, must have in it a seasoning quality. Yet even graceful words will be of no effect unless there is behind them a graceful walk. Believers must walk wisely so that they may talk purposefully.

This part of the personal section which is concerned with the display of the truths for which the apostle has contended centers upon the special precepts which assure it (4:2–6). What Paul has to say at this point concerns the hidden and revealed life of the believer. He directs attention first to the private life of the soul and then to the public life of service.

1. The private life of the soul (4:2–4)

Verse 2: Continue steadfastly in prayer, being watchful in it with thanksgiving: Paul's word here is a strong one. His call is for the Colossians to "cling closely to" and "remain constant" in prayer (Lightfoot). Both thoughts coalesce in the phrase, and both need to be stressed. They are to *continue* in prayer, to "always maintain the habit of prayer" (Phillips). Stick to your praying is what is urged. And for prayer to be a habit, it must be continued in *steadfastly*. The demand for steadfastness is a recurring note in the New Testament, where a variety of words are used to express it.

The tragedy with the nation of Israel was that their hearts were not right with the High God their Redeemer, nor was their spirit "stedfast with God" and "in his covenant" (cf. Ps. 78:8, 37, KJV). But by contrast, the early disciples "continued steadfastly" *(proskartereō)* in the Christian worship and the Christian way (Acts 2:42; cf. 1:14; 2:46). This is the word that Paul has here in Colossians. After the excitement of Acts 2 there comes the quiet worship of Acts 3 (cf. 3:1). They continued on after the dramatic events had passed.

In Luke (9:51) there is a reference to our Lord who "stedfastly" (KJV), "resolutely" (NEB) set his face—*stērizō*—to go to Jerusalem. The verb conveys the idea of resolution and determination. Jesus took to the upward way knowing what awaited him. The steadfast face is the *face which betrays no compromises.*

At the conclusion of his long argument in 1 Corinthians 15, Paul calls the believers to be steadfast (v. 57). In the light of the resurrection certainty, theirs is to be a *life which reveals no cares.* Paul's word for the Corinthians is *hedraios* (cf. 1 Cor. 7:37), which derives from *hedra,* a chair. The idea is that of composure. "Therefore," he says to the Corinthians, do not be disquieted by unsettling doubts. Since Christ is alive, our resurrection is assured. There is no need to become frantic, to rush off in heated anxiety to the séance, to listen for the mutterings of impersonating spirits and be stampeded into a vague belief by the strange knockings in an unlit room. Christ is alive, therefore let your life be composed. Let it settle itself securely on this solid basis.

In 1 Peter 5:8–9, it is urged that the devil be resisted "stedfast in the faith" (KJV). Peter's term *stērigmos* has the thought of solidity. It then came to mean stiff, compact, without breaks. This is the *faith which has no cracks.* Every approach of the evil one must be met with a solid faith; with no breaks in our belief through which he can squeeze or send a fiery dart (Eph. 4:17; 6:16).

Hebrews 6:19 (KJV) speaks of hope "as an anchor of the soul, both sure and stedfast" *(bebaios;* cf. 1 Cor. 1:7; Heb. 2:2; 3:14). Hope is an anchor, valid, trusty and genuine, which holds securely within the veil where Jesus our Forerunner has gone. There anchored within the inner basin of the eternal calm, the ship of life, however tossed, will remain unsinkable in the outer waters until we disembark on the eternal shore. Such a hope is sure and secure: for this hope is an *anchor which causes no concerns*.

Here in Colossians the apostle bids believers continue *steadfastly in prayer*. The word is the same as that which occurs in Acts 2:42. Already in our epistle at 2:3, Paul has referred to the "firmness" (*stereoma*, "stedfastness," kjv) of the Colossians' faith. But this insistence in 4:2 indicates that steadfastness in faith will remain only as long as steadfastness in prayer is maintained. Paul qualifies his insistence further—with continued steadfastness there must go alert watchfulness. Therefore the believer must not only stick at praying but must stay awake when he prays. For we "are apt to do drowsily whatever we do constantly" (Maclaren). Therefore we must "persevere in prayer, with mind awake" (neb). This association of watchfulness with prayerfulness was made by our Lord; and the apostle may well have had that teaching in his mind when he gave this injunction to the Colossians (Matt. 13:33; Luke 21:36; Matt. 26:40, 41; cf. Eph. 6:18). The Christian believer must keep alert. He must not allow his eyes to get so heavy that he can no longer make out the enemy or recognize those who are on his side. Spiritually, then, to be alive is to be alert.

For the seventh time in the epistle, Paul adds a word concerning *thanksgiving* (cf. 1:3, 13; 2:7; 3:15, 16, 17). He himself has mingled thanksgiving with his prayer in chapter 1; he now urges the Colossians to do the same. It is a good thing to give thanks unto the Lord (Ps. 92:1), and the one who offers praise glorifies God (Ps. 50:23). We thank God for *what he has done*, while we praise him for what *he is*. "Thankfulness is the feather that wings the arrow of prayer—the height from which our souls rise most easily to the sky" (Maclaren). "Private prayer, however persevering, is impoverished if it descends to endless asking for things, forgetting *thanksgiving*" (R. E. O. White).

Verse 3: And pray for us also, that God may open to us a door for the word: It was Paul's desire to be remembered in the prayers of the Colossians. And in requesting this remembrance he expresses his confident belief in the efficacy of intercession. He is in prison, but he does not ask that they pray for his release. His one concern is for the success of the gospel of Christ. Apostle though he was, he was not beyond asking for the prayers of the church. And no church is fulfilling its high calling which has no concern for its fellow-soldiers in the common service of Christ. The idea of prayer as a key to unlock closed doors is a constant New Testament theme (cf. Acts 14:27; 1 Cor. 16:9; 2 Cor. 2:12; Eph. 6:19–20). It is not certain, however, whether Paul is thinking of a door of opportunity or a door "of utterance" (KJV) with which to give a ready answer to his accusers. Calvin thinks that it is the latter he has in mind both here and in Ephesians 6:19. At any rate, Paul goes on to describe what he wishes to do with the open door.

To declare the mystery of Christ: He has already said something about this mystery (cf. 1:26–27; 2:2). Here the allusion may be either to the message of the Christian gospel of which Christ is the subject (cf. Eph. 6:19), or else to the preaching of the gospel to the Gentile world which he calls the mystery hid from ages, and the mystery of Christ (cf. 1:26; Eph. 3:4). It seems best to see the phrase as descriptive of "the content of Paul's preaching. Thus 'mystery' is actually understood as a technical term for the message of salvation" (Lohse). The apostle wants scope and speech to proclaim "the unimagined news of God's saving purpose, which no mind could discover unaided, one which no human ingenuity could have invented" (Martin). The Colossians must know it to be his one consuming purpose to tell out the secret of Christ.

On account of which I am in prison: Paul the prisoner! Paul the preacher! It cost him to be a servant of Christ. What costs little counts less. But Paul is not deterred by the circumstances, for he knows that he is where he is for Christ's sake. He does not, therefore, refer to his situation in prison at this point to gain sympathy. He would rather solicit prayer that the gospel may get an opening and a voice right there where he is (cf. Eph. 4:1; 6:19; Phil. 1:13–14). Paul is indeed bound, but he is still God's free man. As guard changed duty with guard, Paul looked for opportunities to share with them the gospel word. For Paul regarded himself as entrusted with the saving message and wished to speak it out boldly. He might be chained, but he is not contained. He is seated handcuffed to a soldier; but he is no less seated in the heavenly places with his Savior. Though down in the dungeon he is up in the glory. And he wanted to bring that glory into the dungeon—to relay the message of Jesus to prison-held men.

Verse 4: That I may make it clear, as I ought to speak: Paul knew very well that the gospel was foolishness to the perishing. But he knew, too, that the word of the gospel could come home with saving effect only if it were spoken with clarity. In other places Paul refers to his compelling duty to proclaim the saving message by such terms as "to announce" (1 Cor. 2:1), "to preach" (Eph. 3:8). Only here does he use the word "to make manifest" *(phaneroun)*. He says to the Colossians, pray for me, "that I may manifest it, may make this Secret large and plain to faith, even as my duty is to speak it" (H. C. G. Moule). Of course, Paul did not forget that the gospel won a hearing not by the mere worldly wisdom of words (1 Cor. 1:17–21;

2:13) but through the power of the Holy Spirit (1 Thess. 1:5). But that did not excuse him, nor does it excuse anyone who would make known the same message, from understanding it as well as he can and making it as clear as he should. Paul requests prayer for himself that he may make the message plain, which he sees as a duty imposed. And this brings him back from referring to himself to the duty of the Colossians, to say something concerning *their* walk and talk in relation to their service. They should live in accordance with their prayers.

2. The public life of service (4:5–6)

Paul talks first, about the Christian's walk.

Verse 5: Conduct yourselves wisely toward outsiders: The word translated *conduct yourselves* is the usual one for "walk" *(peripateō),* and is so rendered in the KJV (cf. 1:10; 2:6; 3:7). The Colossians were once "outsiders" (cf. Mark 4:11; 1 Cor. 5:12–13; 1 Thess. 4:12), and being such they conducted their lives according to the pattern and standards of their pagan surroundings (cf. 3:7). Now they are "insiders" and so must live their lives in harmony with their new position and privilege in Christ. They should "let Christian wisdom rule [their] behaviour to the outside world" (Moffatt, NT). Their Christian zeal must go hand in hand with common sense and practical sagacity. Enthusiasm and moderation are difficult to unite in relation to those outside the faith. "Fervour married to tact, common sense which keeps close to the earth, and enthusiasm which flames heaven high, are a rare combination" (Maclaren). Hard as it is to hold such apparently opposite virtues together, when they are seen displayed they have a magnetic effect. Where they are, the "outsiders" will see something of worth in the "insider"; will see manifest in some measure the mystery of Christ. "But not only does such wise conduct, so that believers use the best means to reach the highest goal, serve as a weapon against vilification and character-assassination, it also has a positive purpose, namely, to win outsiders to Christ" (Hendriksen).

Making the most of the time: The night comes when no man can work. While, then, it is day, the passing season must be turned to account, "letting no opportunity slip by you, of saying and doing what may further the cause of God" (Lightfoot). The word translated *making the most of* is the same as that of Ephesians 5:16 *(exagorazō).* It means "to redeem by the payment of a price" (cf. Gal. 3:13; 4:5). In both passages—here and Ephesians—it has the sense of "to make a wise use of every opportunity for doing good" (cf. Gal. 6:10). Thus the NEB has, "use the present opportunity to the full." If the thought of "redeeming" (KJV) or "purchasing" is preserved, then the interpretation would seem to be "buy up," "buy back," or "buy out" the time "from alien ownership" (H. C. G. Moule). Phillips prefers to see here a call to use our time to the best advantage. At any rate, the special application of the injunction is in relation to the "outsider" with a view of bringing him in. For we "have not acted wisely towards those who are without unless we use every opportunity to draw them in" (Maclaren). What then we are called upon to do is that of "cornering the market in opportunity, or buying back the present time from its evil obsessions into usefulness again" (R. E. O. White).

Paul follows his word on the Christian's walk by saying something about the Christian's talk.

Verse 6: Let your speech always be gracious, seasoned with salt: Christian speech is to be "with grace" (KJV; *charis*). By this Paul means speech which is characterized by "acceptability" or "pleasingness" (Lightfoot). Some, however, understand the term *grace* here in its higher spiritual sense of a gift bestowed (cf. 3:16). In that case the exhortation is to exhibit a speech which is caught from God—words which bring grace to those who heed. In Ephesians 4:29 reference is made to the Christian's talk which imparts grace to the hearer. There the apostle seems to play upon the various meanings of the term, and the same is possibly true here. Certainly helpful talk does indeed convey a benefit upon the hearer. Yet it is graciousness of speech which conveys grace of speech. In Luke 4:22 there is reference to our Lord's speech—the people in the synagogue at Nazareth "wondered at the gracious words which proceeded out of his mouth" (KJV, RSV, cf. Phillips)—at the winsome manner of his speaking. There was something compelling about his every action on that occasion. But not only did the people marvel at the gracious manner of Jesus' speaking, they marveled, too, "at the words of grace" (RV, ASV, NEB) he spoke. Luke would have us understand that there was more in his mind when he wrote these words than the mere aesthetic impression. Christ spoke "with grace" "about grace." "Our glad task is to speak with like attractiveness, avoiding any manner of speaking in public discourse or private conversation which would leave the impression that the gospel message is dull and flat and uninteresting" (Martin).

Paul's word about gracious speech is qualified by the expression *seasoned with salt.* By this he certainly has not in mind the "Attic salt" of Hellenistic ironic wit which might sparkle but could not save. Such wit can only smart the human wound, unlike the wisdom of which Paul spoke which heals the broken heart. In Leviticus, salt plays a significant role; without it the sacrifice was somehow lacking (cf. Lev. 2:13). The rabbis asserted that "the Torah [law] is like

salt." Paul saw this as supremely true of the doctrines of the saving
gospel of Christ. The gospel is like salt to keep the life pure and
wholesome. And Christian talk, when flavored by spiritual wisdom,
is speech savored with salt. So it is a Christian duty to keep conversation free from the taint of moral decay. Yet in view of his following statement, the apostle is counseling not simply the avoidance of
rotten speech but the adoption of reasonable speech. "It is sense
that Paul means by 'salt' " (A. T. Robertson).

So that you may know how you ought to answer every one: Salt
gives a savor to food, bringing out its real flavor. So the Christian
must address himself to the real issues. He cannot be content to talk
in sonorous generalities. What he has to say must fit closely to the
needs and characteristics of those to whom he speaks. For such ac-
ceptableness of speech he will certainly need grace. And it is God
who gives the Christian "the tongue of those who are taught" so
that he may know how to sustain with words the one who is weary
(Isa. 50:4). Therefore would the tongue speak God's word (Ps.
119:172) and tell of his righteousness (Ps. 35:28). So does the mouth
of the righteous talk wisdom, and his tongue speak judgment (Ps.
37:30). Thus will the tongue of the righteous be as choice silver
(Prov. 10:20). With silvered tongue and salted speech, the Christian
will "be always ready . . . whenever . . . called to account for the
hope that is in" him, and will conduct his "defence with modesty
and respect" (1 Pet. 3:15, NEB).

B. Special Persons Who Exemplify It (4:7–18)

Before he bids the Colossians farewell, "the apostle does several
of his friends the honour to leave their name upon record, with some
testimony of his respect, which will be spoken of wherever the gospel comes, and last to the end of the world" (Henry). Yet such a roll
of honor is not characteristic of Paul's letters. Whenever he wrote to
churches where he was well known, he almost studiously avoided
singling out special names. It appears that he might have thought it
invidious to do so. He did not want to leave the impression that
there was in the churches a group whom he regarded as a spiritual
elite. Paul never left us with the idea that he and those associated
with him were in some way better than the rest and more worthy of
God's favor. He was too sensitive a pastor to allow that and too
great a Christian to think it. As he has counseled against partiality,
he will not himself be guilty of it. For the apostle, all who love our
Lord Jesus Christ in sincerity are one in the household of faith (Eph.
6:24). In Colossians, a letter written to a church where Paul was
personally unknown, his reference to particular individuals was not

improper. Throughout, he has made it clear that the church is one body of which Christ is the only Head; but there are those whom he can single out for their service in the gospel on behalf of the Colossians themselves. The section crystallizes around certain names, some of whom are otherwise unknown to us but who embody principles and teach lessons. Paul is continuing his personal section which has to do with the truth displayed; and he can allude to certain persons who exemplify that display.

Verses 7–8: Tychicus will tell you all about my affairs; he is a beloved brother and faithful minister and fellow servant in the Lord. I have sent him to you for this very purpose, that you may know how we are and that he may encourage your hearts: Paul has some consolation in the thought that the way things were going with him was of concern to the church. When they hear about how he and his colleagues are doing (v. 8), and how everything is (v. 9), they will be able to pray with the understanding also (cf. v. 3). Such news Tychicus will bring. The apostle certainly held Tychicus in high regard, as he speaks of him here and in Ephesians (6:21) as "our dear brother and trustworthy helper" (NEB). A native of the province of Asia, Tychicus was chosen as a delegate to accompany those who went with Paul in A.D. 57 to hand over the gifts of those churches to the brethren in Jerusalem (cf. Acts 20:4). He is given a passing reference in 2 Timothy 4:12 and Titus 3:12. Here in Colossians, Paul adds the further commendation by acknowledging Tychicus as a *fellow servant in the Lord.*

Tychicus is sent by Paul as his representative; but he is no less a brother beloved of the apostle; and a brother in Christ with the Colossians. Paul can trust this Tychicus to *encourage.* It is a noble ministry to be an encourager of God's people. David encouraged himself in the Lord (1 Sam. 30:6), but some need others to help them along. Paul uses the familiar word *parakaleō* here, which means literally, "to call alongside." Too few are able to come alongside someone who is finding the way hard and the battle fierce. Too few have the quality of spirit to encourage others. But Tychicus will do so; for Tychicus is "a much-loved brother, a trusty assistant and fellow-servant with us in the Lord's work" (Weymouth).

As is well known, the noun *paraklētos* is used in reference to the Holy Spirit in John's Gospel (cf. John 14:16, 26; 16:16, 17). The Holy Spirit is the true Comforter, the Divine Encourager. And only through him can Tychicus minister comfort to the soldiers and saints at Colossae (cf. Rom. 15:5; 2 Cor. 1:4–7; see 7:7, 13). Tychicus will be the Spirit's agent to bring strengthening and encouragement from God. For both the Ephesians (6:20) and the Colossians, Tychicus comes to encourage the hearts of the believers. The Ephesian church particularly needed to be inspired anew in the inner life, for their love was in danger of waning (cf. Rev. 2:1, 4). The Colossians more especially needed encouraging in their faith. With them there was the danger of losing firm grip on the great truths of Christ which affect Christian living. So they are being urged to persevere in the right way.

As we look at the few references to Tychicus in the New Testament and seek to change the name into the man, we gather that he was well content to take second place to Paul. He could not do what others could who had greater reach of mind and larger opportunities of service. But he was satisfied with his God-given task. Ordinary duties fell to him to carry out, and among them to run Paul's errands (cf. 2 Tim. 4:12; Titus 3:12)—he was in fact the bearer of this letter to the Colossians. As we reflect, then, upon the picture of the man as it is built up from the scattered allusions to him, this lesson for us is "writ large": Tychicus may be "fairly taken as representing the greatness and sacredness of small and secular service for Christ" (Maclaren). The Colossians will welcome Tychicus; and he will come to them to add his own words—his rather secular, everyday words—about the state of Paul's health and the conditions of the prison. They will hear his word and read Paul's letter and perhaps reflect that what Tychicus has to say belongs to the passing, while the apostle's words are abiding. And yet there is the lesson they may learn from his presence and the things he has to tell, namely, that small things done for Christ are great, and fleeting things done for him are eternal. So Tychicus comes among them no less than any other as Christ's servant.

Verse 9: And with him Onesimus, the faithful and beloved brother, who is one of yourselves. They will tell you of everything that has taken place here: Onesimus comes with Tychicus, but for him it is a coming home, because Onesimus hailed originally from Colossae. It is reasonable to link this Onesimus with the runaway slave of the Philemon letter. Irked by his slave conditions, Onesimus had taken off to Rome. There he somehow made contact with Paul, through whom he was converted to Christ. Paul wanted him to go back to his old master, to the Christian Philemon—as a slave, and yet as more—a brother in Christ. The apostle plays on Onesimus's name as he sends word to Philemon pleading the Christian slave's cause. Onesimus means "useful"—but he had become *useless* to Philemon. Now, however in Christ, he is *useful* to Paul, and can yet be to Philemon. So Paul will send him back; he who was "once so little use to you [Philemon], but now useful indeed, both to you and to me" (Philem. 11, NEB).

To the apostle Onesimus is, although still a slave, *a faithful and beloved brother*. How great is this Paul—apostle of Christ, yet brother of slaves! What grace of Christ—that this runaway slave can be so transformed! Onesimus, too, with Tychicus will have something to tell the Colossians. He will add his own story of how he was apprehended by Christ. He has his own testimony to the sheer mercy of God. And if he already knows the content of Paul's letter, he will speak with thanksgiving to the Father who has qualified him to share in the inheritance of the saints in light, for his experience of deliverance from the dominion of darkness and his transference into the kingdom of the Father's beloved Son, in whom he has received a redemption, the forgiveness of sins (Col. 1:12–14). If, then, as Maclaren declares, Tychicus represents the greatness and sacredness of small and secular things done for Christ, Onesimus certainly represents the transforming and unifying power of the Christian gospel.

Verses 10–11: Aristarchus my fellow prisoner greets you, and Mark the cousin of Barnabas (concerning whom you have received instructions—if he comes to you, receive him), and Jesus who is called Justus. These are the only men of the circumcision among my fellow workers for the kingdom of God, and they have been a comfort to me: These three had one thing in common—they broke with the Judaizers to follow the spiritual in Christianity as opposed to the ceremonial in Judiasm. Jewish Christians wanted to keep the new wine of Christianity in the old bottles of the Mosaic law. But the new wine had burst the bottles; yet there were some of the circumcision who refused to discard the tattered skins. Paul takes delight in the presence of these three men. For apart from giving him immediate comfort, they were a constant reminder of the adequacy of his gospel which allowed no partiality. Jew and Greek alike, as well as slave (Onesimus) and master (Philemon), stood on the same platform of need and were open on equal terms to the redemptive grace of Christ.

Aristarchus, whose name figures in Philemon (v. 24), is also mentioned in Acts (19:29; 20:4) as Paul's companion on his trip to Jerusalem for the collection, and on his journey to Rome (Acts 27:2). He is here as Paul's *fellow prisoner* because of his stand for the gospel of Christ.

Mark is better known to us. His story "is an instance of early faults nobly attoned for" (Maclaren). In his Gospel at chapter 14:51 Mark tells his own story of what happened to him on that dark betrayal night. In the midst of the confusion, he abandoned the linen cloth he had thrown about him and fled away naked. That was a rich-textured covering, a kind called *sindon* because it was woven in Seinde in India. Was that the occasion when Mark made his *response* of faith—when he lost his *sindon* to find the Savior? Mark, in whose mother's house was the upper room, knew much about Christ and was perhaps present at the institution of the Last Supper. Maybe he had accepted something of the new way secondhand, as a borrowed creed. But was it on that dark night in the world's history when, jumping from his bed and flinging his *sindon* about him, he caught sight of the face of Jesus in the torchlight, that the light broke in his soul? In Acts 12 there is the story of Mark's *relapse* of faith. At Perga the fight was on for Mark's soul. Recant, said the devil; you lost your *sindon* for Christ; will you lose your life? There at Perga, in the dead of night while Paul slept dreaming of a crown in the glory, and while Barnabas slept dreaming of some new convert to be given a chance, Mark took fright and went home. But here in Paul's letter there is evidence of Mark's *recovery* of faith. Mark is back again in the work of Christ; he has picked up the threads once more. His faith has been renewed, and he is profitable again as regards the work of Christ (cf. 2 Tim. 4:11).

Of the third man nothing is known apart from his sending this greeting to the Colossians. He is one of God's obscure saints; but he no less than others has his name in the book of life and his place in God's scheme of grace for the world. *Jesus who is called Justus*— but it is the Jesus who is called Christ that makes Justus's name significant and stamps him with immortality. And this same Jesus makes any of us of eternal worth and calls us by name. Justus bore the noble name of Jesus; but then so do we all who believe. For we are all called by Jesus' other name Christ—Christians, Christ's men. Justus must have often checked himself before he did or said anything by the fact that he bore the name *Jesus*. And he must often have been challenged by those outside the faith to be true to his name. So we must act with care lest we bring dishonor to him whose name we bear and share.

Verse 12: Epaphras, who is one of yourselves, a servant of Christ Jesus, greets you: We have already been introduced to *Epaphras* in chapter 1:7, as Paul's representative and the one responsible for bringing the gospel to Colossae. There he was referred to as "a faithful minister of Christ." Now, at the end of the letter, the apostle speaks of him again, this time as (literally) "a slave [*doulos*] of Jesus Christ," a title which appears again in Philippians 1:1 in reference to Timothy. Epaphras "is in the Lord's ministry as his obedient servant" (Lohse). Previously he had exercised his calling in introducing the gospel to Colossae; now for some time he had been absent, yet his ministry on their behalf continued, as Paul assures the Colossians.

Always remembering you earnestly in his prayers: Epaphras wrestled for the Colossians, as did Jacob, not to let the Lord go except he bless. Praying cost Epaphras, for Paul states that "he prays hard for you all the time" (NEB). His prayer took time and trouble. He labored *(agōnizomenos)* in his intercession, says the apostle, using a word at the center of which is the idea of conflict and struggle *(agōn)*. Epaphras "prayed in his praying" as did Elijah (cf. James 5:17, ASV margin). Paul knew too well, and Christian experience confirms too sadly, that it is not easy to keep on praying. It needs grit as well as grace. All too soon do knees weaken and minds wander. All too easily, in the thick of the battle, can we lose sight of God and stupidly imagine that success depends on the skill of our swordplay, and our ease of movement. But the battle is the Lord's, and it is prayer that nerves the arm for fight; to fail in this regard is to beat the air and to miss the adversary. But Epaphras's prayer was constant and earnest (cf. Phillips). Such was the manner of it; but here was the matter of it:

That you may stand mature and fully assured in all of the will of God: There can be few prayers of greater intent than this. The burning desire and burdening anxiety of Epaphras was that the Colossian believers might become "mature . . . Christians, in complete obedience to God's will" (TEV). "He bore their souls upon his soul. He yearned with the deepest longing that they might be holy in the sense of a single-hearted and thorough loyalty to the Lord. And he carried this yearning constantly and urgently to God in Christ, resolved to reach Colossian lives by way of the Throne" (H. C. G. Moule).

The background of the two words translated *mature* and *fully assured* is the particular situation that had developed at Colossae which Epaphras himself had communicated to Paul. Both the pastor's prayer and the apostle's proclamation were aimed at counteracting the false teaching which was seeking to undermine the Colossians' faith. Epaphras wanted them to attain perfection *(teleioi)* by becoming full grown and mature in Christ, measuring up to his stature. They must not remain children tossed to and fro and carried about by every wind of doctrine (Eph. 4:13–14). The heretics held out "perfection" as the goal of their secret mysteries. But not so can true maturity come about. Knowing this, Epaphras prayed that the Colossians might *stand mature* in Christ and that in him, too, they might be *fully assured,* "ripe in conviction" (NEB). The rare verb *peplērophorēmenoi* has the meaning "to be sure" or "certain" (cf. Rom. 4:21; 14:5). But its more usual sense is "to be filled" (cf. 1:9, 19; 2:9, 10). It thus recalls once again Paul's polemic against the schismatics, and comes as "a reminder that the Christian needs no Gnostic or legalistic additions to the wisdom and understanding available in Christ" (R. E. O. White). Not through speculative knowledge which they were airing, but by having "their fulness" in Christ, will maturity and assurance "in everything that is God's will" (literal) be theirs. It is for this that Epaphras prays; and this is "the highest service that love can render" (Maclaren).

Verse 13: For I bear him witness that he has worked hard for you and for those in Laodicea and in Hierapolis: Paul gives Epaphras a glowing testimony for his tireless works (NEB), not only as already stated on behalf of the church at Colossae but also for those in the two neighboring towns in the Lycus Valley. The apostle does not state the nature of this work or the difficulties met in performing it. But whatever it was, it was done fully and faithfully out of "deep interest" and concern for their spiritual state (Weymouth; cf. Phillips). In the case of the Colossians, it took the form of preaching and praying; doubtless he did so in both respects for those at Laodicea and Hierapolis. It was a part of Epaphras's hard work to have come to Rome to acquaint Paul with the condition of those churches and the danger threatening their faith. It was compassion for their state without Christ that drove him to tireless effort for them; and it was concern for their state in Christ which sent him off on the long trek to meet the apostle in a Roman prison. Epaphras's whole conduct won him Paul's high commendation; and surely that of Paul's Lord, who welcomed him home after his span of total dedicated service was completed with the words, "Well done, thou good and faithful servant." It must certainly have been so for him; it would be well if it were so for us.

Verse 14: Luke the beloved physician and Demas greet you. We can certainly designate Luke as the faithful; apparently Demas is the failure in the light of 2 Timothy 4:10, 11, where both names occur together again. Luke's long association with Paul in the interests of the gospel is well known. Here he is called *the beloved* doctor. But his ministry was not restricted to his medicine, for he was also Paul's fellow worker (cf. Philem. 24). Luke could minister to the broken-hearted. He carried with him, as well as the tools of his trade, the healing balm of the everlasting gospel. He evidently hailed from Antioch, and seemed to have linked up with Paul's company at the beginning of the voyage to Rome (Acts 27:1). We need not speculate as to how he was converted to Christ. But a real Christian he was. Part of his service in the gospel remains for us in the Gospel he wrote, together with his record of the Acts of the ascended Lord through and for the early church.

Demas, too, has mention, but the brevity of it may suggest that the apostle had noticed the beginning of a movement away from his earlier love and loyalty. In Philemon 24 he is placed among Paul's fellow workers. But by the time 2 Timothy came to be written, Demas's devotion had evaporated. Significant, then, is the contrast in that letter: "Demas has deserted"; "I have no one with me but Luke." And the reason for Demas's departure is then stated: "his heart was set on the world" (2 Tim. 4:10, 11, NEB). Both Luke and Demas are together, but they take opposite directions. Luke follows the upward way, Demas drifts along the downward path. Whether away in Thessalonica where he went Demas repented and returned to the Lord, and before the throne of God will one day join hands and heart again with Luke and Paul, we do not know. But the association of the two names Luke and Demas is a reminder of the possibilities open to us all. With Luke we may remain loyal; with Demas we may degenerate. This lesson we can learn "from these two men who stand before us like a double star—one bright and one dark—that no loftiness of Christian position, nor length of Christian profession is a guarantee against falling and apostasy" (Maclaren). "Let him who thinks he stands, take heed lest he fall" (1 Cor. 10:12).

Verse 15: Give my greetings to the brethren at Laodicea, and to Nympha and the church in her house: Paul now takes his turn to send greetings. He will single out the church at Laodicea for a special word in the next verse—a warning word indeed. But for that he prepares with his expression of good will to them. It is characteristic of Paul, as this very letter illustrates, to indicate his brotherly fellowship before administering his apostolic warnings. Paul wanted to speak the truth in love and to mix his direct warning with divine wisdom.

It is not certain whether the next greeting is for a man or a woman—whether it is for Nymphas (masculine) or, as in the RSV text, Nympha (feminine). Most modern translations consider it to be the feminine name. And there seems no good reason to deny it. This epistle has shown how the gospel puts on equal footing Jew and Greek, slave and free man. If this reference is to a woman, then it also demonstrates what Paul has said elsewhere that in Christ there is neither male nor female (Gal. 3:28). This would not be the first woman who shared with Paul the work of the gospel. Quite a list of women who supported Paul and were his helpers can be compiled from his epistles and the Book of Acts. And it is fitting that they should have a place in the apostle's lists of special greetings. It may well have been that the church at Laodicea met in the home of this "Christian lady" (cf. 2 John 1, Phillips, *Letters*). It was apparently not uncommon for early Christians to meet together for worship, prayer and instruction in convenient homes of other believers. The upper room in the house of John Mark's mother seems to have been the place where the Last Supper was instituted (cf. Acts 12:12). According to Acts 2:46 and 5:42, the first Christians met in houses; and so the pattern was set. Prisca and Aquila used their homes in Rome (cf. Rom. 16:5) and in Ephesus (1 Cor. 16:7) for this purpose; and in nearby Colossae Philemon dedicated his residence to the use of the church. Paul found a welcome in the home of Lydia (cf. Acts 16:15, 40), and at Corinth Gaius acted as host to the church (Rom. 16:23).

Verse 16: And when this letter has been read among you, have it read also in the church of the Laodiceans; and see that you read also the letter from Laodicea: We have no way of knowing for certain what was the *letter from Laodicea* referred to here. It is certainly one from the apostle to the church there. But if it was addressed to them under their own name, it is no longer extant. This supposition is not unacceptable, for there is no reason to suppose that everything that Paul wrote has been preserved. But what has been is sufficient, so that the people of God may be truly equipped for service and adequately fortified in faith (cf. 2 Tim. 3:16–17). Some writers identify the letter with that to the Ephesians, which was evidently a circular letter. But this has been discounted on the score that Ephesians appears to have been a later composition and could therefore hardly be mentioned in Colossians. Other suggestions have been made, but the difficulties involved have rendered them equally unacceptable. Uncertainty must remain. What is clear, however, is that the contents of the two letters were sufficiently dissimilar for Paul to direct that either should be read in the other church.

Reference to the reading of an epistle in the church is significant. The practice was well established (cf. 1 Thess. 5:27; Philem. 2). Paul's letters were, as John Dryden observes, "absent sermons." They were thus early recognized as having a distinctive quality all their own, as being the bearers of God's word to his people. In Paul's words the churches heard the word of Christ, the head of the church. Thus, to hear and heed Paul's epistles was one and the same with letting the word of Christ dwell in them richly.

Verse 17: And say to Archippus, "See that you fulfil the ministry which you have received in the Lord": It is usual to regard Archippus as attached to the church at Colossae, and probably the son of Philemon and Apphia (Philem. 2). But it would seem more natural to associate him with the church in Laodicea; otherwise it is hard to understand why the apostle did not address him directly. If, indeed, Archippus is to be thought of as the minister of the Laodicean church, then the message Paul has for him is of special interest to all God-ordained servants (cf. Phillips). Archippus is to be reminded that the ministry is a boon from God. It has its *source* in God as something *received*. Such is the apostle's high view of the Christian ministry. But he also directs Archippus's attention to the minister's *supply*. His service is received by him *in* the Lord. Here is his sufficiency—his full supply for all its demands, and for every occasion. To fulfill the ministry, one must be filled full of God's Spirit, as was the ideal Minister, God's Servant (cf. Luke 4:18). To make full proof of his ministry, Archippus must "take heed" (KJV), for while the ministry is divine in its source, it is dangerous in its requirements. "There must be diligent watchfulness in order to fulfil our ministry. We must take heed to our service, and we must take heed to ourselves" (Maclaren).

If Archippus were in fact the minister of the church in Laodicea, we must suppose that the message was needed for him. Perhaps Epaphras had to tell Paul that he was becoming lax and languid; so the apostle adds this special word to be given to him. "God ordained you to your work—see that you don't fail him!" (Phillips, *Letters*). But did Archippus really "take heed"? It cannot be said for sure that he did. What is certain, however, is that in a later allusion, the church at Laodicea appears as a complacent church, neither cold nor hot—just lukewarm. And Archippus could well have been the "angel" of that church to which the risen Lord had to speak so strongly (cf. Rev. 3:14–15). That may suggest that Archippus had not taken the message to heart; at any rate, it does suggest that the minister who would fulfill the Lord's service entrusted to him must "attend to the duty" and "discharge it to the full" (NEB).

Verse 18: I, Paul, write this greeting with my own hand. Remember my fetters. Grace be with you: Paul's personal signature would give his letter the stamp of his authority as Christ's apostle, and so be a safeguard against forgery. He wants his bonds remembered by the Colossians, for they must see in the fact that he wrote from a prison cell his great concern for their spiritual welfare. His fetters have not overcome his faith; rather his bonds for Christ have increased his burden for them. Recalling that he is in prison will stimulate their prayer. But he is there as Christ's servant, yet as his apostle, so they will heed what he writes. With a flourish of his chain-bound hand and a stirring in his unbound heart, Paul adds his closing word, *Grace. Grace be with you*—such is Paul's final wish for his readers; and in that one word is included all that is good for them and all that can ever surpass their desires and their deservings. All that God has prepared in the mystery of his glorious gospel, all that Christ has purchased by his sacrifice of love, is contained in that one word *grace*. Deep down beneath the peace that fills the church and the love that floods the believer is the foundation of eternal *grace*.

The word *grace* is as significant at the end of Paul's letter as it is at the beginning (cf. 1:2), for from first to last Paul's theme was grace. In neither place has the term a mere conventional use, for at every mention of this word the apostle is summarizing the essential message of the gospel given to him by the revelation of God. The word *grace* gathers into itself all that Christ is for Christian belief and Christian behavior.

Philemon

INTRODUCTION

Philemon

AUTHENTICITY

The Pauline authorship of Philemon is beyond all reasonable doubt. It has early attestation. And the internal evidence is strong, for historical reality is stamped on every sentence of the letter. Doubt has been cast upon it mainly because of its supposedly un-edifying value. But this judgment has been shown to be false by its great commentators, for example, Jerome, Chrysostom, Luther, Calvin and a host of modern writers. Ernest Renan was right in his assertion that "few pages have so clear an accent of truth; Paul alone, it would seem, could have written this little masterpiece." With the authenticity of Colossians already firmly established as au-thentically Pauline, that of Philemon necessarily follows; for there can be no doubt that the epistle was written by the same hand as well as sent to the same place as the Colossian letter.

OCCASION

When Paul wrote this "little masterpiece" he was a prisoner (vv. 1, 9, 13); thus the letter is linked with Colossians, Ephesians and Philippians as prison epistles. The closer connection between Phile-mon and Colossians is seen in the fact that Onesimus was a native of Colossae (Philem. 11; cf. Col. 4:9). Philemon himself was evidently one of Paul's converts (v. 19). He probably met the apostle at Ephesus, as Paul had not visited Colossae. But the apostle's name was certainly well known in Philemon's household; and when the latter's slave, Onesimus, ran away to Rome he was drawn to Paul's prison lodging where he heard the gospel and came to Christian faith.

It seems natural to infer that this letter went with the one to the Colossians by the hand of Tychicus who, at the same time, handed over the one-time thief-slave to his old master. Onesimus the con-verted fugitive had become dear to Paul in his imprisonment and is spoken of by the apostle in the most glowing terms. He is "his child," "his very heart" and his "beloved brother" (vv. 10, 12, 16). Paul indeed wished to keep him with him because of his helpful ministry (vv. 11, 12). But his service properly belonged to Philemon. The apostle consequently felt bound to send him back. And he writes this letter in the hope of securing for Onesimus the forgiveness of Philemon and the welcome which one Christian brother should give another (vv. 15–17). Paul bases his appeal to Philemon on the love he already shows to all the saints (vv. 4–7, 9), and on a personal request from "Paul the aged and now a prisoner," who has claims on Philemon's service (vv. 9–14, 17, 20). Paul gives vent to a certain wistful humor in his play on the meaning of the name *Onesimus.* "I beseech you for Profitable, who used to be Unprofitable, but now is Profitable . . . . Yes, let me have profit of you . . ." (vv. 11, 20).

SIGNIFICANCE

The importance of this brief letter to Philemon lies in the fundamental principle it enunciates concerning the rights and relationships between one man and another. And it raises the inevitable question of the New Testament attitude to slavery. It was certain that the time would not be long before the problem of the relation of slave to master would arise. Onesimus, now a Christian, is not given the right to be free, so that it is not easy to agree with J. B. Lightfoot that the word *emancipation* trembled on Paul's lips. For in no specific instance did Paul forbid slavery. Yet he set forth principles which were immediately to affect both the slave and the master.

To the slave himself, his worldly position was not to be his primary concern (cf. 1 Cor. 7:21–24). He could be a Christian and live wherever he found himself as a Christian should, even in Caesar's household (cf. Phil. 4:22), or where Satan's seat is (cf. Rev. 2:13).

For Philemon there is this lesson to be learned, that the institution of slavery, which in Paul's day was embedded in the social structure, must be guided by the new and higher principle of the equality and responsibility of all men before God (cf. Col. 3:22–4:1; Eph. 6:5–9).

To be sure, Philemon could assert his "rights," but to do so would be to make a breach in Christian fellowship, and be the rejection of a Christian brother. It is, in fact, these very principles which worked themselves out and at length made the institution of slavery itself impossible, so that the claim is justly made that it was the ethic of the Christian gospel, and not least this letter, which destroyed it. The final implication of Philemon is, therefore, the assertion of human dignity. Paul may not have entered a prohibition of slavery as such, but "what this epistle does is to bring us into an atmosphere in which the institution could only wilt and die" (F. F. Bruce, *Colossians;* see below, commentary on Philem. 12).

OUTLINE

Philemon

COMMENTARY

Philemon

I. SALUTATION (1–3)

In his opening salutation, Paul sets the tone for what he has to communicate to Philemon, his "dearly loved fellow-worker" (Williams). He has a very personal word to give, so he will write as from a friend to a friend. He will not "come to his friend clothed with apostolic authority" (Alexander Maclaren). Rather, he will come with quiet humility as Christ's prisoner. He has a favor to ask of Philemon, whose approval and action he must win. So he will drop all reference to himself as one having a particular divine appointment. which gives him the right to command. Instead, he will have Philemon hear the chains jangle on his arms and let them speak for him. Yet his salutation will include others by name, as well as referring to the congregation of believers which gathers in Philemon's house. And upon them all Paul pronounces the heavenly benediction of grace and peace from God the Father and the Lord Jesus.

Two names in the drama suggested by this note from Paul appear in these verses. For the third, Onesimus, we have to wait until we come to verse 10. But what a strange diversity of personalities in union with Christ are here. "An ex-Jewish rabbi, to whom all Gentiles were once untouchables; a wealthy Gentile patrician, to whom an itinerant Jewish preacher in a Roman prison would normally be an object of contempt, and to whom a runaway slave was a dangerous animal to be beaten or put to death; a rootless slave without hope of human sympathy, or even human justice—in all conscience, humanly speaking, an impossible trio, yet all three are caught up through their common allegiance to Christ into an entirely new relationship where each acknowledges the other as one of God's adopted sons, and a brother for whom Christ died" (William Barclay, *Bible Handbooks, Philemon*).

Verse 1: Paul, a prisoner for Christ Jesus, and Timothy our brother: Paul associates with him in his postcard to Philemon Timothy as *our brother* in the faith of the gospel (cf. 2 Cor. 1:1; 1 Thess. 1:1; 2 Thess. 1:1; Phil. 1:1; Col. 1:1). And truly a brother he was, because bound with the apostle in the bundle of new life in the supreme brotherhood of Christ (Heb. 2:11, 12); and, therefore, together with Paul a partaker of a heavenly calling (Heb. 3:1). Timothy's brotherhood with Paul "was born not out of human stock or urge of the flesh or will of man but of God himself" (John 1:13, JB). Yet he was a brother of the most persistent and practical kind. From the time that he linked up with Paul in their common interest in the gospel Timothy stood with the apostle and stuck by him through occasions rough and smooth. In season and out of season, Timothy proved himself to be Paul's faithful "colleague" (NEB; cf. Rom. 16:21, NEB). In Timothy's friendship the apostle clearly took a special delight and seems to have taken every opportunity to bring his name to the fore. To Paul, Timothy is a brother indeed, sharing a spiritual affinity and empathy with the apostle in his imprisonment. Apparently later he himself suffered a like experience (cf. Heb. 13:23).

In Paul's estimation Timothy was certainly, as his name means, "honoured of God"; and in that divine honor Paul was glad and great enough to share. The glimpses we have of Timothy's story in the New Testament show us a man who had a profound capacity for faith and love. He hailed from Lystra, the son of a Jewess by a Greek father (Acts 16:1), and was evidently converted through Paul to be his "son" in the faith (cf. 1 Tim. 1:2, 8; 2 Tim. 1:2). On account of Jewish opposition, Paul had him circumcised (Acts 16:3). Timothy shared in Paul's missionary strategy (cf. Acts 17:14, 15; 18:5; 19:22; 20:4; 2 Cor. 1:19), and sometimes he represented the apostle on special ministry (1 Cor. 4:17; 16:10; Phil. 2:19; 1 Thess. 3:2, 6). Timothy became one of the trusted leaders of the church and was the recipient of two special communications from the apostle concerning the doctrine and work of the gospel.

Although Paul brings Timothy's name into the opening salutation, the note to Philemon is nevertheless Paul's own. From verse 4 on, he uses the personal pronoun only, for he knows that he, and he alone, can win Philemon's good will by appealing to their common faith and continuing fellowship. Yet a petition from one suffering for Christ and the gospel "surely would be tenderly regarded by a believer and minister of Christ, and especially when strengthened too with the concurrence of Timothy, one eminent in the church" (Matthew Henry).

Because he wants from the beginning to reach Philemon's heart, Paul describes himself at the opening of his letter as *a prisoner for Christ Jesus*. Here is "a captive pleading for a slave" (Graham Scroggie). What a position this is for one armed with authority as an apostle of God! But Paul is careful here not to invoke his apostolic authority. He does not want Philemon to slavishly obey a command; rather he would have him lovingly fulfill the dictates of Christian brotherhood. So he will "entreat rather than command" (Lightfoot; cf. vv. 8, 9). Thus Paul shows himself as a model of Christian tact. He refers to himself simply as *a prisoner* of Christ Jesus, believing that that, if anything, will touch Philemon's heart, and with all but irresistible force produce a response to his appeal. Philemon can hardly refuse Paul's request by failing to put into action the love he professes for his friend in prison.

Yet Paul does not employ the designation merely to induce Philemon to do what he requires of him, for that would rob Paul's use of it of all spiritual worth. There is something deeper here in Paul's reference to his imprisonment—"the accents of inartificial spontaneousness" (Maclaren). In these words of salutation is the profound music of an unconscious pathos; they are all the more appealing because, while they strike the right notes, Paul seems quite unaware of how right they are. Paul never felt himself hard done by because of his imprisonment for the sake of the gospel. And he refers to it here not just to solicit sympathy but to stimulate spirituality. As our English word *strain* can mean either a tension or a tune, so Paul never allowed his tensions to cancel his tunes. He is a prisoner; but he does not permit the harsh prose of his prison stories to empty him of the high praise of his prison songs.

Paul calls himself a prisoner *for Christ Jesus;* that music drowns his moan (cf. Acts 16:25). The apostle is a prisoner—not of Jerusalem, not of Rome, but of, or for, Christ Jesus. He sees beyond his manacled wrists to a higher authority who has allowed him to be where he is. He ignores all subordinate agencies and looks to the true author of his captivity (Maclaren). He is a *prisoner* for *Christ Jesus*. There is no contradiction here. It does not mean that Christ is helpless in the affairs of men and nations. The apostle was sure that Christ is Lord of all and that his "hand moves the pieces on the board" (cf. Col. 1:15–20).

Paul is, it seems, literally a prisoner at the time of writing to Philemon (cf. vv. 9, 10). And that tells us something of the *cost* there may be for those who profess the name of Christ. The apostle considered "his imprisonment as the fate that is in store for the messenger of the gospel—that is, part and parcel of the commission given to him. The messenger of the Kyrios must suffer like his master to whom he owes obedience" (Eduard Lohse). Others, however, regard Paul's reference to his imprisonment for Christ Jesus to be either metaphorical (H. C. G. Moule, *Colossians and Philemon;* cf. Col. 4:10), or figurative (Reitzenstein; cf. Luke 13:16). Although neither idea is likely here, the imprisonment does speak to us of the *commitment* there must be on the part of those who would be Christ's followers. For to follow Christ is to be one with him, bound to him, imprisoned in him, not having a righteousness of our own, but controlled by his mind and will. Once Paul was Rome's free man (cf. Acts 16:37–39; 22:25–29; 23:27), but he knew he was then imprisoned (cf. Rom. 6:16–19). Now, however, he is Christ's imprisoned man but knows himself to be free (cf. Rom. 6:18; 8:2; Gal. 5:1).

To Philemon our beloved fellow worker. Certainly Philemon was the addressee, not as has recently been asserted, Archippus (John Knox). By referring to Philemon as "our dearly loved fellow-worker" (Williams), he is immediately "reminded that he belongs to a community of mutual love" (Lohse; R. P. Martin, *Colossians and Philemon*). Paul had many friends whom he could address with the added appellation *beloved* (cf. Rom. 16:8; 9:12; 1 Cor. 4:17; Eph. 6:21). But here in Colossae are Epaphras, his *"beloved* fellow servant" (Col. 1:7), Tychicus and Onesimus, *"brethren beloved"* (Col. 4:7, 9), and Luke "the *beloved* physician" (Col. 4:14). Among them Paul puts Philemon. He, too, is beloved; for he "is loved by Paul, by Timothy, and by every believer who has heard of him. He is loved by Christ and has the characteristics of a brother" (William Hendriksen). As a Christian, Philemon lived a life of love and manifested it in his actions. Hardly then can he deny that love to a slave whom Paul calls a *beloved brother* (cf. v. 16). Philemon was both a good man in himself by the grace of God, and a good servant of Christ Jesus, showing his love in loyalty to those who were co-workers with him in the gospel. Other versions qualify the term *beloved (agapētos)* by adjectives such as "dearly" (KJV; cf. "our dear friend and fellow-worker," NEB). Such a reading of *agapētos* is usual in the KJV (cf. Rom. 12:19; 1 Cor. 10:14; 2 Cor. 7:1; 12:19; Phil. 4:1; 2 Tim. 1:2) and should be retained here. Philemon, like Daniel of old, was a man "greatly beloved" (cf. Dan. 9:23; 10:11, 19).

Philemon is also regarded by Paul as his *fellow worker,* a designation earned by others of the apostle's company (cf. Rom. 16:3, 9, 21; 2 Cor. 8:23; Phil. 2:25; 4:3; Col. 4:11; 1 Thess. 3:2). Maybe Philemon had aided the apostle during the latter's long stay in Ephesus and followed on in the work after the apostle's departure. But not just on that account does Paul speak of him so: he is still for him a fellow worker as he continues to be active in the local fellowship and in the common work of proclaiming the gospel by living word and loving deed. True, Philemon's work is not on the scale of Paul's. Yet the apostle does not reckon it of lesser significance for Christ than his own. Rather, in his large-hearted way, he lifts Philemon's humbler service out of its narrowness and limitation by uniting it with his own. Philemon's sphere may be restricted, and his much wider, but for Paul they are equally fellow workers for the same Lord.

Verse 2: And Apphia our sister and Archippus our fellow soldier, and the church in your house: Paul runs on to include in his opening salutation, and perhaps in the general contents of the letter, the names of *Apphia* and *Archippus*. Although the name Apphia was quite common, it is assumed as a safe inference from the connection of the names that she was the wife of Philemon (Lightfoot, Lohse). As mistress of the home, concerned with domestic duties, it seems inevitable that Paul would include her in the discussion about the reinstatement of a runaway slave. She was not, of course, designated *our sister* by being so literally or physically, as Mary and Martha were sisters of Lazarus (John 11:1), nor yet metaphorically (cf. 2 John 13), but spiritually. "Apphia is 'our sister' in the sense in which Timothy is 'our brother,' namely, as belonging to the family of faith" (Hendriksen). A slave is called "a brother" and a woman "a sister"—how the gospel has made all such distinctions void. The old world was parted by gulfs deep and wide. Even in the most enlightened Jewish circles women were of little account; in his morning prayer the Jew gave thanks that God had not made him a Gentile, a slave, or a woman. The disciples themselves in the early days could hardly believe that Jesus would talk with *a,* with any, woman (John 4:27). But now "in Christ" there is neither male nor female, slave nor freeman (cf. Gal. 3:28). So to the apostle, Apphia is *our sister;* one with him in the bonds of Christ Jesus.

Archippus, mentioned in close conjunction with the other two, may have been their son. But all we know for certain about him is limited to the reference here and to Colossians 4:17 (see commentary). Paul considers him as *our fellow soldier:* a title in fact given to only one other person in the New Testament, namely, Epaphroditus (Phil. 2:25). It is a designation of high intent. Philemon is "our fellow worker;" Archippus is "our fellow soldier." The "fellow worker" tells of achievement; "fellow soldier" speaks rather of endurance; but every Christian is called to be both (Phil. 2:25). In some way Archippus was "a fellow combatant of the apostle" (Lohse); he was with Paul "our comrade-in-arms" (NEB).

It is thought by some that Archippus took the lead against the Judaizers in Colossae during the absence of Epaphras, and was the overseer of the church there (cf. Col. 4:16, 17). In this reference to himself as a fellow soldier, Archippus will find encouragement. If indeed he was the son of Philemon and Apphia, he would still have been a young man. And at this time Paul was well on in years (cf. v. 9, KJV). How beautiful, then, "that the grizzled veteran officer should thus, as it were, clasp the hand of this young recruit, and call him his comrade" (Maclaren). Archippus, we think, was Paul's representative in Laodicea. So the word the apostle has for him there (Col. 4:17, see commentary) will come as a warning. The ministry he has received is finally from the Lord. This Archippus must recognize, and make sure that he doesn't fail his Lord (Col. 4:17; cf. Phillips, *Letters*).

The greeting comes, too, to *the church in your house*. In days when church buildings were not available as they are today, it seems to have been the custom for the believing community to gather in homes large enough to accommodate them. Such hospitality was a feature of the early Christians, and the giving of hospitality for the sake of Christ was considered part of the Christians' way of love (cf. Rom. 12:13; 1 Tim. 3:2; Tit. 1:8; 1 Pet. 4:9). So Philemon's home served as gathering place for the local fellowship of believers much as did that of Aquila and Priscilla in Ephesus (1 Cor. 16:19) and Rome (Rom. 16:3–5). At Laodicea, Nympha put her home at the disposal of the church (Col. 4:15), as did Gaius at Corinth (Rom. 16:23). The house-church was, then, the usual meeting place for the early believers. But as the believers multiplied, more spacious buildings were required, so the transition to the present type of church premises was gradual. In fact, the oldest known church building unearthed by archaeologists typifies this transition, for it appears to be a modified, once privately owned dwelling. The house was built in A.D. 232–33 at Dura Europos in eastern Syria on the Euphrates. In its transformed condition it consists of a chapel designed to hold a hundred worshipers.

Philemon had a church in his home. Our English word *church* comes from the Greek *kuriakē* meaning "of or *belonging to the Lord*" (cf. *kirk*, Scottish; *kirche*, German). And so we have the picture of Philemon and Apphia conducting their home as ultimately belonging to the Lord, to be ruled by him and used for him. In such an atmosphere, all ties and tasks were considered sacred. Here husband and wife dwelt as heirs together of the grace of life, with their household ordered in the ways of the Lord. From this remote valley there thus comes a lovely picture of what a Christian home should be, in which common duties and social joys are hallowed and serene.

Verse 3: Grace to you and peace from God our Father and the Lord Jesus Christ: Here is the grand climax of Paul's salutation—a heavenly benediction upon all, for the *you* is in the plural—upon Philemon, Apphia, Archippus, and the community of faith which meets in Philemon's house. There is no greater word in all the vocabulary of the gospel than this word *grace (charis)*. The common

Greek greeting is *chairein* (cf. Acts 15:23; 23:26; James 1:1); but here, as always, Paul uses his own special word *charis,* and so unites, with an enriched content, the Greek and Hebrew form of salutation—grace and peace (see comment on Col. 1:2).

Grace comes first in the apostle's thought. Paul suggests by this priority at the outset of his writing that all that he has of the blessings and bounties of Christ's new order was due to the unmerited favor of God. And with grace goes *peace (eirēnē); grace* is antecedent to *peace;* for it is as a result of grace that *peace* is realized and restored. *Charis* "denotes the love of God manifested in the form of pardon towards sinful men; and peace, *eirēnē,* the feeling of profound calm and inward quiet which is communicated to the heart by the possession of reconciliation" (F. L. Godet).

Paul never got away from his awareness that it was God's loving action in Christ which brought him into fellowship with God and brotherhood with all believers. So the peace was for him not only peace with God but peacefulness in relation to one another. "Grace in God's heart, and 'peace' in ours" (Scroggie): that is the way of God's dealing with men. Thus does " 'grace' refer to the action of the Divine heart, and 'peace' to the results thereof in man's experience" (Maclaren).

By thus uniting the Greek and Hebrew form of salutation, the apostle blends the ideals of good which the East and West have desired for those to whom they wish the highest favors, and, at the same time, he makes clear that whatever men of every century and circumstance hope for as their greatest blessings can only be found in God and reached through Christ. For the grace and peace are *from* God and the Lord Jesus Christ. They are communicated to us, coming "away from" *(apo)* God and the Lord Jesus Christ. And in coming from God and the Lord Jesus they find their way to us. In the Greek text the preposition is not repeated. This placing of both names under the government of one preposition implies the mysterious unity of the Father and the Son, while conversely, in a parallel passage in 2 John 3, by employing two prepositions, the distinction between the Father, who is the fontal source, and the Son, who is the flowing stream, is suggested.

Paul can, therefore, desire for Philemon and the rest no greater blessing than the peace which flows from grace. Peace with God, of course—that first. But with it, too, peace with our own selves so that we are no longer, like Brutus, with ourselves at war. By the grace that flows into our hearts, bringing with it the assurance of God's forgiving and healing love, there is created an inner calm. For our nature, hitherto churned like a troubled sea by conflicting emotions and competing desires, is hushed, "and birds of calm sit brood-

ing on the charmed wave" (John Milton, "On the Morning of
Christ's Nativity"). Of this one thing we are certain, to change the
figure, that nothing "but a heavenly power can make the lion within
lie down with the lamb" (Maclaren).

But how is Paul's elliptical form of salutation to be read—as a
wish or a desire, an assurance or a prayer? Possibly as all
together—as a *votum cum affirmatione,* to quote J. A. Bengel's
comment on the parallel greeting in 2 John referred to above. Paul's
words are at the same time a desire assured of certain fulfillment and
a wish inspired by prayer (cf. v. 4).

II. THE REMEMBRANCE WHICH INSPIRED PAUL'S
THANKFUL SUPPLICATION (4–7)

In these verses Paul lets Philemon know how much his spiritual well-being and well-doing have caused him to give thanks to God. And with his constant praise, there goes his continual prayer that their fellowship in the common faith of the gospel "may deepen the understanding of all the blessings that our union with Christ brings us" (v. 6, NEB). Paul then discloses how much he is encouraged by Philemon's love, and how that love, so generously displayed, cheers the hearts of God's people. "The apostle's thanksgiving and prayer here for Philemon are set forth by the object, circumstance, and matter of them, with the way whereby much of the knowledge of Philemon's goodness came to him" (Henry).

Verse 4: I thank my God always when I remember you in my prayers: Paul has special sources of information of how things had been going with Philemon and the believing community which gathered in his house, all of which brought new occasions for his prayers of thanksgiving. There was Epaphras, leader of the church in Colossae and himself a Colossian, now with the apostle (cf. v. 23) who would have been able to give Paul many details concerning the congregation and Philemon's hospitality and generosity. Then there was Onesimus, the fugitive slave, from whom Paul would have learned more of Philemon's kindly conduct and Christly character. And at every mention of his name, Paul would lift his heart in thanksgiving for a life so evidently affected by the saving influences of the gospel.

Philemon was for Paul the occasion of thanks to God: literally, "I give thanks *(eucharistō)* to God *(tō theō)*." Central in the Greek word for "to give thanks" is the word for "grace" *(charis;* cf. *charin echō*—"I have grace," i.e., "I thank him," 1 Tim. 1:12; "I thank God," 2 Tim. 1:3). The relation between *charis* and *eucharistō* is of the very closest. It is a grace to be grateful; and it is also *of* grace. Paul gives thanks "to God." To God, no less, does he attribute Philemon's faith and love. "To God be the glory, great things he has done"; that is for Paul the tone and test of true thanksgiving. To such a God Paul can pray with joyous confidence and can put in the personal pronoun *my*. To the apostle, God was not a distant, unbending and reluctant deity whose concern has to be purchased and love gained in some extraneous way. Paul knew and taught, not that he was loved of God because Christ died; rather it was the other way. It was because God loved him that Christ died for him, even while he was yet a sinner (Rom. 5:8). He had come to know the love of God in Christ, and in that love of Christ he could rejoice that he was loved of God. In Christ's love he was enfolded in the love of God: thus can he say, I thank *my God*. "It is the privilege of good men, that in their praises and prayers they come to God as *their God*" (Henry).

Paul thanks God *always* when he remembers Philemon in prayer. The adverb *(pantote)* is usually construed with the main verb to read, "I thank my God *pantote,* that is, 'always,' when at prayer he thinks of Philemon" (Lohse). Paul's prayers for Philemon are no less times of praise. His supplications to God on Philemon's behalf brought to mind some new reason for thanksgiving (see on Col. 1:3–5). But there is a further implication here; the hope that Philemon's response to Paul's request concerning Onesimus will afford him an additional reason for thanksgiving. The specific cause for Paul's thanksgiving prayer follows.

Verse 5: Because I hear of your love and of the faith which you have toward the Lord Jesus and all the saints: Some have supposed that by the use of the verb *I hear (akouō)*, Philemon was as yet unknown personally to Paul since it is used in his letters addressed to communities he had not visited (cf. Col. 1:4; Eph. 1:15; see Rom. 1:8). But this view does not seem to hold here, as it does not in the case of the Ephesian reference, because Philemon was evidently converted through Paul's witness (cf. v. 19) and must have met the apostle elsewhere, almost certainly in Ephesus. Perhaps for some time there had been no direct contact between them, and Paul's knowledge of how it fared in recent days with Philemon came to him only indirectly. At any rate, it was by hearing of Philemon that Paul's prayers for him were inspired and his thanksgiving increased.

What Paul heard about Philemon concerned his *love (agapē)* and *faith (pistis).* The fact that in other passages faith, as the source from which love springs, comes first, has occasioned much discussion. Most commentators consider it to be an instance of the grammatical structure known as chiasm, or inverted parallelism (Lightfoot, M. R. Vincent, H. C. G. Moule, Hendriksen, Martin). The idea is that of a crisscross structure in which, in the present case, the first word of the sentence relates to the last, while the second and third agree. Thus the *love* which Philemon exhibited is for *all the saints,* and the *faith* exercised is *toward the Lord Jesus.* The reason for Paul's use of the structure is then explained somehow as follows. The first and predominant thought in Paul's mind as he writes is of Philemon's love. This, however, immediately suggests a mention of faith as the source from which it springs. But the idea of faith at once suggests a reference to its object, the Lord Jesus. Then at length Paul comes back to the deferred sequence, the range and comprehensiveness of Philemon's love encompassing all the saints. This "arrangement then is an echo of the talks which had gladdened the Apostle" (Maclaren).

This explanation has certainly several advantages. It permits the sense of faith as trust, or confidence, to be given with the preposition *pros* (toward) the Lord Jesus (cf. 1 Thess. 1:8). It explains the variation in the use of the preposition *eis* (to) before "all the saints"—"there is a propriety in using *pros* of the faith which inspires *towards* Christ, and *eis* of the love exerted on all men" (Lightfoot; cf. Rom. 5:8; 2 Cor. 2:8; 2 Thess. 1:3; Col. 1:4). It explains why "love . . . for the saints," "as a composite phrase comes both first (for emphasis) and last in the sentence, since compassion and generosity rest on and are proof of Philemon's Christian standing as a believer in the Lord Jesus" (Martin).

A few commentators, however, contend that the words are not to be taken chiastically. Rather, they would take the word *pistis, faith,* in the sense of faithfulness—your love and faithfulness toward the Lord Jesus and all the saints. Although *pistis* can be given this meaning (cf. Rom. 3:3), it is generally agreed that it cannot be allowed this connotation here; both (1), because in conjunction with "which you have towards the Lord Jesus" it requires its proper theological meaning (Lightfoot), and (2), because in connection with "love," *pistis* always means faith (Lohse).

Others, while refusing the chiastic arrangement of "love and faith" on the score that the appearance of the phrase in a relative clause prohibits it (Lenski), would still give to the term *faith* its theological meaning. The point is then made that the *sou* (*your;* "thy," KJV) placed before love (*tēn agapēn*) modifies both nouns—"your (thy) love and your (thy) faith," and that the relative clause does not simply modify "faith"; "which (love and faith) thou hast towards the Lord Jesus and for all the saints" (R. C. H. Lenski). Or as translated by Phillips—"for I have heard how you love and trust both the Lord Jesus himself and those who believe in him."

It was the exhibition of love and faith by Philemon which gladdened the heart of the apostle. Philemon's love for the Lord Jesus was certainly genuine. For by Christ the love of God had been shed abroad in his heart by the Holy Spirit, so that in love for Christ, God is loved. The one who thus loves God is known of him (1 Cor. 8:3). Philemon discovered as a reality of his own experience that in love for God "everything that happens fits into a pattern for good" (Rom. 8:28, Phillips). It was in the outflow of this love for the Lord Jesus that Philemon's love encompassed *all the saints*. Such love was something quite astonishing in Philemon's days when the barriers which separated class from class were far more formidable than they are even in these days. But "the new faith leaped all barriers, and put a sense of brotherhood into every heart that learned God's fatherhood in Jesus." (Maclaren). Yet Philemon's love for all the saints was not a gushing affair which soon evaporated when events got too hot. It was the news of Philemon's practical goodness, his generosity and his hospitality, which cheered Paul in his prison cell. For Philemon had truly shown himself to be a benefactor of the brotherhood, and his love for all the saints was not spent in waving the "paper money" of words and promises. It was a love cashed in the hard coinage of kindly deeds. But it was certainly a love that had its source and foundation of goodness and fruitfulness of character in faith. "This love for God's consecrated children has its root, as always, in faith towards the Lord Jesus" (Hendriksen). Only in true faith can love be true. This is the "work of faith and labor of love" (1 Thess. 1:3). Yet "love and faith" are "from God the Father and the Lord Jesus Christ" (Eph. 6:23). That which is exhaled from the heart and drawn upwards by the savor of Christ's own self-sacrificing love is faith; when it falls to earth again like the gentle rain from heaven which causes the good seed of tenderness and pity to sprout forth, it is love. So are faith and love wedded, and they cannot ever be divorced. They belong together; consequently "a loveless faith is cruel, and a faithless love is sentimental" (Scroggie).

Paul focuses attention on the true object of faith, the Lord Jesus. The choice of these names here would seem to be deliberate. He is *Lord* with a lordship which is absolute. When Paul was confronted with the living Christ on the Damascus road, his immediate reaction was to acknowledge him as Lord. And it became clear to him as he went on to proclaim the gospel of Christ's lordship, that "no one can say 'Jesus is Lord' except by the Holy Spirit" (1 Cor. 12:3). This lordship of Christ was thus for Paul the decisive factor in the church. The church is his (Rom. 16:16, etc.), as it is God's (1 Cor. 1:2; 11:22; 15:9, etc.). Here is a relationship which does not detract from God but which rather exalts Christ to the status of deity. It is from this conviction of Christ's absolute right as Lord that all the ethical demands and urgings of the New Testament derive. The believer in Christ is related as a slave to Master, and his highest ideal is to be made captive "to the obedience of Christ" (2 Cor. 10:5, KJV). This lordship of Christ is all-embracing: over Jew and Gentile, rich and poor, slave and master. He is the same Lord to all who call upon him (Rom. 10:12, 13). To his lordship all will be subject (Eph. 3:11; Phil. 2:11; etc.). To call upon the name of the Lord Jesus Christ was virtually a synonym for Christian. To do anything for his sake is the true norm of service to God (cf. Acts 9:16; Rom. 15:30; 2 Cor. 12:10). By the application of the term *Lord (kurios),* the uniqueness of Christ as standing in the place of the Jehovah of the Old Testament is made manifest (Rom. 10:12; cf. Joel 2:32). For Paul, the title *Lord* had a lofty significance. It had ceased, in fact, to be a title and had become the sacred expression of a personal devotion to God encountered in Christ into which went the gratitude, the love and the loyalty of his redeemed being.

But the Lord is at the same time Jesus, the man; truly man and fully man. And in that manhood of the Master, Philemon should see every man; should see Onesimus the runaway slave from the standpoint of his new manhood in Christ.

The true object of faith is, then, the *Lord Jesus,* at once fully divine and truly human. Christian faith sees his divinity in that humanity and his humanity around that divinity. A faith which professes the humanity only is maimed, and a faith which looks only to the divinity is strained. To grasp his humanness alone is not sufficient. There is nothing here for faith's foothold and love's flow. For all that is human is not enough for the humanness of all. At the same time to leave the human and look far off to some distant being "on the limits far withdrawn" will not do. We are taught that the Word came to be flesh and to tarry among us that we might see his glory (John 1:14, cf. 17:24) and behold in his face the glory of God (2 Cor. 4:6). A divine being too remote for contact we may believe in but cannot converse with. But "the far off splendour and stupendous glory of the Divine nature becomes the object of untrembling trust, when we have it mellowed to our weak eyes by shining through the tempered medium of His humanity" (Maclaren).

Verse 6: And I pray that the sharing of your faith may promote the knowledge of all the good that is ours in Christ: This verse links up closely with what has gone before, as Paul's praise leads him into prayer. But this is characteristic of him (see comment on Col. 1:3–5). Verse 5 here gives the cause of the apostle's thanksgiving, as he states the purport of his intercession. He has just mentioned Philemon's love for "all the saints." That love went out in helpful regard, both spiritual and temporal, for them. It is the burden of Paul's prayer that Philemon may once again exhibit the same attitude of liberality and the same genuine character of faith with respect to

Onesimus, who stands in need of his forgiveness and help. Such sharing of his faith will promote *the knowledge of all the good* that flows from union with Christ, and will be for Christ's glory. Paul is confident that his prayer will be answered, that Philemon will act out of Christian charity, and that he himself will be "delighted and encouraged by your love" (v. 7, NEB).

While, however, some such general meaning may be given to the passage, there are a number of problems arising from the significance to be given to the Greek words which make it "the most obscure verse in this letter" (C. F. D. Moule). So terse and difficult is it that "all exegetes try to approximate its meaning by paraphrase" (Lohse). A few of these issues need allusion here.

The word *koinōnia,* rendered *sharing* in our version ("fellowship," NEB), has indeed this meaning (cf. 2 Cor. 8:4; Eph. 3:9; Phil. 1:5; 2:1; 3:10). But it can also be translated as "participation" (cf. 1 Cor. 10:16; 2 Cor. 6:14; 13:14). The question is, then, which is the more appropriate word here. Each term has its advocates. Lohse opts for the meaning "participation," and comments: "Philemon shares in the common faith. This share of faith he possesses should be active as the 'faith working through love' (Gal. 5:6) insofar as he realizes that the blessing bestowed on the believer should now appear in concrete acts of love." "This word means 'fellowship,' " declares Lenski (cf. NEB). He then amplifies: " 'Of thy faith' is the subjective genitive as the predicate shows: 'may be active or energetic.' Philemon's faith puts him into fellowship with all the saints (v. 5)." The choice is therefore between participation in faith or fellowship in love. But maybe there is no need to opt for one against the other, for the one who truly participates in faith will have sincere fellowship in love.

The phrase *en epignōsei* (literally, "full knowledge") raises the question how the *en* is to be understood: *by* the full knowledge or *in* the full knowledge. The latter "makes it difficult to arrive at an intelligible meaning for the entire sentence" (Hendriksen). Accepting then the former and rendering it as "by the clear recognition," the text may be read: "that the sharing to which your faith gives rise may be energetically stimulated for Christ by the clear recognition of all the good that is ours in Christ." Lightfoot, however, opts for the *in:* "in the perfect knowledge of every good thing." He then gives the exposition: "This *epignōsis,* involving as it does the complete appropriation of all truth and the unreserved identification with God's will, is the goal and crown of the believer's course. The Apostle does not say 'in the possession' or 'in the performance' but 'in the knowledge of every good thing': for, in this higher sense of knowledge, to know is both to possess and to perform."

Difficulty has also been found in the precise meaning to be given to the phrase *all the good (panta agathou)*. The neuter is used, as in classical Greek, as an abstract noun—"every good"; that is, "everything good." But is the *good* that which comes as a boon to be enjoyed, or is it right deeds to be done? The former fits the context best here and is followed by most commentators: *the good* are "the blessings that our union with Christ brings us" (NEB). " 'The good' ([ta] agatha) is the salvation that has been offered in preaching (Rom. 10:15)" (Lohse). It means "everything good for our salvation," "what we possess in Christ" (Lenski).

It is God who begins such a good work in the believer and who will bring it to completion at the day of Christ (Phil. 1:6; Rom. 8:28). For, "Every good endowment that we possess and every complete gift that we have received must come from above, from the Father of all lights, with Whom there is never the slightest variation or shadow of inconsistency" (James 1:17, Phillips, *Letters*). The blessings of God are good because he always wills what is good (Rom. 12:2). Therefore we can trust "that in everything God works for good with those who love him, who are called according to his purpose" (Rom. 8:28). It is indeed the very goodness of God which leads to repentance (Rom. 2:4).

But the good which is bestowed must be expressed. For the new life is God's workmanship created in Christ for good works (Eph. 2:10; cf. 2 Cor. 9:8; 2 Tim. 3:17). This then is the Christian's aim—"good should be your objective always, among yourselves and in the world at large" (1 Thess. 5:15, Phillips; cf. Rom. 15:2; Gal. 6:10). We are not to be overcome by evil, but rather to "use good to defeat evil" (Rom. 12:21, NEB). "Therefore, if Philemon recognizes 'the good' that God has given and that consequently is 'in us' *(en hēimin)*, he will also comprehend the will of God and heed the admonition of the apostle: 'so that your good deed might not stem from compulsion, but from your free will' (v. 14)" (Lohse).

There still remains for consideration the last words of the sentence, *in Christ*. This phrase should most certainly be rendered as "for Christ" (Hendriksen), or "unto Christ, i.e., leading to Him as the goal" (Lightfoot); or, "for the glory of Christ" (Lohse). The preposition is *eis (Christon)*, not as in verses 8 and 10 *en (Christō)* where it is rightly rendered "in Christ" (cf. v. 20, *en Kuriō*, "in the Lord").

It is Paul's purpose to focus his conclusion on the fact that all active workings of faith, according to the knowledge of the good which has been bestowed upon us, should have Christ's glory as its goal and aim. The words express the condition on which Christian fellowship, like all acts of Christian love, can be divinely energized,

tin). For by ending with the emphatic word *brother,* Paul's deep gratitude for and heartfelt delight in Philemon's love shows him to be no cold-blooded stoic. Paul's emotions were greatly stirred and he did not seek to hold them in check. He knew how to sorrow for others and to rejoice with them; in both he allowed his whole soul to be outpoured in the overwhelming love of Christ (cf. Rom. 9:2, 2 Cor. 4:14).

Here, too, is strategy. *Brother* (cf. v. 20) Philemon is to Paul, as is Timothy (v. 1). But as Philemon reads on, he will learn that Onesimus is now to the apostle "a beloved brother" (v. 16). Will Philemon take that in? Will he who has been "fellowshiping with slaves" take back Onesimus, not only as a slave but as a brother? Paul believes that it will be so. This word *brother* comes, then, as "a fitting climax, showing how deeply the apostle loves the man whom he here addresses, how highly he esteems him, and how completely he trusts him" (Hendriksen).

In our version, however, the words *my brother* do not come at the end of the sentence. They are central in it and are followed by Paul's further statement about the effects of Philemon's love.

Because the hearts of the saints have been refreshed through you. "These final words suggest the unexpected good which good deeds may do. No man can ever tell how far the blessing of his trivial acts of kindness or other processes of Christian conduct may travel" (Maclaren). The word translated *hearts* here is *ta splagchna* (also in vv. 12, 20), which refers to "the nobler viscera, regarded as the seat of emotions" (Lightfoot; cf. comment on Col. 3:12). The term has special reference to the innermost feelings which give rise to the tenderer affections such as kindness, compassion, benevolence. (It is generally translated in the KJV as "bowels"; cf. Acts 1:18; 2 Cor. 6:12; Phil. 1:8; 2:1; Col. 3:12; but once, in 2 Cor. 7:15, as "inner affection," which gives the true sense of the term.) Paul rejoices that the community of faith, the saints *(hagioi),* have been refreshed in their innermost being by Philemon's love.

And *refreshed* they are, declares the apostle, using the infinitive form of the verb *anapauō,* which means literally "to cause or permit one to escape from any movement or labour in order to recover or collect his strength" (Thayer; cf. 1 Cor. 16:18; 2 Cor. 7:13; see Mark 6:31; 14:41; Matt. 11:28; 26:45; etc.). By Philemon's love, the saints, including his slaves, were given " 'relaxation, refreshment,' as a preparation for a renewal of labour or suffering" (Lightfoot). In this, Philemon exhibited something of his Master's spirit. Those who have found rest in Christ ("relief," NEB) for their souls (Matt. 11:28), have need of times for refreshment and renewal (Mark 6:31; cf. 9:2).

It has frequently been pointed out that verses 4–7 contain a

number of words which reappear with effect in the following verses.
First here is the supreme term "love" *(agapē)* verse 4, which comes
again in verse 9—"for love's sake," and in verse 16—"a brother beloved"; "prayers" *(proseuchōn)* in verse 4 again in verse 22; "fellowship" or "partnership" *(koinōnia),* verses 6 and 17; "the good,"
verses 6 and 14; "heart(s)" verses 7, 12 and 20 and "brother,"
verses 7 and 20.

III. THE REASON WHICH OCCASIONED PAUL'S TACTFUL COMMUNICATION (8–14)

In these verses Paul comes to the main purpose of his writing. But even now he does not blurt out his desire all at once. Rather he weighs his every word with the greatest care and gradually leads up to his special request: the reinstatement of a runaway slave and the recognition of him as a brother in Christ. Perhaps in our changed social context we can hardly take this in. There was, on the whole, little consideration given to runaway slaves at the time. In fact there is evidence that the greatest efforts were made to find them and bring them back to their masters who were left to punish them at their discretion. There is extant in Alexandria, dating from the middle of the second century B.C., the copy of a warrant issued for the apprehension of a slave named Hermon who fled the service of a certain Aristogenes. The man's particulars are detailed, his race, age, height and so forth. The further information is appended that he was accompanied by another runaway named Bion who belonged to Callicrates, for whose return a reward is offered.

It seems that recaptured slaves were subjected to a good deal of cruelty. Of interest therefore is the famous letter of Pliny the Younger to Sabinianus, in which he intercedes for a *libertus*—a freeman—who had fled from Sabinianus and come to Pliny for help. Pliny discloses that the *libertus* is full of remorse and would return to his master but fears his anger. Pliny pleads the runaway's cause, contending, on his behalf, that clemency is more to be desired than rage. Sabinianus is reminded that the *libertus* is but a young man and that he truly is sorry for his action, having shed many tears. A subsequent letter from Pliny thanks Sabinianus for heeding his request and not meting out punishment.

Paul is about to enter his plea for a runaway slave. "He, however, does not say that the master should exercise the Stoic virtue of clemency and show himself to be mild-mannered. Rather, Paul speaks to him in terms of Christian love and faith" (Lohse).

These verses allow us to reconstruct in some detail the story of Onesimus, the runaway slave of Philemon, and thus they present the

[173]

occasion of Paul's writing. Evidently Onesimus, a Phrygian slave of
Philemon, had wronged his master, possibly by robbery (cf. v. 18),
and had fled the home. Somehow he got to Rome where he came
under the influence of Paul, through whose ministry he was converted. The apostle developed a deep affection for him (v. 10), and
took delight in his dedicated service (v . 13). Aware, however, of his
social responsibilities as a Christian, Paul wants Onesimus to return
to Philemon; a decision in which Onesimus evidently shared, realiz-
ing that "no true Christian can ever attempt to evade his obligations."

So Paul sent Onesimus back to Philemon with this accompanying
letter in which he urges Philemon to receive, forgive, and reinstate
Onesimus "as more than a slave—as a dear brother . . . and as a
Christian" (v. 16, NEB). Yet the apostle refrains from giving Philemon a direct command. He prefers to use the language of entreaty
(vv. 8–10), and alludes, with a touch of humor, to the pragmatic fact
that Onesimus, who had belied his name in the past and was *unprofitable* will now, as a Christian, be true to it and be *profitable* in
Philemon's household (v. 11). Paul testifies that Onesimus has indeed proved this already in the service he has rendered looking "after me . . . here in prison for the Gospel" (v. 13, NEB). But the ultimate decision concerning Onesimus he will leave with Philemon (v.
14). The only requirement is that he fulfill the commandment of love
which is the sole norm for his conduct in this affair, as in all others.

*Verse 8–9: Accordingly, though I am bold enough in Christ to
command you to do what is required, yet for love's sake I prefer to
appeal to you:* The particle *dio, accordingly,* forms a loose link with
the preceding words of Paul's thanksgiving prayer (vv. 4–7). In the
light of what the apostle has learned of Philemon, he knows that he
could exercise his apostolic authority and secure his obedience.
Philemon is the kind of person who delights in loving and sharing
and so refreshes the hearts of God's people. "A man like Philemon
would not be offended when he is frankly told what he ought to do.
This is a sincere compliment to Philemon. Not every Christian is
ready to bow to direction from others: we, too, feel that we cannot
frankly tell them what is the proper thing for them to do in a given
case. Philemon is of a higher type" (Lenski).

On the apostle's part, he was aware of his authority—the partici-
pial clause is concessive: "although I have the right to command,
yet for love's sake I prefer to appeal to you." There were occasions
when Paul had to exert his authority as an apostle of Christ (cf.
Rom. 1:1; 1 Cor. 5:3; 9:1; 2 Cor. 10:13, 14; 12:12; Gal. 1:1; etc.).
But here, such is his confidence in Philemon's character and knowledge of his conduct, he can waive this authority and appeal to

Philemon's love as a genuine Christian. It is enough to learn from this attitude adopted by the apostle in the present situation that "it is no disparagement for those who have power to be condescending, and sometimes even to *beseech,* where, in strictness of right, they might *command;* so does Paul here, though an apostle: he entreats where he might enjoin, he argues from love rather than authority, which doubtless must carry engaging influence with it" (Henry, italics mine).

In being Onesimus's advocate Paul did not, of course, renounce his right to command what is fitting *(to anēkon),* but "the reference to authority is made to flash before Philemon's mind for just a moment, only to recede entirely to the background when the spotlight is turned on the most dynamic motivating power in the entire universe, namely, love" (Hendriksen). Yet even here, while Paul renounces his use of apostolic authority, he interjects the repudiation of the right which is still his as deriving from himself. It belongs to him only "in Christ." "His own personality gives him none, but his relation to his Master does" (Maclaren).

The apostle's desire is that Philemon should act freely *"for love's sake" (dia tēn agapēn).* The reference here is not, however, specifically to Paul's love, or even that of Philemon, but "to the love which governs the Christian's dealings and association with one another" (Lohse, so Lightfoot). On this fact of love, the greatest of God's gifts (cf. 1 Cor. 13:31–14:1a), Paul bases his ultimate appeal of how Onesimus should be treated by Philemon. He thus puts the "whole matter solely on this highest plane of pure love, intelligent and purposeful Christian love" (Lenski). This is the grand and sacred principle which bids the apostle set aside his authority; and this same grand and sacred principle is to be Philemon's norm of reference as he decides what course of action to take concerning Onesimus. Such love obliterates, in the sacred bonds of Christian brotherhood in Christ, the hard and harsh distinctions of inferior and superior which find their expression in laconic imperatives and silent obedience. Maybe, then, the contention is not altogether true that authority is the weapon of the weak man. Certainly Paul was never such when speaking on behalf of Christ. At the same time, the other side of the contention is fully true, namely this, "Love is the weapon of a strong man who casts aside the trappings of superiority, and is never loftier than when he descends, nor more absolute than when he adjures authority, and appeals with love to love" (Maclaren). "Such ever was love's way: to rise, it stoops."

Verses 9–10: I, Paul, an ambassador and now a prisoner also for Christ Jesus—I appeal to you for my child, Onesimus, whose father I have become in my imprisonment: We have waited until now for the first mention of "the objectionable name" (Scroggie). It has taken 145 words in the Greek out of a total of 335 to get to Onesimus's name. Yet these previous words have not been mere verbiage; every one of them was carefully chosen. Elihu, in the Book of Job, takes 52 lines to say that he is going to speak! But then he was a young man, and Paul at the time of writing to Philemon is an old man (cf. v. 9, RSV marg., Phillips), and that may be the reason for it!

The apostle now brings in personal considerations to reinforce his entreaty of Philemon on behalf of Onesimus. These are his age and his imprisonment. So he enters "a simple personal appeal from Paul the old man, in prison for Christ Jesus' sake" (Phillips).

Several commentators contend, by an appeal to Ephesians 6:20, that the RSV and NEB rendering of the noun *presbutēs* as *ambassador* is to be preferred (so Lightfoot). "The sense requires Paul's invoking of his authority as an ambassador" (Martin). But this surely is precisely what the apostle has eschewed. Certainly the rendering of the word as "ambassador" is admissible, but here it "has not congruity in its favour, and would be a recurrence of that very motive of official authority which he has just disclaimed" (Maclaren). This consideration is, it seems to me, decisive against the translation of the RSV (H. C. G. Moule).

It seems, then, that the KJV translation, "being such an one as Paul the aged" should be retained. "Therefore, in saying that he is a *presbutēs,* Paul is alluding to his age. Paul is not employing his apostolic authority here; he is speaking to Philemon as an elderly man" (Lohse, so Hendriksen). It does not strengthen the case for the rendering *ambassador* to reply that because only men of years and experience were sent to fulfill this office the designation should stand here. The fact of the matter is that the idea of ambassadorship is quite out of harmony with the present connection; and no commentator has been successful in working it into the apostle's thought here in any convincing way (Lenski).

Paul is referred to in Acts 7:58 as "a young man." But since then several years have gone by; and now the apostle, according to generally accepted calculation, was about sixty years old. Today, sixty is hardly old enough to warrant the description of "old man." But in Paul's time, life expectancy was much less than now. And besides, "Paul had lived dangerously" (D. E. Hiebert). He had spent his life carelessly in the service of Christ and bore in his body the marks of the Lord Jesus (Gal. 6:17; cf. 2 Cor. 2:23–33), so that "the weakness of age was aggravated by the helplessness of bonds" (C. F. D. Moule). Paul had so given himself to the work of his Lord that he had "o'er-informed his tenement of clay."

The propriety, however, of this reference to his age as the ground of appeal to Philemon has been questioned. But it is surely most cogent. For it was a day when deference was given to age. And, besides, Paul had accumulated many years of service and could speak out of a rich and rare experience in the work of the gospel: "from such a person one might well take a frank and open order that is given in Christ's name but not so readily from a younger man, a beginner in the work" (Lenski). "Years bespeak respect; and the motions of such, in things lawful and fit, should be received with regard" (Henry).

Paul's further consideration comes in his allusion to the fact that at the time of his writing he is *a prisoner also for Christ Jesus* (cf. v. 1). As such "he shares in the weakness and humiliation of Christ, for whose sake he is now suffering" (Lohse). The emphasis 'may be allowed to fall here, first, on the apostle's reference to himself as a *prisoner*. He could have resented his situation or boasted in it—become either hard or haughty. But Paul did neither. Rather his love grew in his cell—a love for his Lord that went out to a bedraggled slave. He does not, then, allude to his position as a prisoner to direct attention to his own condition. He holds up his fettered wrists to win the heart of Philemon and to make it almost impossible for him to reject Onesimus. All that Paul desires is that Onesimus be given a place in Philemon's heart, that his compassion born of love be permitted to override his clamor for justice.

Equally must the emphasis fall on the words *for Christ Jesus*. With that name every situation acquires a new perspective and purpose. Philemon will not fail to notice that name, for he, too, professes a like devotion and obedience thereto. Paul is then a prisoner for Christ Jesus. As aged in the service of Christ Jesus, and a prisoner for the sake of Christ Jesus—such are the grounds of Paul's further entreaty. The plea is not, therefore, just pathetic; it is also majestic.

Paul's whole concern is for *my child, Onesimus*. So once again he uses the verb, "I beseech" (*parakalō*, cf. v. 9) on his behalf. The possessive adjective Paul uses (*tou emou*) is stronger than the plain pronoun *my*, and could be translated "my son." Onesimus is to Paul "my own *child*" (*teknou*), his own spiritual offspring begotten in Christ during Paul's imprisonment. In the short period of their association, Paul has become his spiritual father (cf. 1 Cor. 5:15). Maybe Philemon will consider how much longer Onesimus had been in his service without ever coming to know the Savior. Yet what may have startled Philemon even more is the fact that someone like Onesimus has been found of the Lord. Perhaps, before his flight, he had seemed to Philemon an unlikely target of the grace of God. Yet as a runaway slave, and in utter disgrace, he had been sought and found by Christ Jesus. The story of Onesimus is thus a reminder that "Christianity knows nothing of hopeless cases. It professes its ability to take the most crooked stick and bring it straight, to flash a new power into the blackest carbon which will turn it into a diamond" (Maclaren).

In the Greek text, it should be noted, the name Onesimus has the unusual placing of being the last word in the sentence. It appears as though the apostle was hesitant to mention it. There may have been lingering in his mind the thought that, perhaps, in spite of all he has said by way of tactful preparation, Philemon may not yet be quite ready for his request. So he will focus attention, not first on the name of his runaway but on one whom he can introduce as *my own child* whose spiritual *father* he has become while here under lock and key.

At the same time, Paul may have also anticipated an objection which would spring immediately to Philemon's mind as he came to the name Onesimus. It is as if the apostle could hear Philemon saying, "So, that is it! He wants me to receive back that ungrateful, thieving, ne'er-do-well Phrygian. How could he. . . ?" But Paul has checked Philemon's further reaction by his placing of Onesimus's name, and by then hastening on to play the name in agreement with Philemon's indictment while indicating in the same breath that the Onesimus who fled is different from the one to be received back again.

Verse 11: (Formerly he was useless to you, but now he is indeed useful to you and to me): Here is Paul's parenthesis with a pun—a play on words which find their contrast in the "was once," "but now" of Onesimus's experience (cf. Rom. 6:21; Eph. 2:12, 13). The contrast marks the difference that the acceptance of the gospel makes in a life. Onesimus had run away from Philemon, but run into Christ. And what he "was once," he is not "now."

Once he was *useless (achrēston)*, but *now* he is *useful (euchrēston)*. The name Onesimus, deriving from *oninēmi*, means "the useful one." So Onesimus, the useful one, was once useless to Philemon; but now he is useful both to you, Philemon, and to me, Paul. In past days Slave Useful was anything but that. He neglected his duties, was a pilferer, and eventually ran away. In every respect he belied his name. Then he was *achrēston* (useless). But now in Christ he is a "new man" who will prove himself *euchrēston* (useful) to Philemon when he is given leave to return, as he has already been to Paul. The apostle has evidence enough of Onesimus's usefulness as one born anew. There need be no fear on Philemon's part that Onesimus will be useless to him again. "Surely never were the natural feelings of indignation and suspicion more skilfully soothed, and never did repentant good-for-nothing get sent back to regain the confidence which he had forfeited, with such a certificate of character in his hand!" (Maclaren).

The word here translated *useless (achrēston)* is one of five in this short writing which do not occur anywhere else in the New Testament. The other four are: "free will" *(hekousion)*, v. 14; "I will repay" *(apotisō)*, v. 19; "your owing" *(prosopheileis)*, v. 19; "some benefit" *(onaimēn)*, v. 20. The other term of Paul's antithesis, *useful (euchrēston)*, is found twice in 2 Timothy. And both can be taken to illustrate what had become true in Onesimus's experience. He had purified himself of what was ignoble, and become "a vessel for noble use, consecrated and useful to the master of the house, ready for every good work" (2 Tim. 2:21). And as Mark (v. 24; see comment on Col. 4:10), restored after his desertion of Christ's cause, proved himself "very useful in serving Paul" (2 Tim. 4:11), so had Onesimus become after opening his heart to the redeeming influences of grace.

Verse 12: I am sending him back to you, sending my very heart: By using the epistolary aorist for the verb translated *I am sending,* Paul is underscoring that the returning of Onesimus is a definite act on his part. In sending him back, Paul is actually meeting the requirements of the law. The apostle wanted to fulfill his legal obligations when they did not go right against his loyalty to his Lord. He sought to be a law-abiding citizen and to render unto Caesar the things that are Caesar's, as well as to God the things that are God's.

But there was also a spiritual reason for Paul's return of Onesimus. Christianity is no escapism. It does not seek to cushion off believers from the harsh realities of life in a perverse world. Onesimus had run away from his service in Philemon's house. To that sphere he must return. For "one of the surest evidences of the presence of grace in the heart is the resumption of neglected duties" (Scroggie).

Onesimus is, however, going back supported by Tychicus (cf. Col. 4:7–9), and fortified by two noble writings of the apostle: a letter to the church at Colossae, which gives a high view of Christ in whose love and forgiveness they are bound together; and this postcard to Philemon, with its very personal plea to him regarding its bringer—his once useless runaway slave, but now a brother in the faith. "Surely, never did a runaway return to his master in better company!" (Hendriksen).

In returning Onesimus, Paul avers that he is sending back one who has become part of him; "yes, *him,* who is *my very heart.*" The word translated *heart* we have encountered already (cf. v. 7), and will do so again (v. 20). With the departure of Onesimus, says the apostle, there goes "part of myself" (NEB, C. F. D. Moule), "part of me" (Norlie). So useful and dear had Onesimus become to Paul that his leaving was like tearing from him some vital organ necessary for his continued living. Paul and Onesimus were bound together in the tender mercies of Christ. Apostle and slave, one in the brotherhood of faith; that will surely do more, in the long run, to destroy slavery than any prematurely instigated revolt would have done. Philemon is the first called upon to accept those principles which will someday work themselves into the social conscience of men in general to abolish a terrible evil.

As we noted in the commentary on Colossians 3:22, Paul belonged to a society in which slavery was an accepted institution. Rather than deny its existence or try to abolish it, Paul gives the churches to which he writes the principles that will one day make slavery impossible. (See commentary on Col. 4:1, and the further commentary on Philemon.)

Verse 13: I would have been glad to keep him with me, in order that he might serve me on your behalf during my imprisonment for the gospel: The thought had evidently crossed Paul's mind of keeping Onesimus with him, so useful had he become to him. He was, he informs Philemon, "desiring with himself" (literal) to do so—he would very much have liked this, but then, "the will stepped in and put an end to the inclinations of the mind" (Lightfoot). He would have detained Onesimus but knew that he was Philemon's to retain. Yet, if it had been possible to keep him, Paul tells Philemon, he would have regarded his service as being *on your behalf,* for "he could have done what you would have done" (Phillips). Indeed, had Onesimus been able to stay, he would have served the apostle "instead of you" *(huper sou),* Philemon.

What Paul, then, is assuming with "marvellous generosity" (Maclaren), is "that Philemon had been wishing that he himself could render such service to Paul; and also that, prevented by distance from doing so, Philemon had he but known all the circumstances, would have been only too happy to substitute the services of Onesimus for his own" (Hendriksen). But, of course, Paul quickly realized that he cannot act on such an assumption; Onesimus must return to Philemon.

The one reason why the apostle would have kept Onesimus is that he might be of service to him in his *imprisonment for the gospel.* Only for the gospel's sake was Paul in prison; and only on this account did he wish for the ministrations of Onesimus. The KJV reads, that "he might have ministered unto me in the bonds of the gospel." Paul himself is in bonds (cf. v. 10) which imposed certain restrictions upon him (cf. Col. 4:18). Yet he did not allow his chains to hinder his chances of witness; for imprisoned as he was, he was able to reach Onesimus for Christ (v. 10; cf. Phil. 1:13, 14). Now Onesimus is in bonds, but his bondage brought him perfect freedom. Paul is in bonds, literally, *for* the gospel, Onesimus is a free man spiritually in bonds *in* the gospel.

In this verse, then, Paul has informed Philemon of his passing wish to have retained Onesimus. But to have done so would have been neither legally justifiable nor spiritually proper. Paul wants to show "what regard he has for civil rights, which Christianity does by no means supersede or weaken, but rather confirm and strengthen" (Henry). The situation requires Philemon's action.

Verse 14: But I preferred to do nothing without your consent in order that your goodness might not be by compulsion but of your own free will: Paul's final determination is, then, made clear. He will defer to Philemon's cognizance and consent. The view of some commentators that Paul is hinting that he wants Philemon to send Onesimus back to him

can hardly be sustained. For Paul was actually expecting an early release (cf. v. 22) and hoped to renew fellowship with Philemon and
Onesimus in the near future. All that the apostle intends in this verse
is to underscore for Philemon's consideration how useful Onesimus
has become. "For what Paul says is wholly in the interest of
Onesimus; Philemon is to know how highly Paul had learned to prize
this converted slave" (Lenski).

Of course, Paul expects a "good deed" *(to agathon)* of Philemon
which he will regard as a "kindness" (NEB, Williams), a "favor" (NIV,
cf. Phillips). The expression is quite general and leaves open the question of how precisely it will be expressed; "for love is resourceful
enough to find the right way to accomplishing the good" (Lohse). But for
the deed to be "good" it must be "spontaneous and not forced" (NIV, cf.
Phillips). So the apostle will not impose even his apostolic restraint on
Philemon. Nor indeed does he want there to be the least suspicion of
any. That is why he introduces the "delicate addition" (Maclaren), "not
. . . as it were of necessity" (KJV). "St. Paul does not say *kata anagkēn*
but *hōs kata anagkēn.* He will not suppose that it would really be by
constraint; but it must not even wear the *appearance* (hōs) of being so"
(Lightfoot). "Not of constraint, but willingly"—here surely is the principle of all Christian action. "Good deeds are most acceptable to God
and man, when done from freedom" (Henry). " 'Must' is not in the
Christian vocabulary, except as expressing the sweet constraint which
bows the will of him who loves to harmony, which is joy, with the will of
Him who is loved. Christ takes no offerings which the giver is not
glad to render" (Maclaren; cf. 1 Pet. 5:2; 2 Cor. 9:17; see Exod. 25:2;
35:5, 21, 29; 1 Cor. 29:5; Isa. 1:19; Ps. 110:3; etc.).

IV. THE REFLECTION WHICH INCREASES PAUL'S HOPEFUL EXPECTATION (15–22)

Here is Paul in a Roman prison writing to commend a runaway slave to his master in far-off Asia Minor. And this once good-for-nothing is here with him, a changed young man, rendering to the aged apostle useful service. Paul must have reflected often on the strange chain of events which brought them together in the capital of the empire. Can he read the whole concurrence of events as a display of the mysterious movements of divine providence? Yes, "perhaps." The apostle will not, however, be too dogmatic here, for on this issue he has not eavesdropped on the secret counsels of God. It occurs to him that "there has been a purpose" in Philemon's loss of his slave (v. 15, Phillips); but, still, he can only say, "perhaps this is why you lost him for a time" (NEB). The great apostle is thus humble enough to admit that he did not know all the purposes of God whose thoughts are higher than his, and his ways past finding out. We, who know far less of God than Paul the apostle, often profess to have special information from on high beyond that which God has already made known. But we ought "not to be in too great a hurry to make sure that we have the key of the cabinet where God keeps his purposes, but content ourselves with "perhaps" when we are interpreting the often questionable ways of providence, each of which has many meanings and many ends" (Maclaren).

Yet Paul trusts that his reflection of the "maybe" of God's ways in the actual events of Onesimus's life—those which led him to Rome and to faith in Christ, and to service on Christ's behalf—will help Philemon to have him back, not just as a slave but as a brother beloved (v. 15). Besides, if Philemon considers Paul his partner in the gospel he will most surely act the partner's part (v. 17, 18). And if Onesimus has wronged Philemon in any way, the apostle will see to it that it is put right (v. 19). To deal kindly with Onesimus is tantamount to dealing kindly with himself. Such is the underlying spirit of Paul's hopeful expectation of Philemon's action in the matter, which is capped by the moving consideration, "Now brother, as a Christian, be generous with me, and relieve my anxiety; we are both in Christ!" (v. 20, NEB).

Verses 15–16: Perhaps this is why he was parted from you for a while, that you might have him back for ever, no longer as a slave but more than a slave: In these words Paul suggests what may be believed as the probable providence of God in bringing Onesimus and himself together: that although they were separated for a while, Philemon might have Onesimus back as a brother beloved forever. This *perhaps* might have been God's way of it; and maybe Philemon will read it so.

Paul says *perhaps (tacha,* cf. Rom. 5:7) for even he, an apostle of God, can here speak only tentatively. Well does he know that for the most part God's providential ways are veiled from even the most enlightened spiritual eyes. "St. Paul will not encourage us in a rash and presumptuous confidence, when we endeavour to interpret in detail God's providence in this life by the light of the next" (H. P. Liddon). For the professor of an "over-confident, 'verily,' 'verily,' often dwindles to a hesitating "perhaps' " (Maclaren). Yet, if Paul wonders about the reason why Onesimus was separated from Philemon, he was certain that his wronging of his master and subsequent flight were not directly inspired of God. God had indeed used his waywardness for Onesimus's good, as in his overall purpose he can utilize every man's evil for the fulfillment of his grand design which is beyond our comprehension. "Observe, the wisdom and goodness and power of God, in causing that to end so happily, which was begun and carried on for some time so wickedly" (Henry). Paul sees the hand of God in the movements of Onesimus's life and detects, as in a mirror dimly, the hidden purpose of God behind and within the incidents which caused such grievance to Philemon. He thus uses the passive verb *was parted (echōristhē)* rather than the active "he parted," while at the same time avoiding the harsher term "he fled," since this "would appease Philemon by a more euphemistic phrase" (Lightfoot).

This parting, Paul affirms, was but *for a while,* or literally, "for an hour," *(pros hōran;* cf. 2 Cor. 7:8; Gal. 2:5). "It was only a brief moment after all compared with the magnitude of the work wrought in it" (Lightfoot). For eternal consequences were in that "hour." Much of divine significance can happen in a short time, and the passing moment can determine the future millenniums. For Philemon his temporary loss was eternal gain. The relationship between him and Onesimus as a mere slave would have been, however long, of very brief duration. But now Onesimus is returning to Philemon in the faith of the gospel to be his *forever.*

Verse 16: As a beloved brother, especially to me but how much more to you, both in the flesh and in the Lord: For a short time the slave had been parted from his master, but now he is united to him forever as a *brother.* In the flesh, as has been observed. Philemon has a brother for a slave; in the Lord he has a slave for a brother. Slave—brother;

what a juxtaposition we have here! This is a revolutionary and revolutionizing idea that two such men can be mentioned in the same breath as belonging to one another. *Slave*—such is Onesimus to Philemon *in the flesh; brother*—so is Philemon to Onesimus *in the Lord.* Here earthly and heavenly relationships intertwine. And this relationship remains not only within the church in the house, but equally in the house outside the church. It is far too possible, and much too easy, for some Christians to happily regard their Christian subordinates "in the Lord" on Sunday and then to treat them as merely related "in the flesh" for the rest of the week.

At this point, some have supposed that Paul should have suggested, or even required, Philemon to free Onesimus from the bonds of slavery. But the apostle knew better. It was not for him at that time to make a frontal attack on the inhuman institution. What he does do is to inject into the situation, which was not in his power to abolish, the dynamism of Christian love. In time this principle will work itself into the fabric of society, to become an accepted dictum of nations infused by the Christian ideal—that every man is of worth in himself, as created in the image of God—and so will make impossible the enslavement of one man by another.

Meanwhile, Paul allows that Onesimus "in the flesh" is still his master's slave, but "in the Lord" that earthly relationship is superseded forever. In the situation as then prevailing, the slave must do what is right for his master and the master treat his slaves justly and fairly (see commentary on Col. 3:22–4:1). In this way Paul puts a new face on slavery by regarding the human conditions as unimportant in contrast with a person's desire to fulfill his Christian vocation (Martin).

The phrase *especially to me* is thought by some commentators to be somewhat illogical, on the score that, if the apostle refers it to himself as the most prominent example of all those to whom Onesimus is now a beloved brother, how can he add, *how much more to you?* The usual solution is to take the adverb *malista*, which is superlative in form, as elative, so giving the meaning *especially*, as in our translation (or "immensely—[what about intensely?]" Hendriksen). The comparison is then heightened by the *how much more (posō mallon)* which follows. This construction does give good sense and is generally accepted. Onesimus had become more than a slave in relation to Paul. He was a beloved brother *especially*. If Philemon will receive Onesimus back, he will be even more a brother beloved to him because, although still his slave, he will act in that capacity as a beloved brother, because of the Lord. So will Philemon be twice blessed by him in the brotherhood of faith. For this brotherhood of Onesimus the Christian slave will be made actual in the

temporal concerns of everyday life as well as having its scope and
strength in the spiritual and eternal realities of the Christian fellowship.

*Verse 17: So if you consider me your partner, receive him as you
would receive me:* Paul at last now completes the sentence which he
began at verse 12, and which he broke off to introduce other
thoughts which would, as it were, prepare Philemon to receive the
apostle's request the more favorably. Yet even now he prefaces the
words of his actual appeal with one further powerful inducement,
namely, the tie that exists between Philemon and himself. For some
time the real purpose of his writing has been quivering on his lips.
At last he comes out with it, but in the context of the most gracious
tactfulness.

Philemon can hardly repudiate partnership with the apostle in the
gospel; indeed, Paul has already felt able to address him as "our beloved fellow worker" (v. 1). The partner here is the *koinōnos,* one
who shares common interests as a comrade in the same endeavor.
However, when Paul calls himself a "partner," he is not referring
either to business transactions or simply to ties of friendship. For
"their 'fellowship' *(koinōnia)* is grounded in their belonging to the
Lord" (Lohse).

Wedged in the middle of the sentence is the pivotal request Paul
has to make of Philemon regarding Onesimus: *receive him (pros-
labou auton),* he asks. The verb *proslambanō* occurs in the New
Testament only in the middle voice, with emphasis falling on the
pros—"to take to one's self." (See footnote on Col. 1:6 re middle
voice.) So Priscilla and Aquilla took Apollos to themselves and ex-
pounded to him the way of God more accurately (Acts 28:26). In
other passages it is translated as "welcome" in the RSV (cf. Rom.
14:1, 3; 15:7). Yet it is more than merely to give a hearty welcome
to a person on arrival. It is to grant another access to one's heart, to
take him into abiding friendship and fellowship. God and Christ are
said to have received *(proslabesthas)* those who were formerly estranged but have been united to them in the grace of the gospel (cf.
Rom. 14:3; 15:7). For Philemon to *receive* Onesimus is, then, to do a
godlike deed. For it *is* a godlike thing to "welcome *[proslambanes-
the]* one another, therefore, as Christ has welcomed *[proselabeto]*
you, for the glory of God" (Rom. 15:7).

Paul requests Philemon to receive Onesimus *as you would receive
me.* The apostle is sure that Philemon would certainly welcome him
and grant him open access to his heart. In this way Paul identifies
himself with Onesimus and lets Philemon know that the welcome he
is sure he will extend to Onesimus will be considered as love show-
ered upon himself.

Verses 18–19a: If he has wronged you at all, or owes you any-thing, charge that to my account. I, Paul, write this with my own hand, I will repay it: Paul states the case hypothetically, but he knew well enough that it was a fact. Onesimus had done his master an injury, probably he had stolen from him, and fled to escape punishment. He may have made a clean breast of it to Paul; or, at any rate, if that were not so, the apostle had well-grounded suspi-cions as to his previous behavior (cf. Tit. 2:9, 10). Certainly his wrongdoing was serious and did not merely involve his fleeing Philemon's home and depriving him of service (Lenski). If that were all, it is hard to account for Paul's *if.*

In verse 15, the apostle choose to say that Onesimus "was parted" from Philemon instead of the harsher, "he ran away," so as to "keep some thin veil over the crimes of the penitent, and not to rasp him with rough words" (Maclaren). For the same reason the apostle prefers here the milder word *wronged (ēdikēsen)* instead of the harsher "stolen" (cf. 1 Cor. 13:4; James 5:20). The term is, however, common enough in the New Testament to express in gen-eral some unspecified wrong done by one person to another (cf. Matt. 20:13; Acts 7:24, 26, 27; 1 Cor. 6:7, 8; 2 Cor. 7:2, 12; Col. 3:25).

The wrong done by Onesimus involved him in a debt. And it was not magically removed by Onesimus's becoming a Christian, for "the new life does not cancel old debts" (Scroggie). Such debt, in Paul's mind, stood in the way of Philemon's taking Onesimus back, if not into his household, certainly into his heart. Now Philemon's stolen money has been squandered and he has nothing wherewith to pay. At this point, it seems, the apostle took the pen from his amanuensis and interjected a promissory note—"put that down to my account. Here is my signature, PAUL" (NEB). Regarding Onesimus's debt, Philemon is to "reckon it in" (Lightfoot) as Paul's—Paul will take full responsibility for it. Such is Paul's "cer-tificate of indebtedness," *(hos cheirographa,* cf. Col. 2:14). The "one thing that Paul desires is the removal of anything whatever from the mind of Philemon that might hinder him from genuinely re-ceiving Onesimus as a child of Paul's" (Lenski).

Some commentators have speculated whether indeed the apostle could pay, and doubt has been cast on his sincerity. Most certainly Paul was not signing a contract he could not, or would not, honor: "the fact that Paul drew attention to his own signature shows that he intended Philemon to treat his IOU seriously" (Donald Guthrie, "Philemon"). The word rendered "I will repay" *(hapotisō)* is a judi-cial term by which Paul knew himself to be bound. And evidently, at this time, the apostle had the wherewithal to meet the demand. He had his times of prosperity, as well as of poverty (cf. Phil 4 :12, 17, 18). Acts 24:26 records how Felix detained him, hoping that money would be given to him by Paul for his release; while Acts 28:30 contains the information that while imprisoned in Rome, "he lived there two whole years at his own expense." Paul was not, therefore, making an empty gesture to Philemon regarding Onesimus's debt. He was prepared to pay what was owing, and to fulfill his own injunction and "contribute to the needs of the saints" (Rom. 12:13; cf. Gal. 6:2).

The term rendered *charge that to my account* is, as noted above (see commentary on v. 11) one of five *hapax* (single occurrence) terms in the letter, "and perhaps the singular phrase may be chosen to let another great Christian truth shine through" (Maclaren). Onesimus was in debt to Philemon. But then are we not all in debt to One greater than he? Indeed, we are (cf. Matt. 6:12; Gal. 5:3). All we can do is acknowledge the bill—the debt owed; and accept our bankruptcy—we have nothing to pay, no means of meeting God's just demands; and then apply to the Bank. For he who has in justice demanded payment has in love paid it—"paid it all, long, long ago." That is, in simplest terms the meaning of what the great Thomas Chalmers was fond of referring to as the "great atonement." What Paul did for Onesimus on the plane of the human and the temporal to bring about reconciliation between him and Philemon, Christ has done for us in the realm of the divine and the eternal (cf. Heb. 9:28; 1 Pet. 2:24; cf. also 2 Cor. 5:18, 19; Eph. 2:16; Col. 1:20, 21). Or, to state the fact in the much quoted comment of Luther: "Even as Christ did for us with God the Father, thus also doth St. Paul for Onesimus with Philemon; for Christ also stripped Himself of His right, and by love and humility enforced the Father to lay aside His wrath and power, and to take us to His grace for the sake of Christ, Who lovingly pleadeth our cause, and with all His heart layeth Himself out for us. For we are all His Onesimi to my thinking."

Verse 19b: To say nothing of your owing me even your own self: These words pick up the idea expressed in verse 18. From the thought of Onesimus's debt Paul passes to recall Philemon's greater debt he owes to him. In what is termed a *paraleipsis,* a construction in which one deliberately protests against saying something which he nevertheless says, Paul reminds Philemon that there can be a greater debt owing than stolen money or lost time. Philemon, in truth, owes Paul his "very self" (NEB). It had crossed Paul's mind that maybe there was no need to say this to Philemon; and yet, he had better say it. And it was altogether proper that he should. For all that Philemon was as a Christian he owed to the apostle. Paul was his spiritual father, who had begotten him in the gospel, "and to whom therefore he owed his being" (Lightfoot). Philemon's forgiving the pecuniary debt of a poor penitent, for Paul's sake and at his request and for which he has taken full responsibility, is not so great an indebtedness as that of Philemon's to Paul; "here is more *per contra*—thou owest me even thine own self besides" (Henry).

Yet while Paul reminds Philemon that he is a debtor to the one by whom he was brought to faith in Christ, Paul himself always regarded himself as a debtor to all men for the sake of the gospel, both to live as a new man in Christ (Rom. 8:12), and to proclaim abroad the saving message of faith (Rom. 1:14).

Verse 20: Yes, brother, I want some benefit from you in the Lord: At this point Onesimus disappears from the scene, and Paul's final plea to Philemon is based altogether on the consideration that "such an act of love will do my old heart good" (Phillips, *Letters*). Once again the apostle uses the term of endearment, *brother* (cf. v. 7) to express that intimate spiritual relationship in which he and Philemon are one. It is because of this very bond of brotherhood that the apostle can confess with a heavily accentuated "I" *(ego): I* am the one who "would like to make profit of thee in the Lord!" (Lenski).

Although denied by some few commentators, it is not unlikely that the word *onaimēn*—a second aorist optative from *oninēmi* (only found here in the New Testament) meaning, "to have joy or *benefit*" involves a play on the name Onesimus. If this is so, then the thought goes something like this: what Onesimus has been to me and is going to be to you, I want that you should be to me. He is your Onesimus, your profit; will you, Philemon, be mine? And the benefit that Paul would have of Philemon is *in the Lord.* This is at once the power for its accomplishment and the test of its validity.

Refresh my heart in Christ: Here Paul states what he desires from Philemon, the profit he would make out of him. The word *refresh* points back to verse 7. Philemon has refreshed the hearts of the saints. Paul wants to be included in the circle of those to whom Philemon has brought such great benefit. He will, however, be specific. He has only one desire: to be refreshed *in the Lord.* The phrase expresses the element or sphere in which all is done, as well as the element or sphere in which the apostle is refreshed. The phrase *in Christ* is a specific Pauline one, and is almost a synonym for "Christian" (so NEB). To be in Christ is for Paul an equivalent for the whole meaning and measure of the gospel. So, for example, the apostle uses the expression eleven times in the first fourteen verses of Ephesians 1. " 'In Christ' gives the picture of Jesus as an organism to which Christians belong as its parts. Such a phrase underlies the fact, (a) Christians owe all to Jesus and are nothing without him, and (b) Christians are tied up together in one fellowship, and so belong to each other" (G. H. Thompson).

At the end of the two short sentences that comprise this verse, Paul places the phrases, "in the Lord" *(en kuriō)*, and "in Christ" *(en christō)*. "The Kyrios demands that all, who are one in Christ, deal with each other in 'love' *(agapē)*. With this in mind, Paul once again requests that Philemon refresh his heart in Christ" (Lohse).

Verse 21: Confident of your obedience, I write to you, knowing that you will do even more than I say: Paul anticipates Philemon's compliance with his request regarding Onesimus. He is indeed sure that Philemon will go the second mile; that he will do more or "better" (NEB) than he asks. "High Heaven rejects the lore,/Of nicely calculated less and more" (William Wordsworth, *Ecclesiastical Sonnets*, pt. 3, 43). Paul's confidence of Philemon's obedience is based upon what he already knows and has heard about him from Epaphras and Onesimus. It was an obedience "in the Lord," "in Christ," that he always exhibited. So the apostle has no fear but that he will do not only what he requests of him but will far exceed it. The word *obedience* must not be given a stoic reading, especially in the present context: *"hupahoē* is not what we call 'obedience,' i.e., to a command. Paul has given no command. The word means 'hearing and heeding' what is said to a person and thus matches 'the things I say' " (Lenski). What Paul desires of Philemon is the "obedience of faith" (Rom. 1:5), which even now has become "known to all" of Philemon's circle (cf. Rom. 16:19). The obedience of which the apostle speaks is *"gospel-obedience.* It is the harkening to the demands of God as expressed in the gospel (cf. Rom. 10:16; Phil. 2:12; 2 Thess. 3:14). It is, therefore, more than heeding *Paul's* advice and granting his request. It is exactly the gospel as proclaimed by Christ that demands that those who have benefited shall also show kindness to others" (Hendriksen).

Verse 22: At the same time, prepare a guest room for me, for I am hoping through your prayers to be granted to you: The apostle uses the adverb *hama* which denotes the coincidence of the performance of two acts together (cf. Col. 4:3; see Acts 24:26; 27:40; 1 Tim. 5:13), and thus links up with what has gone before. Paul is confident regarding his request concerning Onesimus. Yet this *at the same time* is one further nudge towards the same end. "There is a gentle compulsion in this mention of a personal visit to Colossae. The apostle would thus be able to see for himself that Philemon had not disappointed his expectations" (Lightfoot). So the apostle shows not only his tact but his trust; his conviction that Philemon will not only do the more than he has asked (cf. v. 16), but will even add his favor also, and prepare a guest room for him. He will not just go the second mile but will add a third also.

Here, as in Acts 28:23, Paul uses the word *xenia,* meaning "hospitality," "entertainment shown a guest," or "guest room" (the verbal form is found in Acts 10:6, 18, 23, 32; 21:16; 28:7), not *kataluma* (cf. Mark 14:14; Luke 22:11), which means literally "a place of resting." It certainly was not the apostle's intention to take it easy. His wish was for a base from which to spread abroad the gospel. It would doubtless have suited Paul's purpose if the guest room were a "small roof chamber with walls," like the one prepared by the woman of Shunem, so long as it had a bed on which to rest, a table on which to write, a chair at which to kneel, and a lamp by which to read (cf. 2 Kings 4:10).

Not only, however, did Paul's words suggest his anticipation of Philemon's response to his request concerning Onesimus, but they also suggest his own anticipation of his near release from prison. The apostle expresses great hopes that through their prayers he will be returned to Philemon as well as Onesimus.

The *prayers* in which he takes consolation are not, however, those of Philemon alone, since here the second person plural reappears. Included in the company of intercessors are Apphia, Archippus, and the church meeting with Philemon in his house: "For the cry of the community presses on God and can bring it about that the prison shackles be loosed and the Apostle regain his freedom" (Lohse). He has already told Philemon that he has not been forgotten in the apostle's intercession (cf. v. 4). And he would have him and those with him engage in spiritual warfare on his behalf (see on Col. 1:3, 9).

Once again Paul puts the issue in the language of love's sweet tact. He does not say baldly, "I hope to be released from my sore imprisonment," but, "I hope that, in answer to your prayers, God will grant me to you" (NEB). Yet the apostle does allow that all this is in the hands of a higher providence. Here his "I hope" *(elpizō)* is like the "for perhaps" *(tacha gar)* of verse 15. Paul believed strongly in the efficacy of prayer, yet he had a right understanding of its limits and provisos. He does not see prayer as a sort of Aladdin's lamp which anyone can operate at will when once the trick has been learned. Paul wants the prayers regarding his imprisonment conditioned on the threefold proviso, "Hallowed be thy name; Thy kingdom come; Thy will be done." These are the main hinges on which one may hang his own petitions or "festoons," as C. S. Lewis calls them.* "The criterion of true prayer is that it should be the expression of nobleness in the man who prays. It is the spiritual

---

*C. S. Lewis, *Letters to Malcolm, Chiefly on Prayer* (London: Geoffrey Bles, 1964; New York: Harcourt, Brace & World, 1964).

nature reaching upwards" (James Hastings). Petitionary prayer is indeed essential to the fulfillment of God's program and purpose. It is "part of the soul's response to the challenge and invitation to it to become *through* co-operation with Him a personality more and more fitted *for* co-operation with Him; it is one of the things by which, under earthly conditions, the soul grows in stature as a son of God and in readiness for that which in its consummation transcends earthly conditions altogether" (H. H. Farmer, *The World and God*). We do not seek in prayer to drag down the divine will to the level of our own; rather does the man of prayer seek to lift up the human will to the divine.

Prayer is not, then, inevitable in bringing about a desired result. The church prayed for Peter and he was delivered (cf. Acts 12:6 f., 12); and doubtless, too, the church prayed for Stephen that he might be delivered, but it was not to be. This, however, does not mean that such prayers were to no purpose. Rather, "Petitions for outward blessings, whether for the petitioner or for others, are to be presented with submission; and the highest confidence which can be entertained concerning them is that which Paul here expresses: 'I *hope* that through your prayers I shall be set free' " (Maclaren).

V. BENEDICTION (23–25)

At last Paul has made his request of Philemon and is about to take his leave. But before he does he must add a few lines of greeting from those of his circle of friends in Christ who seemingly are known to Philemon, who share the apostle's sorrows and hopes and are, in varying degrees, one with him in his thoughts and tasks. It may appear surprising that in a work so brief Paul mentions the names of ten other persons. But, then, such allusions to his fellow workers may be regarded as "important in showing how much Paul respected the principle of collegiality in the Christian mission" (Martin). Of the ten, five have appeared already in the early part of the letter: Timothy, Philemon, Apphia, Archippus, and, of course, Onesimus. Here in the benediction are the names of five others who figure, to a greater or lesser extent, in the story of the early church.

Verse 23–24: Epaphras, my fellow prisoner in Christ Jesus, sends greetings to you, and so do Mark, Aristarchus, Demas, and Luke, my fellow workers: Epaphras is naturally mentioned singly and specifically as a Colossian (see commentary on Col. 4:12). In Colossians he is referred to as "a servant of Jesus Christ"; here it is "my fellow prisoner in Christ." And he is literally in prison with Paul as "Christ's captive like myself" (NEB). The name of Marcus— Mark—comes, too, in Colossians, as does that of Aristarchus (see commentary on 4:10). It is strange that Luke, the man who wrote more of the New Testament than anyone else, was a Gentile, not a Jew, and that there are only three references to him in the whole of the New Testament (Col. 4:11–15; Philem. 24; and 2 Tim. 4:11). From the last reference in 2 Timothy we see him still faithful as the evening shades close around the apostle. Only Luke the faithful remains with Paul. Colossians tells us that Luke was a doctor, which may account for the sort of Gospel which he wrote. It has been said that a clergyman sees men at their best, a lawyer sees them at their worst, while a doctor sees them as they really are. A good doctor can diagnose a man's illness, yet is not repelled or disgusted by it, but desires to heal and to help. So Luke sees Christ as the Great Physician, and he himself as a good doctor sees human need with clarity and treats it with compassion, as his Gospel so abundantly illustrates. We need add nothing to the story of Demas beyond what is said on Colossians 4:14, except to stress again the contrasting directions followed by each. From Luke we may gain inspiration, for with the passing years his faith in and passion for the gospel grew stronger. But from the account of Demas there is warning. For as he grew older he became colder, till at last the record reads, "Demas, in love with this present world, has deserted me and gone to Thessalonica" (2 Tim. 4:10).

Verse 25: The grace of the Lord Jesus Christ be with your spirit: With this benediction Paul brings his brief word to Philemon to a close. At the beginning of his letter he has invoked grace upon Philemon and his house "from God the Father and the Lord Jesus Christ." Here at the end he comes to the word *grace (charis)* once again and conceives of it as Christ's own gift. For in Christ all the stooping, saving, and sustaining love of God is concentrated and poured forth. "Grace is the best wish for ourselves and others; with it the apostle begins and ends" (Henry). *Grace* is thus Paul's final benediction for his readers; in that one word there is included all that is good and true for them in the household of Philemon, all that can ever surpass their desirings and their deservings.

This grace has as its sphere of operation the spirit of man. "Grace in the spirit spiritualises the whole man" (Jerome). It is on man's spirit that the Spirit of God impinges to witness with his spirit that he has become a child of God (cf. Rom. 8:16) and works outward to encompass the whole being. The term *spirit (pneuma)* is found 146 times in the Pauline epistles and covers broadly the meaning of the Old Testament word *ruach,* except that the sense of "wind" is not in Paul and the idea of "life" or "breath" is almost entirely absent. Two main thoughts are then associated with Paul's use of the word. First is the psychical sense. In about half the passages with this meaning, the word refers to the higher nature of the Christian man and can hardly be distinguished from the activity of the Divine Spirit. There are, therefore, statements, for example in Romans 8, where it is not easy to say whether the word should have a small "s" or a capital—whether, that is, the reference is to the renewed spirit of the redeemed man or the Divine Spirit within the believing man (cf. Rom. 8:4, 5, 13; cf. 1:9; 7:6). But for the rest, the term certainly connotes an element in man's natural life (cf. 1 Cor. 2:11; etc.). Paul does not teach that man by nature is without *pneuma.* The human spirit is not a gift super-added to man when he believes. It is a reality of man's personality, a constituent of his nature, a distinguishing mark of his being. It is that element in man in which he is most akin to God. It is the nonmaterial part of man which relates

him to the eternal world. Man's spirit is the higher aspect of man,
the Godward aspect which provides that point of contact in his nature for the regenerative action of God's Spirit. Into the spirit of
Philemon and his circle Paul would have the grace of the Lord Jesus
Christ enter, and there abide, in a union more close and a communion more real than human words can express or physical illustration
can clarify.

Why, it has been queried, has such a brief writing, a "Note" as
Renan calls it, a mere postcard, concerned with a trivial everyday
matter which could be settled, it is supposed, without reference to
religious issues, been granted a place in the canon of Holy Scripture? We are almost tempted to reply, "But why not?" There is
quite a consensus of high estimation regarding the tone and quality
of its writing. It has but 335 words (Nestle-Aland text; 334 in
Westcott-Hort text), and yet it "far surpasses all the wisdom of the
world" (Franke): and thus "stands unrivalled" (Lightfoot). But not
on account of such opinions was its place assured in the canon from
the beginning. True, the fact that it was the work of an apostle of
God was a decisive factor. But even so, it is not just the word of
Paul expressing mere humanitarian good advice on personal and in-
terpersonal problems. It comes as a word of God on the narrower
conditions of domestic, as well as on the wider issues of social, life.
It has its permanent place in the Scriptures of God as a divine word
to be heeded just because it is a divine receipt for healing.

Dealing as the letter certainly does with ordinary and routine affairs, it is yet throughout "saturated with Christian thought and feeling" (Maclaren); and thus "showeth a right noble, lovely example of
Christian love" (Luther). It is "penetrated with the noblest Christian
spirit" (F. C. Baur, *Paul the Apostle of Jesus Christ)*, though in it,
Paul "handleth a subject, which otherwise were low and mean, yet,
after his manner he is borne aloft unto God" (Calvin). And, consequently, on the wings of his words, in this short letter we, too, can
like the eagle, mount heavenward.

BIBLIOGRAPHY

Abbott, Thomas K. *The Epistles to the Ephesians and to the Colossians.* The International Critical Commentary. Edinburgh, 1897. Reprint. Naperville, IL: Alec R. Allenson.

Alexander, Gross. *The Epistles to the Colossians and to the Ephesians.* Bible for Home and School Series, New York: The Macmillan Co., 1910.

Alexander, W. "Philemon." In *The Speaker's Commentary.* Edited by F. C. Cook. London: John MacMurray, 1881, p. 819–44.

Ashby, E. G. "Colossians." In *A New Testament Commentary.* Edited by G. C. Howley, et al. London; Grand Rapids, MI: Zondervan Publishing House, 1969.

Baggott, Louis J. *A New Approach to Colossians.* London; Naperville, IL: Alec R. Allenson, 1961,

Barnes, Albert. *Notes on the New Testament: Thessalonians, Timothy, Titus and Philemon.* Edited by Robert Frew. Reprint. Grand Rapids, MI: Baker Book House, 1951.

———. *Popular Commentary: New Testament.* Vol. 8, Ephesians-Colossians. London: n.d.

Barry, A. *The Epistles to the Ephesians, Philippians and Colossians.* A Bible Commentary for English Readers, edited by C. J. Ellicott, vol. 8. London, 1861.

Beare, F. W., and MacLeod, G. Preston. "Colossians." In *The Interpreter's Bible,* edited by George A. Buttrick, vol. 11. Nashville: Abingdon, 1963.

Beet, Joseph A. *A Commentary on Paul's Epistles to the Ephesians, Philippians, Colossians, and Philemon.* London: Hodder and Stoughton, 1890.

Bengel, Johann A. Translated by A. R. Faussett. *Gnomon of the New Testament.* Vol. 4. Edinburgh: T & T. Clark, 1958–59.

Bruce, F. F. See Simpson, E. K., jt. auth.

Calvin, John. *Commentaries on the Epistles to the Galatians, Ephesians, Philippians, and Colossians.* Translated by T. H. Parker. Grand Rapids, MI: Wm. B. Eerdmans, 1948.

Carson, Herbert M. *Commentary on the Epistles of Paul to the Colossians and Philemon.* London: Tyndale Press; Grand Rapids, MI: Wm. B. Eerdmans, 1960.

Chrysostom, John. *The Homilies of St. John Chrysostom on the Epistles of St. Paul to Timothy, Titus and Philemon.* Oxford: John Henry Newman, 1853.

Drysdale, A. H. *The Epistle of St. Paul to Philemon.* Reprint. Devotional Commentary Series. London: Religious Tract Society, 1906.

Eadie, J. *A Commentary on Colossians.* London, 1856.

Eales, S. J. "The Epistle of Paul to Philemon." In *The Pulpit Commentary,* edited by H. D. M. Spence and J. S. Exell, vol. 21. Reprint. Grand Rapids, MI: Wm. B. Eerdmans, 1959.

Ellicott, C. J., *A Critical and Grammatical Commentary on Philippians, Colossians and Philemon.* London & New York: Longmans, Greer & Co., 1865.

Erdman, Charles R. *Commentaries on the New Testament Books: Colossians and Philemon.* Philadelphia: Westminster Press, 1933.

Guthrie, Donald. "Colossians." In *The New Bible Commentary Revised,* edited by Donald Guthrie, et al. London: Inter-Varsity Fellowship, 1962; Grand Rapids, MI: Wm. B. Eerdmans, 1970, pp. 1139–53.

————. *New Testament Introduction: The Pauline Epistles.* London: The Tyndale Press; Chicago: Inter-Varsity Press, 1961.

————. "Philemon." In *The New Bible Commentary Revised,* edited by Donald Guthrie, et al. London: Inter-Varsity Fellowship; Grand Rapids, MI: Wm. B. Eerdmans, 1970, pp. 1187–90.

Harvey, H. *Commentary on the Pastoral Epistles, First and Second Timothy and Titus; and the Epistle to Philemon.* An American Commentary on the New Testament. New York: The American Baptist Publication Soceity, 1890.

Hendriksen, William. *Epistles to the Colossians and Philemon.* Grand Rapids, MI: Baker Book House, 1964.

Henry, Matthew. "Philemon." *An Exposition of the Old and New Testaments,* vol. 3. London: Westley and Davis, 1835.

————. "Colossians." *Commentary on the Whole Bible,* vol. 6. Reprint. Old Tappan, NJ: Fleming H. Revell, 1961.

Hiebert, D. Edmond. *Titus and Philemon.* Everyman's Bible Commentary Series. Chicago: Moody Press, 1957.

Knox, John. *Philemon among the Letters of Paul.* Rev. ed. Nashville: Abingdon, 1959; London, 1960.

Lange, John P., ed. *Lange's Commentary on the Holy Scriptures.* 12 vols. Grand Rapids, MI: Zondervan, 1950.

Lenski, Richard C. H. *The Interpretation of Colossians, Thessalonians First and Second, Timothy First and Second, Titus and Philemon.* Columbus: Lutheran Book Concern, 1937.

Lightfoot, J. B. *Saint Paul's Epistles to the Colossians and to Philemon.* London and New York: The Macmillan Co., 1880. Reprint. Grand Rapids, MI: Zondervan, 1957.

Lohse, Eduard. *A Commentary on the Epistles to the Colossians and Philemon.* Edited by Helmut Koester. Philadelphia: Fortress Press, 1971.

Maclaren, Alexander. "The Epistles of St. Paul to the Colossians and to Philemon." In *The Expositor's Bible,* edited by W. Robertson Nicoll. 6 vols. London, 1890. Reprint. Grand Rapids, MI: Wm. B. Eerdmans, 1947.

Martin, Ralph P. *Colossians: The Church's Lord and the Christian's Liberty.* London: Exeter, 1972; Grand Rapids, MI: Zondervan, 1973.

————. *Colossians and Philemon.* New Century Bible Series. London: Oliphants; Greenwood, SC: Attic Press, 1974.

Moffatt, James. *Grace in the New Testament*. London: Hodder & Stoughton, 1931.

Moulden, J. L. *Colossians*. Pelican Commentary Series. London, 1972.

Moule, Charles F. D. *The Epistles of Paul the Apostle to the Colossians and Philemon*. Cambridge: University Press, 1957.

Moule, H. C. G. *Colossian Studies*. London, 1898.

————. *The Epistles of Paul the Apostle to the Colossians and to Philemon*. Reprint. Cambridge Bible for Schools. Cambridge: University Press, 1952.

Murphy-O'Connor, J. "Colossians." In *The New Catholic Commentary on Holy Scripture,* edited by R. C. Fuller. Rev. ed. London: & New York: Thomas Nelson, 1969.

Peake, A. S. "The Epistle to the Colossians." *The Expositors Greek Testament,* vol. 3. Grand Rapids, MI: Wm. B. Eerdmans, n.d.

Robertson, A. T. *Paul and the Intellectuals: The Epistle to the Colossians*. Reprint. Nashville: Broadman Press, 1976.

Scott, Ernest F. *The Epistles of Paul the Colossians, to Philemon and to the Ephesians*. Moffatt New Testament Commentary. New York: Harper & Bros., 1930.

Scroggie, W. Graham. *A Note to a Friend (Paul to Philemon)*. London.

Shaw, R. D. *The Pauline Epistles*. Edinburgh: T. & T. Clark, 1903.

Simpson, E. K., and Bruce, F. F. *Commentary on Ephesians and Colossians*. New International Commentary, edited by F. F. Bruce. Grand Rapids, MI: Wm. B. Eerdmans, 1965.

Synge, Francis C., ed. *Philippians and Colossians*. Torch Bible Commentary Series. London, 1951; Naperville, IL: Alec R. Allenson.

Thayer, Joseph Henry, ed. and trans. *Greek-English Lexicon of the New Testament*. Rev. ed. 1889. Reprint. Grand Rapids, MI: Zondervan Publishing House, 1962.

Thompson, G. H., ed. *The Letters of Paul to the Ephesians, to the Colossians, and to Philemon*. Cambridge Bible Commentary Series. Cambridge: University Press, 1967.

Turner, G. A. *Colossians*. The Wesleyan Bible Commentary, edited by C. W. Carter, et al. Grand Rapids, MI: Wm. B. Eerdmans, 1965.

Van Oosterzee, J. J. "The Epistle of Paul to Philemon." In *Lange's Commentary on the Holy Scriptures*. Translated from the German with additions by Dr. Hackett.

Vincent, Marvin R. *A Critical and Exegetical Commentary on the Epistles to the Colossians and to Philemon*. Reprint. Edinburgh: T. & T. Clark, 1950.

Williams, A. Lukyn. *The Epistles of Paul the Apostle to the Colossians and to Philemon*. Cambridge Greek Testament. Reprint. Cambridge: University Press, 1928.

White, R. E.O. *Colossians*. Broadman Bible Commentary, edited by Clifton J. Allen, et al. Nashville: Broadman Press, 1970.

DATE DUE